Bearin's
The Book

Bearin's
The Book

Twenty Years of Bulkhead Wisdom,
Quiet Smiles, Belly Laughs, and
Good Ol' Salty Tears

Brian Robbins

North Wind Publishing
Belfast, Maine

North Wind Publishing
P.O. Box 8
Belfast, ME 04915
northwindpublishing.com

Published 2011
Copyright 2011 © Brian Robbins

ISBN-10 0-9830780-5-X
ISBN-13 978-0-9830780-5-0

Library of Congress Control Number: 2011902751

Edited by *Commerical Fisheries News*
    www.fish-news.com/
Cover Photo of author by Rick Martin
Text Design by North Wind Design & Production
    www.nwdpbooks.com

≈

For Tigger —
My wife, my best friend, my one true love—
and the best navigator one could ever hope to share
the voyage with. I could quote a million song
lyrics that would all fit the bill . . . but maybe
"Thank you" and "I love you" say it best.

≈

Contents

Author's Note &
Some Thanks

≈

I struggled for quite a while with the best way to lay this collection of selected *Bearin's* columns out. Split up the fact and the fiction? What about the reflections and memories of friends and family? Road stories here and offshore stories over there? And what about Monroe Sinclair? I mean, other than Eddie Pluggs, nobody's going to want to be in the same category as Monroe, right?

Leave it to my wife Tigger to put things in the proper perspective. "Don't take this wrong," she said, "but this is most likely going to be a bathroom book for a lot of people."

"Are you saying it should be printed on soft, 2-ply paper?" I asked.

"No, no," she said, shaking her head. "I mean, it's probably one of those pick it up, read a chapter, and put it down books."

"And flush," I said.

"And wash your hands," she added. "Don't forget to wash your hands."

Sounded good to me. So with that in mind, I simply laid the chapters down as they ran in *Commercial Fisheries News*, beginning with 1988 and ending up 20 years or so later. Out of the 200-and-something columns I'd written during that period, here are 65 that I happen to like the best.

One thing I should point out, though: if you borrowed this book from someone else, just remember that they've most likely been reading it in the bathroom. I mean, this isn't some cheap attempt to sell books—I'm just thinking that for health reasons, it might not be a bad thing to have your own copy. Just a thought.

Now comes the hardest part of the whole cussed book.

The problem with making a list of thank-yous is you're never going to get it right. Somebody is going to be left out. I know that; I dread doing this; I already feel bad; and I apologize to whomever ahead of time.

The fact of the matter is, I should thank everybody I've ever known in my life, because you're all in these stories one way or the other. So are a bunch of folks I've never met, from Johnny Cash to Keith Richards and from John Steinbeck to R. Crumb.

But we have to start somewhere.

Thank you to . . .

Marm and Pa for all their love, humor, and wisdom; Stevie—my brother and my hero; Jess, Cass, and Jeremy—I could be no prouder and I love you so much; all my family—who happen to all be either good storytellers or wicked listeners, which works out well; Clare Grindal and the late Margaret Vaughan for letting a teenage boy on Deer Isle, ME know it was okay to like to write back in the 70s; my shipmates, road pals, and boat shop friends up and down the coast— yes, Joe, even you—some of whom are mentioned in these pages, but have all provided inspiration; Peter and Paul, my fellow Horseshoe Crabs, for musical therapy; Randy Olson (Doc Urchin) and Steady Eddie Leydecker for changing our world with "Salt of the Earth"; Janet Robbins (no relation—she checked) at North Wind Publishing; and everyone—every last one of you—who ever told me, "You oughta write a book." Remember: I know where you live.

It goes without saying that this book would not exist without 20 years' worth of columns to choose from; and those columns wouldn't have been possible without the help of all the good folks at *Commercial Fisheries News* I've worked with over the years—from the early days when someone would have to interpret what I'd scrawled on yellow legal paper and type it out to Steve Curtis graciously leaving a light on for my return. In particular, I want to thank Robin Alden for bringing me aboard back in 1988 and Susan Jones, who has had to put up with every single one of these words over the years and always—*always*—understood what I was trying to say.

And then there's Rick Martin.

I always have to remind myself that Rick is the publisher at CFN. I tend to think of him more as a friend, a shipmate, and if not a brother, then at least a mildly-twisted-but-dearly-loved cousin. And where he comes from, that's pretty close.

Brian Robbins
February 2011

Introduction

"Humor is the good natured side of a truth."
—Mark Twain

≈

And so begins the debate.

Are Eddie Pluggs, Monroe Sinclair, and the rest of the band of slightly-off-the-bubble characters who inhabit Brian Robbins's mind and many of his *Bearin's* columns in the pages that follow, real or fictional?

Robbins is not saying.

But to his loyal legion of readers who have been following *Bearin's* in the pages of *Commercial Fisheries News* for more than 20 years, the people, the situations, and the general weirdness that often ensues, are all very real.

Folks often tell me they see themselves, or someone they know, in the *Bearin's* crew. And the situations, along with many of the characters, I know to be grounded in Robbins's many years of experience as a working commercial lobsterman before he "came ashore," as they say, in the late 1980s.

While *Bearin's* has been and continues to be a reader favorite in the pages of CFN, a monthly newspaper for commercial fishermen across New England, the themes of Robbins's columns touch a much broader audience.

Over the years, Robbins has treated readers to a mix of humor, satire, and wry—sometimes poignant—observations on life, death, and the often strange ride we all take in between.

His columns on the birth of a child, the passing of a friend or loved one, or the new-found respect for the wisdom of a parent—touch us in places we don't visit often enough.

Honesty.

That's it.

If I had to sum up the body of work that follows, and all I know and love about my friend who created it, I would tell you it's all real and it's all honest — even the exaggerated, made-up stuff.

That's good enough for me and I bet it will be for you too.

Enjoy!

Rick Martin
Publisher, *Commercial Fisheries News*

Chapter 1

Josh & Dottie: The Rowboat

For the first few years of Bearin's—before Eddie Pluggs arrived on the scene—there was Josh Bollard. Josh was sort of an offshore freelancer, I guess; respected by every skipper he sailed with and answering to none on a steady basis. When we first got to know him, he was a life-long bachelor, but . . . things happened, as we shall see.

Imagine it: back in 1988, I figured 50-something was a good age for a crusty old character. Uh-huh.

≈

Joshua Bollard looked at himself in the mirror one more time and shook his head.

"There's somethin' the matter with you—no doubt about it," he said. "What a sight: big bellied, spindly legged, damned hair lookin' like you'd been through a line gale. Who the hell'd want ya?"

Digging through his limited wardrobe, Josh had discovered he didn't have anything (except his funeral suit) that was completely free of traces of the boats he'd worked aboard. Paint here, a grease stain there; a rip in a shirtsleeve, a fray in a pants leg "I give up," he finally announced to the cat eyeing him from the top of the bureau.

1

Josh settled on a pair of faded corduroys and a khaki shirt that only had a few drips of copper paint on it from the Ulysses haulout.

"Best I can do with what I got to work with," he said, then turned to the big black and white cat studying him.

"What are you gawkin' at? Go hunt a friggin' mouse or somethin'. Leave me alone!"

The cat jumped down off the bureau, paused just long enough to bat the cover from a bottle of Bay Rum aftershave under the bed, then scurried down the hall of the trailer.

"Cussed cat!" Josh yelled after him from down on the floor, trying to retrieve the Bay Rum cap. All he got for his efforts was a handful of dust balls and a good thump on the top of his head from the bed frame.

Josh sat up and leaned against the nightstand, rubbing his skull. A welt was already rising.

"Why am I friggin' around with all this?"

He knew the answer all too well.

It was Dottie Nickerson.

It was funny how he'd been a fairly frequent visitor to the tavern for years and had known Dottie as the bartender all that time. He'd been good friends with her late husband, and in fact, had fished with him on a couple of the scallopers.

Nice people. Good friends.

Josh had shared plenty of laughs with Dottie. She'd wiped up the rings his glass had left on the bar, along with the smears and spills from thousands of others through the years.

But now, all of a sudden (and damned if he knew why), Josh found himself hanging around the tavern more often in between his trips as a fill-in on various boats in town.

And it wasn't the drinking. In fact, the other night he'd somehow made a single beer last from eight o'clock till midnight, just sitting and talking to Dottie behind the bar.

That told him something. He wasn't sure what, but he supposed that it was what must have drove him to asking Dottie about going for a walk, or maybe a row in his old peapod this evening.

"So here I am," Josh thought, "all nerved up like some school boy goin' to a damn prom or somethin'. Fool."

He wearily climbed to his feet and stuffed what clothes still lay on the bed into his seabag. Josh would be leaving on a trip in the morning, on the 90' fish dragger *Alexandra*.

"Probably oughta just take my bag now, go aboard, get into my bunk, and lay to till mornin'. Never mind makin' a fool outta myself in front of half the town."

Josh paused with the duffel's handle in his grip. He closed his eyes and made a tow through his scalp with his free mitt. There was a bottle of Canadian whiskey in the kitchen cupboard and . . .

"Nope!" Josh scaled the bag onto the bed and headed down the hall bound for the front door. "Of all the things to dub up, I ain't dubbin' up this one!"

He stomped down the front steps of the trailer with great resolve, and stepped right into a mud puddle, filling one of his shoes.

≈

Dottie Nickerson—even in the rowdy, smoky confines of the tavern—always looked, well, matronly.

Tonight she was downright lovely. To Josh, clomp-clomping down the sidewalk with one soaked foot, she couldn't have looked any better.

"Evenin', Josh," Dottie called to him from her

porch where she was picking dead leaves from summer flowers in the window boxes.

"Hey there, Dot," Josh answered, struggling to sound casual. "I ain't early, am I? 'Cause, you know, if I was, I could always take another turn around town or maybe go over to the tavern for Willy's shift or even, if yer busy or somethin', I oughta . . ."

Dottie had made her way out to the sidewalk and now stood in front of Josh. His ramblings trailed off weakly.

She smiled at him. "You couldn't have come at a better time. Josh. Let's go for a walk."

Josh took a swipe at his forehead and came away with a sleeve full of sweat. "Yeah . . . let's go for a walk, Dot."

He spun around toward the shore and struck out, Dottie almost having to trot to keep up with him.

Off they went with over 100 years of life between the two of them—Dottie smiling, Josh looking a bit glazy, and a wet, squeaky shoe sounding a cadence.

≈

It was a good summer for herring. The purse seiners had come up with dandy sets for several nights running.

Darryl Owsley was braced off in the pilot's chair of his 50' seiner *Utopia*, feet up on the bulkhead, staring at a chart of the bay.

It was getting ready to talk to him.

Darryl was good at purse seining—the best by most opinions—but a trifle odd-acting at times. He was prone to deep conversations with his electronics, and seemed to regard the charts with the awe one would reserve for crystal balls and ouija boards. But he was cool under pressure and good with his crew—a class act.

A quick glance at the clock told Darryl that the

crew ought to be right along and they could cast off. Then he spotted something that sort of tickled him.

Josh Bollard was untying his old, but well-kept peapod from the float at the head of the town pier — and damned if that didn't look like Dottie from the tavern in the stern.

Darryl chuckled out loud.

"Well, sir—ain't that somethin'. I like *that*," he told his color recorder.

≈

Josh had been rowing for almost half an hour, first along the shore, now out into the harbor.

With every pull of the oars, the town spread a bit further out, full of vehicles and figures. Josh wondered how many times he'd watched this same view go out of sight as he headed out on a trip, or welcomed the sight of the town's lights, steaming up the bay in the middle of the night.

"It's been a long time since I've seen the village from out here, Josh," Dottie spoke softly. "Years. Lord, I don't know how many."

"Yeah, well . . . it's there," said Josh, then thought to himself, "What the hell does *that* mean, 'It's there?'"

Josh knew that his mind was boggling up and the sweats were getting worse. It was time to get his words up on deck.

"Dot," he began, "I kinda wanted to . . . let you know about somethin'."

"Yes, Josh?" Dottie turned to face him and smiled again. What was all this damn smiling about, any-ways? thought Josh. It wasn't making anything easier.

"Well, Dot, I've been thinkin' about stuff," Josh began.

The oars began to slow. Josh stared down at his wet shoe. "I don't know . . . I got a knack of gettin' things twisted around wrong and sometimes I think

I'm better off just stayin' out there," Josh waved an arm down the bay, "'cause of how I look at stuff. But, Dot, honest . . . I ain't what I'd call a bad fella."

He glanced up at her. Dottie was still smiling.

"You know, Dot, there's been people come and gone in my life . . . different reasons . . . some's my fault, some weren't . . . but sometimes you get to thinkin' and feelin' stuff that ain't like anything you felt before and . . . and . . . you know that . . . that . . ." Josh's head dropped to his chest, "Aw, hell—never mind."

And that's when it happened. Dot slid off her seat and leaned forward, her face a foot or so away from Josh's.

"Listen to me, Josh Bollard," she began. "You've spent 50-odd years pretending you didn't know how good of a person you were, and I guess it's about time you admitted to it. I've seen you up and seen you down and you're still a good man, no matter where or how you stand. And as far as I'm concerned, Josh— you're special. You're an old bear sometimes, a *silly* old bear, but you're special to me."

Josh couldn't remember afterwards but he was pretty sure Dot gave him a kiss on the cheek about that time. He knew for certain that was when he lost the oar overboard.

≈

The *Utopia* was just easing out through the harbor.

The charts had spoken.

Darryl had to shade his eyes to the sun setting on the water, but could still make out clearly the sight of the woman and the big man in the peapod, going round and round in circles—and laughing.

"Now that's nice," Darryl told his plotter. "More power to 'em."

Chapter 2

Sterno:
Maalox, Music,
and Mystery

Ah, yes . . . the cooks. Every one of them was special. Sterno was, like, special with extra hot sauce. (The "medicated balm" story is immortalized in the "Salt Of The Earth" movie that Stevie, Pa, and I were in. I still flinch at the smell of lanolin.)

By the way, any mention of "Snyder" in this book—or Viceroys—is a reference to Steve Snowden, a long-time shipmate and friend. They come no better than Snyder.

≈

His name was Sterno, and for a short time, he was our cook. He showed up with spring's coming and left as the fall winds began to gust up.

I'd like to be able to say that knowing Sterno changed our lives or drove us to greater heights of achievement or something like that, but it didn't.

Actually, he almost killed us with his cooking, insisted on smoking black, foul-smelling cigars in his bunk, and sometimes acted bad.

7

But, man, could he play the harmonica.

I can see Sterno now the day he applied for duty, looking sharp enough to scratch a match on. *I* thought he looked sharp, anyway. Snyder the engineer, being a good judge of character, thought he looked like trouble. My brother Stevie, the skipper, thought he looked like a cook, and that's all that counted.

Sterno was hired.

For the most part, Sterno's past remained a mystery while he sailed with us. Every now and then, he'd slip something out in the course of conversation, like the quality of bread in your average jail or how fast certain makes of cars would go in reverse.

Apparently, Sterno had lived for a while with a lady who was a roller derby pro. He'd get kind of choked up when he'd tell us about the night she crashed out through the wall of the arena and got hit by a passing bus.

Besides what he brought to the galley situation, Sterno was quick with his hands, making him pretty handy out on deck at stuff like unsnarling rope. He attributed this to years of handling live reptiles. We didn't ask why.

Sterno's cooking always had a distinct "south-of-the-border" bite to it. This not only stuck in my mind, but I'm sure there's big hunks of scar tissue still stuck to my insides as well.

Above all, he was truly one of the best harmonica players I've ever heard. Many a time, regardless of the weather, Sterno would come out on deck after supper and serenade us with "Stardust" or "Under the Double Eagle" while we all laid on the platform, doubled over with cramps.

It was a nice touch.

Truth be known, we spent a *lot* of time out on deck, as I remember, apart from the cramps. Sterno

kept the galley stove going wide-open most of the
time, which made going below and staying for any
length of time damn near impossible. On the other
hand, we didn't have much trouble with dampness in
the fo'c'sle while Sterno was aboard.

He stayed with us through the spring and most
of the summer. It was sometime in August, I think,
when the end came. We left the boat (and Sterno)
down in Portsmouth, NH and chartered a small plane
home to Stonington, ME. He had insisted on staying
down to keep an eye on the boat, plus he was thinking
about buying a car.

Our return flight a few days later ended up being
cut short. A rainy, foggy mess caught us about halfway
down and we had to land in Portland.

We took a chance and called the Pier II, where
the boat was berthed. Why yes, they told us, Mr.
Sterno was right there, and sure, he'd drive right up to
Portland and pick us up.

Thirty minutes later the roar of an unmuffled
engine could be heard approaching, coupled with
a steady WHACKOWHACKOWHACKO
WHACKO that sounded just like somebody beating
on an empty 55-gallon drum with a sledge hammer.

We ran to the front door of the terminal just in
time to witness Sterno's arrival. A large black car,
some sort of Chrysler, I think, was headed right for
the building on two wheels. At the last second, the car
ran aground on the curb and slammed back down on
all fours, lurching to a halt.

As the smoke and dust settled, there was Sterno at
the wheel, flashing us a "thumbs up" sign.

Reluctantly, we climbed in with our seabags.
Nobody spoke as we roared off. Actually, talking was
quite a chore, as the drive shaft seemed to have a bad
bend in it. With every revolution, it would beat up

against the floorboards, making that loud WHACK-OWHACKOWHACKO sound, and jolting everybody up out of their seats.

"Little loud, but it keeps ya from fallin' asleep at the wheel!" Sterno bellowed as we weaved our way down the interstate.

"Honest—don't you think there's something wrong with him?" Snyder hollered in my ear.

"Former trophy winner at Daytona!" Sterno informed us as he concentrated on a controlled skid out around a line of tractor trailers.

"We're takin' the boat home from now on," said my brother after we got done kissing the ground upon our arrival in Portsmouth.

The next trip was Sterno's last. He seemed sort of disillusioned with shipboard cooking. Things took a turn for the worse when we caught him dipping into an institutional size jar of medicated balm we kept on hand. Sterno was using it for cooking grease. We knew something was up.

Things finally came to a head on his last watch on the way in. I came up topsides and found him sipping on a bottle of after-shave at the wheel.

"Sterno," I said, "what's wrong? You, uh, don't seem like yourself."

"Ah, Byrum," he replied, eyes wet with emotion and Aqua Velva, "it's time for these feet to be movin' on. I'm sorry, but old Sterno's gotta fly. I'm a ramblin' man, Byrum, a ramblin' man."

That was all that was said. After unloading, when we got ready to leave Portsmouth, Sterno stayed behind with his car.

I can see him now, sitting on the wharf and waving us goodbye while softly playing "On the Wings of a Snow White Dove" on the harmonica. We all felt

kind of choked up until Snyder came topsides and announced that his after-shave was missing.

Ah, Sterno, wherever you are, old dog, God bless
ya. Maybe you did act up a little bit now and then—
but your breath always smelled good.

Take care.

Chapter 3

The Amazing Grace: Eb Saves the Day

The fictional Amazing Grace *stories that I wrote between 1988 and 1990 were a way of splicing the Maine Lobster Boat races into deeper matters, like overcoming adversity and good conquering evil—you know, stuff like that.*

Good ol' Colby Young down in Corea, ME tells a story from years ago about a boat he had that was repowered overnight for a race the next day. I'm sure Colb was a total hands-on part of the procedure, though—rather than passed out in the back seat of a Delta 88 like Eb.

≈

"Gawd . . . ain't she pretty!"

The tallest man amongst the group on the wharf shook his head in admiration and let fly a jet of tobacco juice to emphasize his point, clear over the heads of the rest and into the water.

The men stood in silent wonderment at the work of art before them.

The Amazing Grace was roaring through the channel with just about two-thirds of the length of her bilges out of the water. The bellow of her big V-8 gas engine combined with the cleanliness of her lines as she sliced her way through the thoroughfare brought goose pimples to the onlookers' skin.

They loved her—and for good reason, as she was the product of their combined efforts. Add up a winter and spring's worth of missed suppers, gouged knuckles, more than a little cash outlay (and a whole lot of heart), and there you had it: the challenger for the crown of "World's Fastest Lobster Boat."

Abe, the tobacco-chewing elder, actually owned the hull. The rest, Burt (who closely resembled a grumbly circus bear), Philmore (a stringbeanish wheeler-dealer), and the always-grease-smeared mechanic of the group, Walter, had all contributed in their respective ways.

From the rebuilding of the old wooden hull—now so shiny you'd swear she was fiberglass—to the placement and fine tuning of the big-block Buick engine, they'd worked together with total dedication.

Not to say that the project hadn't had its problems along the way. There'd been the incident when Philmore had hit Burt over the head with an oak trap runner during a disagreement about refastening techniques. (Luckily, the sill was pretty worm eaten and didn't do much damage.) Then there was the time when Abe got mad over the propeller size Walter came up with and climbed up on the roof of the boat shed, refusing to come down. He just sat up on the peak well into the night, staring out over the bay. They finally coaxed him down with a fresh bag of Beechnut chewing tobacco.

But things have a way of taking care of themselves and now the men were standing in perfect harmony watching the fruit of their labors.

And she was truly beautiful.

"I might be in love," said Burt.

"She couldn't go no easier," added Philmore.

"I can see Lester Junior smilin' from here," said Walter. Lester Junior had the wheel, his shock of burnt red hair standing on end. It had been unanimous that Lester should be the skipper and have the honor of the trial run, as he was the best boat handler. Besides, the others wanted to see the *Grace* in action.

And now they stood on the wharf, bonded by all they'd gone through to witness this moment.

They had absolutely no warning whatsoever before the fruit of their labors soiled its britches.

With a dull KAWUMPH, followed by belches of flame and billows of smoke from her twin stacks, the *Amazing Grace* gradually lost her headway and settled in the water. Lester Junior could be seen beating his fists and forehead against the bulkhead and screeching bad words at the top of his lungs.

The onlookers were frozen in place. Their bright and shiny personal heaven had just gone black, black as the evil-looking smoke now just feebly putt-putting from the *Grace's* pipes.

Abe, visibly shaken, spit weakly onto his own feet and broke the silence.

"He should have cut her back on the throttle a little. Pushin' her too damn hard too soon. Plus, that friggin' propeller—"

"That's right—start right in on the propeller again," said Walter, throwing his arms in the air. "I *knew* that was comin'! Listen, there weren't nuthin' wrong with that propeller and -"

"CUT IT OUT!" yelled Burt, stepping between the two. "This is no time for that crap. We're in this together, remember?"

They all did a bit of throat clearing and mumbling, but things did ease up a bit as the men waited for Lester Junior to row the *Grace* ashore with a dory oar.

"Looks bad," Lester Junior hollered from his berth by the pot hauler.

"*How* bad?" yelled Philmore. They had to wait for Lester Junior to cross to the other side of the *Grace*. Presently, his bright red hair appeared around the far corner of the windbreak and he took a bite with the oar.

"*Real* bad. Never seen nothin' like it. Looks like a friggin' bomb went off inside 'er. Lotta oil and—"

His words were drowned out by the appearance of a big, noisy yellow car at the head of the wharf. A bushy blonde head popped up above the roofline, from the driver's window on the far side. It was Eb, who'd ridden to Boston on a fish truck the day before to—in his own words—"Find me a hot vehicle."

It looked like he'd done it. Eb was driving a hybrid of style and performance—a once-elegant Delta 88 with air-shocked rear end, half-a-fathom-wide tires all the way around, massive sidepipes, and an air scoop as big as an oversize country mailbox riveted to the hood. He blew the Oldsmobile's horn in greeting and gunned his engine.

Philmore waved his arms like an umpire making a big call. "Shut that damn mess down, Eb! Don'tcha got no respect for the dead?"

"She'll go 140!" yelled Eb, rocking the Delta with a punch of the accelerator.

"—and both valve covers blew off." Lester Junior was still eulogizing as he closed in on the shore.

"I kin get rubber in all four gears!" Eb proudly announced and blew the horn again for effect.

"SHUT *UP*, EB!" Abe spat on the Oldsmobile's hood with a vengeance. Eb shrunk into his seat and his sidepipes settled into a low rumble. Abe turned to the slowly-approaching *Amazing Grace* and cleared his throat.

"Can we save her, Jr.?"

Lester Junior was now just sitting on the rail waiting for the Grace's bow to ground on the beach.

"No way."

These two words struck the men right in their hearts. It was over. The boat races were tomorrow—there was no time, no way.

The dream was pooched.

"Well," said Burt, staring at his feet, "maybe next year. We could always -" His words were lost, as Eb, unable to contain himself, began revving his engine again.

"WILL YOU CUT THAT OUT?" Burt hollered at the big old car, rocking on its suspension with each kick of the accelerator.

About that time, something magical happened—a sort of silent telepathy among Burt, Abe, Philmore, and Walter. A bystander might have said that the men seemed to take on the cunning look of a pack of wolves. They slowly spread out into a semi-circle as they approached Eb, still revving up his Delta 88 with a blissful look on his face.

Philmore made the first move. He stealthily withdrew a pint of whiskey from a jacket pocket as he patted the Olds' hood scoop.

"Boy, this sure is a pretty car, Eb," he said. "You've had a big day, huh?" He leaned in through the driver's window and rubbed Eb's shoulder.

Eb punched the accelerator and nodded his head. "Best day of my life."

"Well, I'd say a celebration was in order," said Philmore. "What say you shut that beast down and have a little slat?" He offered up the pint.

Eb slacked off the gas pedal, letting the Delta's roar die to a gurgling rumble before shutting it down.

"Well . . . why not? *One* can't hurt, right?"

The wolf pack closed in.

≈

The operation was completed just as the sun broke the horizon the next morning.

The men thought it was a nice touch that Eb was in the back seat of the Delta for most of the procedure, snoring loudly in a deep, intoxicated slumber.

The engine compartment of the big car was now empty and the *Amazing Grace* was rumbling with new life. There would be no test runs, as they didn't dare to push the big Olds engine any harder than Eb already had on the way home from Boston. It didn't matter now, anyway; they had what they had and the race would tell it all, one way or the other.

"You done a good thing, Eb," said Philmore to the twitching, drooling heap in the back seat. "Whether you know it or not."

Late that morning they guided an unsteady Eb down to the water's edge to watch the lobster boat races. Eb's pounding head and spells of dizziness only substantiated his friend's arguments that he shouldn't try to drive, and that it was best to leave the Delta 88 in the shade of the boat shop.

Sometimes the actual fulfillment of dreams can happen all too quickly. The time that it took the *Amazing Grace* to leap clear of the rest of the pack, skim the length of the course, and roar across the finish line in first place wasn't very long on the stopwatch. But each second, each sight, each sound, and each smell were branded in the men's minds to stay. With the victory announcement over the VHF came handshakes and hugs all the way around.

Eb rubbed his gory-looking eyes and grinned. "Gawd," he announced shakily in a cracked rasp, "think what she'd do if she had a engine like my Olds!"

Abe swallowed a cheekful of tobacco and went into a bad gagging fit. While Burt was leading Abe over to the tall grass, Philmore turned his attention to Eb.

"How's about we go get a beer to celebrate?" he said in his most wolf-like voice.

≈

The final step of the operation was completed about midnight. The slamming of the Delta's hood raised Eb from his slumber, once again in the back seat.

It struck him that his unselfish friends had fed him more alcohol in the last 24 hours than he'd seen in all his adult life put together.

Eb slowly rose up and peeked over the back of the driver's seat, only to find Burt at the wheel, ready to fire the big Delta up.

"Ready to go home?" Burt smiled. "I'll drive ya there and Philmore can pick me up."

"Yeah, thanks," croaked Eb. "Boy, I'm sorry I wasn't much help through all this . . . "

"Oh, hell, boy—you done yer part," said Abe, standing alongside the big yellow Buick. He arced a jet of juice a good 20 feet into the beautiful summer night.

Chapter 4

Early (Awful Early) Days of Boat Building

This column from fall of 1988 marks one of the few times I have ever been asked to attempt to write to a theme (in this case, for that year's "Boat Building Focus"). That'll show 'em.

≈

The first fishing boats were built out of necessity. For a long time, folks had been content to stand on the shore and heave rocks into the water, hoping to knock passing fish unconscious and have them float to the surface. Then, hopefully, wind and tidal action would combine to drive the numbed creatures up onto the beach.

Needless to say, this wasn't the most productive of methods. Highliners rarely got into double figures for the year in number of fish killed.

Wading helped, but not much. Inventive minds dallied with swimming, but this ran up against its own stone walls, so to speak; there were only so many rocks you could carry and still float.

A major breakthrough came about when, after a primitive clambake, one of the partygoers tossed a corncob into the ocean. The splash attracted the attention of several others and they couldn't help but notice a wonderful phenomenon—the corncob was floating.

This really stirred up the crowd on the beach in good shape.

"OOOOGA! WAOOOOGA!" pointed one tall fellow. (Which translates to "Good Lord, it rides the waves!")

"BAMABAMA! JIM DANDY!" exclaimed another, a bearded lad with a high forehead. ("A way to go farther and fish harder!")

"WIZZO! BANGO! HOOT NANNY!" hollered a third. (Imagine what she'd do with a big V-8!") At this point in maritime history, oars hadn't been invented, let alone engines, so nobody had one living clue as to what he was talking about.

Anyhow, plans were made and the head craftsmen worked day and night for a solid week.

The first problem they faced was finding a 20' long corncob. It was agreed by all that this was impractical and that they should go ahead and make their own facsimile.

Good move.

They figured on chiseling it out of stone.

Bad move.

On the day of the big launching, a massive crowd gathered on the shore at high tide.

The granite cob was positioned at the top of a grassy slope that dropped sharply away into deep water. There was a small scuffle over who would ride the cob down the ways, the honors finally going to the original designer, the head stonecutters, and one awfully large, foul-smelling brute who threatened to pound the tar out of anyone who argued with him.

The launching signal was given and the blockings were removed.

The cob didn't budge. Its crew rocked back and forth in their seats, trying to get a little motion started, but this accomplished nothing.

Some in the crowd were beginning to get restless and mouthy (as they often do at launchings), and the big, ugly, self-appointed mate could take it no longer.

He swung down off the granite cob, braced his backside against its stern and heaved.

Nothing happened. And the crowd really started to hoot and holler.

The foul-smelling giant growled, took a deep breath—and began to repeatedly slam his rearend into the cob.

Slowly at first, then with ever-increasing speed, the granite shape slid down the slope and rocketed off the bluff.

Being made of rock, naturally, it sank.

Things could have been a lot worse, though. As was the custom in those days, each of the cob's crew, like everyone else at the launching, had a goat bladder, full of spirits, on a string around his neck. These brew-filled bladders floated, of course, keeping the men from drowning.

A law was passed on the spot. If anyone got near the water, let alone on or *in* it, without a goat bladder full of alcohol, they'd get a beating. No ifs, ands, or buts about it.

Sort of a zero tolerance measure, I guess.

Well anyway, as is the case in all things (hopefully), the aspiring mariners learned from their mistakes. The problem, they decided, wasn't so much the design as the materials used.

Many different ideas were tried and rejected. Leaves, egg shells, hay, and old loin cloths all took their turns and failed miserably as construction materials.

Again, it took a clambake to get the answer.

Late in the festivities, one of the partygoers was overcome with emotion. She jumped to her feet and began dancing around the fire, twirling a flaming tree limb.

(Unbeknownst to all at the time, this exhibition would evolve into a popular half-time show at the Super Bowl.)

This made some folks nervous. They wrestled the burning stick away from the dancer and threw it out into the bay.

The fire went out.

And the limb floated.

"WOOKA!" exclaimed one onlooker ("Holy cow!") as he slapped his forehead.

"COOBA! LAMPOONA!" cried another. ("Of course—big stick!")

"DABAMMO! WIGGY! WIGGY!" yelled a third, but he was chasing the dancer across the sands and really wasn't paying attention to the matter at hand.

Regardless, there was another serious effort put into getting a vessel ready for fishing, this time with a wooden hull.

A midnight launching was planned for this version—if things didn't go as they hoped, the craftsmen didn't want to expose everybody to another dose of failure.

So, in the heavy heat of a summer night, a group of loin-clothed figures could be seen dragging their latest creation down to the shore. Apart from occasional grunts, the men were silent.

At sunrise, people awoke to the sounds of singing and laughing coming from the water. Heads peered from the doorways of caves, curious as to what was going on.

They were amazed at what they saw.

Out in the middle of the bay were half a dozen men—the midnight launchers—waving their goat bladders in the air, standing in a 40' long, hollowed-out tree trunk.

They had done it. The first fishing boat was ready for sea trials.

It really was ready too, for the ingenious crew had already rigged the craft for fishing.

Rather than loading up with softball-sized boulders, these pioneers of fishing had come through with an impressive display of engineering. An immense slab of granite was balanced on the stern, with long lines of woven animal skins made fast to the huge stone. The idea was to make a big set—increase the productivity—and then haul the rock back up. They figured to be able to knock a large number of fish unconscious if they were bunched up.

As the crowd cheered from the shore, the fishing crew moved aft and made their first set. With a mighty heave-ho, the slab was launched clumsily off the stern and overboard, with the coiled skin line paying out rapidly behind.

There hadn't been much thought put into depth of water in regards to length of line. In fact, nobody had even considered the matter.

But as luck would have it, the granite slammed into the bottom just as the line snubbed up, with its end wrapped completely around the dugout. There was a sharp jolt, which took the crew off their feet, then silence.

Apparently the skin line couldn't have been much shorter, as the craft's stern was hauled down to within 2" of being under.

The crew got to their feet and shook themselves off. Well, they figured, that would be something to remember next time—allow for plenty of slack.

There were no unconscious fish floating on the surface, but no matter—this was, after all, just a shakedown cruise. The men eased back aft with an eye on the freeboard situation, and gave a hearty tug on the line, planning to haul the slab back up.

No go.

The granite had mired itself in the muddy bottom. All the crew succeeded in doing when they pulled, was to half fill the craft as the rails went under. They ran back to the bow to let the stern up and tried to think things out.

They definitely had made a boat to work from, and this was good.

The rock, as a fishing device, left something to be desired—this was obvious.

Unwittingly, they had invented the mooring, but this was of little consolation right at that moment.

Besides, they had no means of propulsion. Somebody mentioned a V-8 again ("WIZZO! BANGO!"), but it was agreed by all that it was a stupid idea, as they still hadn't invented an oar.

So that was it.

The men hollered ashore for somebody to get their act together and invent: an oar; a knife; a bailing dish; and monofilament.

Then they took their goat bladders and sat down in the bilge of the half-sunk dugout.

Making history took a lot out of a guy.

Chapter 5

Josh Bollard: Coffee in a Plain Cup

Another visit to Josh Bollard's world. By October of 1988, everyone around the water-front seemed to know about Josh's feelings for Dot Nickerson. But the main focus of this one was that feeling of waiting . . . waiting . . . waiting for the right chance to swing around between seas.

≈

". . . And for the Gulf of Maine, more than 25 miles offshore, tonight, winds southwest 25 to 30 knots, becoming northwest by morning and diminishing to 15 to 20 knots. Average seas 8 to 12 feet tonight, diminishing with the wind shift by morning."

Edward "Sparky" Hanson stuck his head out through the hauling station window and gave a yell to the crew on deck.

"Holler when you got them traps tied down in good shape and I'll swing her around!"

Josh Bollard nodded his head as he leaned out over the starboard rail and fed the loose end of a coil of rope in through a scupper. After making the end fast, Josh hove the coil up over the forward tier of four-foot lobster traps to the man waiting by the opposite rail.

Hanson was holding the 55' Nicola into the wind, giving the crew a chance to lash down the last of the gear they'd taken on.

Sparky planned to swing and run with the wind, jogging along until daybreak. Barring a weird twist in the weather, they should be handy to the Nicola's inner gear by then and could set the trawls they had aboard on that same bottom. Hopefully, the wind would be hauled into the nor'west by then, flattening things out and giving them a decent day to finish their trip.

Sparky, looking back aft, couldn't help but laugh and shake his head. That Josh Bollard was a good man on deck, no doubt about it. It didn't matter that he was just going as a fill-in—or that he was a good 20 years older than the next oldest man on the crew (Sonny Howard, who'd just turned 30). Josh knew his stuff.

Sparky himself was 20 years younger than Josh, but had already paid his share of dues. Hanson had been offered a skipper's berth at 23 and had the Nicola built when he was 28.

Nobody could question the fact that he'd earned his keep, although waitresses still questioned his age. It didn't make much sense that you could come in off a trip and still have to show your drivers license before you could get a beer, but it happened a lot. Baby-faced for life.

Sparky grinned, watching Josh. The man could just show up with his seabag and immediately fit into place. Any boat that had Josh aboard for a trip or two benefited, as he had a way of working with others that kept things flowing well, usually leaving some better way of doing things behind.

Plus, thought Sparky, Josh set a good pace. The frustrating part was, the old bear would make a perfect mate on any boat, but he wouldn't make a commitment.

"Give me a holler when you need a man for a trip or two," Josh'd say. "That's one thing. But don't be buying me a coffee cup with my name on it . . . that just ain't my way."

"Oh well," thought Sparky as he tapped the weatherglass fastened to the overhead. "Maybe he'll rub off on the gang, if nothing else."

The glass was rising . . . the weather report might be somewhere near right, it seemed. The Nicola was pitching a little harder into the sou'west chop as the wind picked up, but would run along easy with it once they swung around.

The wheelhouse door opened and in stomped the crew off the deck, dripping wet and puffing. First was the kid, Willy Pierce, who was trying to make the adjustment from high school baseball hero to deckhand on an offshore lobster boat. By the second day of the trip, Willy had fastened one eye on Josh and was absorbing the man's moves.

Sonny Howard was next, teeth clenched on an upside-down corncob pipe, soaking wet but still burning. Sonny filled the door almost as well as Josh, Sparky thought—between the two of them; oil clothes and all, you'd have a good quarter-ton.

Josh, as always, was last off deck, glancing back at the gear one more time.

"Look all right?" asked Sparky.

"Give her hell," said Josh.

"Tied on in good shape," added Sonny. "They ain't going anywhere without us." He blew sodden pipe gunk into a paper towel.

Sparky leaned sideways in the captain's chair and bellowed down the companionway.

"Cook! Hey—COOKIE!"

A pale, round head wearing a hairnet popped into view, one eye slightly bigger than the other, but both blinking equally fast. A pudgy hand with a big ball of gauze on the thumb shot up in a salute.

"Aye-aye captain!" said Melburn Healy, known to all as "Cookie." Sweat ran down into his eyes, speeding the crazed snapping action of the lids.

Sparky slowly shook his head, thinking that it does take all kinds, but this one was definitely a rare breed of cat.

"Cookie, will you stop that 'aye-aye' crap? Now listen—is everything secure down there in the galley of doom? 'Cause what ain't will probably end up in a heap on the floor when we turn. You need a minute to get squared away?"

The face beneath the hairnet whitened a bit more and one eye closed completely.

"NO SIR! Ready for any given course change!"

Sparky nodded, thinking that maybe he should see about having Cookie put in some sort of a home when they got in. Cooks were odd enough as a rule, but this one was stuck in limbo somewhere between the King's Navy and "Star Trek."

"How'd you cut yer thumb, Cookie?" asked Josh, unwrapping a soaked towel from the neck of his oil-coat.

Melburn's expression eased up a bit. He wasn't as hyper around Josh, and had even made halfway-stable conversation during Josh's watch the night before. Cookie started to speak when Sonny Howard broke in.

"Probably cut it on the lid of the lard can," said Sonny as he stepped out of his barvel. "That first 50-lb. can must be used up by now. It's been four days."

With that, the Nicola made a leap and the cook lost his balance on the companionway stairs and disappeared from sight.

"All right . . . here we go," said Sparky. He watched the seas, waiting until they were coming down off the backside of one to begin his swing, laying on the power.

The Nicola laid over to starboard as she came about. Josh was braced in the aft doorway, watching the pile of traps. He was confident about their lashing job, but . . . well, stuff happens.

They were just about through their arc when the next sea struck. The Nicola took it solidly on her quarter, lifting her rump a little, but getting more of a washing than anything.

Then they were around and running with the wind. The Nicola had proven herself in a following sea many times, being full enough forward to run easy and stay up, without ever offering to dig her bow in and broach. "I think it could blow a friggin' hundred," Sparky had said before, "and you'd never know it. Button her up and let her go."

Willy and Sonny had shed their gear and were down in their bunks within minutes, leaving Josh and Sparky in the wheelhouse.

Sparky glanced over at the big man tucked into the far corner. Josh was watching the horizon, idly rubbing his right shoulder. Sparky knew that the old bear was stiff at the end of a trip, but never made a noise about it.

"Maybe Dottie rubs his shoulders for him," Sparky smiled to himself. He knew that Josh had been seeing her for a while. They made a good pair, too, but Sparky didn't feel as he could ever say that to Josh.

A strong stench wafted up the companionway about then. Sparky sighed and leaned over toward the opening.

"COOKIE!" he yelled. "I'd say yer friggin' burn an' serve rolls was pretty near done! And once you get the flames out, how's about a cuppa coffee for me and Mr. Bollard!"

Sparky could see Josh out of the corner of his eye. The big man was still looking out the window, but now had a good grin on.

"Aw hell," Sparky said to himself, "so maybe he doesn't want a cup with his name on it. But if he ever did . . ."

> "Our forecast, updated at 11:30 PM for the Gulf of Maine, calls for southwest winds diminishing and becoming light northwest by morning. Average seas 6 to 8 feet the remainder of tonight, becoming 2 to 4 feet after the wind shift."

Chapter 6

Scalloping with Pa

I've written many words about my father, Steve Robbins Sr., since his passing in 1995. I'm glad I wrote some to him before then, as well.

This column from Christmastime in 1988 was a way of saying thanks.

≈

It's that time of year again, isn't it?

The air's heavier and the wind packs that much more wallop.

The holidays have struck, with their way of getting you thinking about a lot of things you don't usually take time for.

And, scallop season has opened in Maine waters.

Looking back, I can see where my father was probably relieved when my brother decided to rig over the 44' offshore lobster boat he used to have for inshore scalloping.

Pa ended up putting in plenty of time getting us rigged up, showing us how to work the gear, and just plain fishing (and putting up) with us.

But now that I think about it, I know that he enjoyed doing all that a hellish lot more than sitting up nights at home during the few offshore lobster trips we could get in during the winter, listening to crackly static on the VHF, waiting for some word from us.

I can't remember what the turning point was in the decision to rig over—maybe there wasn't any one thing. It could easily have been just the sum total of beatings we'd gone through in previous winters.

The frigging boat was tough enough—no question there. She simply wasn't big enough for Crowell Basin in the middle of January. There can be some pretty days on the water that time of the year—and then there's the rest of them.

Anyhow, I remember Pa latching right on to the idea of us rigging the *Shirley & Freeman* over for scalloping.

"Oh, she'll make a dandy nubber," he said. "Main thing is getting the gear to work with."

And with that, he sort of took charge.

There was a lot of running around done over the next few weeks. Pa advised us on what we'd need for materials to build the gear from—and laid down some basic rules.

"Rig her heavy enough to take the odd strain. The times you get into scrapes is when stuff breaks," he said.

The hard part about following Pa's ideas was that he'd be standing outside explaining something and, to get his point across, begin sketching stuff in the dirt with a stick. That was all right, I guess. But if you didn't quite get it all the first time (and sometimes we're talking about a good 20 minutes' worth of drawing), you'd have no option but to sit there and think things out until you *did* have it down. (Or, you could try to lift the plot of dirt with the drawing on it in a shovel to take with you.)

Anyhow, thinking was easier than shoveling, so we tried to learn as we went along. Or at least have a pencil and paper handy.

Pa thought the best setup for us would be a single-drum winch with a bitt head for the tackle fall.

"You got the rope right in your hands," he explained, "and if you've got to go up or down a little or a lot—it's right there."

Keep it simple. Keep it rugged. That's what Pa maintained—and it didn't let us down.

Once officially rigged, there was a spell of getting acquainted with this new way of life. It took a little bit to get used to all that rigging up over our heads (lobster traps don't often come plummeting down out of the sky). We learned to handle the gear while keeping one eye out for all the what-ifs. (There's a difference between confidence and cockiness.)

When we were actually getting the drags to fish, of course, then there were the shucking lessons.

I'd always heard folks tell stories of Pa whittling out scallops, and keeping a shell in the air steadily. Somehow it hadn't meant much until I tried it myself.

I remember us standing at the dumping box the first time I was going to cut. I watched Pa go in between the scallop shells with the knife blade, make a couple of quick and smooth motions—the shell was flying, and the meat was in the dish.

I gave it a go and managed to crack the shell, rip the nub into two ragged chunks, and drop the biggest part of the rim in my shelling dish.

That wasn't right.

Pa maintained that it was to a man's advantage to be fairly big to begin with (well, look at him, what else would he say?) and have plenty of clothes on, as you would in the winter months, anyway.

Then you could strike the famous "Nubber's Stance": boots slightly spread, body sort of braced back, belly out, with the scallop resting hinge-first against your chest.

Pa would demonstrate, whittling along smoothly and steadily while talking.

I got so I could flip the rim and shell with the same

swipe, like he did, but it was still frustrating. I'd have to bear down and concentrate to make any kind of time, while Pa would be braced back, cutting along at a good clip while telling stories or pointing out marks on the shore.

I guess the best thing about those times was that I'd never really had a chance to work with my father before. When I was little, I bailed a few dories out and stayed aboard the boat now and then during the seining summers. But those days were over and Pa had gotten out of the business by the time I was really old enough to work.

So at that point, I went fishing with my brother and we went our way. The chance to stand shoulder to shoulder and work along with my father never came until those scalloping winters.

But the chance was worth waiting for. There were lessons learned about doing—and there were "doings" that were lessons in life.

And, of course, there was some stuff that was plain foolishness—done just for the sake of laughter—and that was all right, too.

By the second season, I'd gotten familiar enough with the gear to take the boat myself, off and on. As it goes, there were some poor days and some good days. Pa didn't go that year, but looking back, now I know that it was his influence that made it happen for me. And he was always there for the occasional scrapes.

So, as I said back at the beginning, I guess now I understand a little more about some of my father's reasons for going through all that with us. And *for* us.

Maybe it's as good a time as any to say thanks, Pa.

You're as good a shipmate as anybody could be.

And—oh yeah—Merry Christmas.

It's that time of year again, isn't it?

Chapter 7

Eddie & Ross:
Morning Rituals

This column from the April 1989 issue of CFN introduced us (me too) to lobsterman Eddie Pluggs—although we didn't even find out his last name at that point.

If you're going to go inshore lobstering, you have to be able to get up in the morning. It doesn't matter what you feel like; it doesn't matter what's worrying you; you need to get your act together and go. The day's going to come, with or without you.

Morning rituals help.

≈

If Ross sat by his kitchen window, he could see the glow of the pickup truck's headlights a good minute before Eddie reached his driveway.

And at quarter to four on this late-winter morning, Ross saw the light.

With a grunt, he got to his feet and ran through his usual leaving-the-house-early-in-the-morning check-list:

Mr. Coffee had spewed out his mandatory 2-½ cups and was shut off. That was good.

Ross' lunch pail was packed—a sandwich made

from last night's meatloaf, two deviled eggs, a slab of Velveeta, and an apple. That was good.

Woof the family dog had been out to do his duties and was now curled up on the living room sofa chewing one of the kid's dolls. That *wasn't* so good, but Eddie was in the driveway now and it was time to go.

Ross zipped up his snowmobile suit, hit the light switch, and stepped out into the early-morning bite. His turned-down hip boots swish-swished as he walked out to Eddie's waiting truck.

Ross opened up the passenger side door and swung in. He got the door closed just in time to miss clipping off his mailbox as Eddie backed out into the street at half-throttle.

The same thing had almost happened the previous morning. Actually, the same thing had almost been happening now for a solid ten years, since Ross had started going as sternman for Eddie. No greeting, not even a nod, just a rocket-like launch from the driveway and then a full-bore dash down to the shore.

It was time to go to haul.

Eddie had gouged out a peephole in the frost-covered windshield with the plastic cap off a can of belt dressing. Ross couldn't see out of his side at all. It was better that way.

They skidded through town, Eddie grinding gears and cranking the wheel back and forth. Ross was braced off in the corner trying to get a Viceroy lit. The first stab with the lighter almost caught his hat on fire and the second, his nose. By the third try, though, they hit a smooth stretch and the cigarette was lit.

The wipers were just starting to cut through the windshield's crust when Eddie wheeled into the parking lot and slammed the brakes on. Off with the headlights, kill the ignition. The doors opened and shut in unison and both men were headed across the slush-covered gravel to the head of the ramp.

Ross was down on the float first. He stopped and bent, hiked up his boots, took one last drag on the Viceroy, and then flicked it overboard. He jumped aboard the rowboat and began to bail.

Eddie would now utter his first words of this and every morning: with the first swipe of the oars, the port one would pop out of its oarlock—the one with the broken yoke.

Eddie pushed out from the float. He plugged the oarlocks into place, then slipped the oars into them. He dug the blades in and pulled. The port oar popped out. "Dammit, gotta fix that . . ." Eddie said, resetting the oar and beginning again, a little gentler this time.

"Yeah," said Ross. That was all that was required. He lit another cigarette.

In a minute or so, they bumped easily alongside the *Mr. Kelp*, Eddie's 38' lobster boat. Ross grabbed the lunch pails and set them up on the washboard, purposely built wide enough to accommodate a dinner box sideways.

Then Ross ducked.

The first few days he'd gone, Ross had gotten clipped on the ear by Eddie's hip boot as he swung aboard. That was Eddie's way of getting aboard and Ross' head was in the way.

He learned to duck.

Eddie was disappearing through the cabin doorway as Ross' feet hit the platform. He tucked the lunch pails in a safe corner first, then grabbed the mooring's buoy line and made fast the rowboat's painter. Ross was headed up onto the bow just as the *Mr. Kelp*'s diesel came to life.

CHAAAAAAWUMP!

CHAAAAAAWUMP!

Eddie always let the engine roll over a couple times, regardless. Then would come the PSSSSST-PSSSST of the ether can.

CHAWAWAWA-BARPBARPBARPBARP!

The diesel snarled and snapped at being woken up by the starting fluid, but soon settled into a steady rumble.

Eddie was back up by the wheel. When Ross heard the pilot window swing open, he wrestled the pennant up over the bitt and cast off, ducking again to clear the spotlight's beam.

Eddie swung the *Mr. Kelp* around and idled in toward the bait shed as Ross made his way down off the bow. Oil pants were next. Ross slipped into them quickly, had his gloves wrung out and on, and was taking the top off the bait box by the time they bumped the spilings.

A dollop of tobacco juice exploded on the rail, followed by a roar from above: "How many and what flavor?"

The men looked up to see Dudley the bait man, backlit by the glare of the dock's big floodlight. He was easily as big around as one of the 55-gallon drums of redfish in the shed and not much taller. He was foul-tempered, naturally abrasive, and chewed bagfuls of Beechnut at a clip, but kept a clean bait house and knew his stuff.

Ross, squinting in the floodlight's brightness, hollered back, "2-½ cuttings! 3-½ redfish! Good stuff!"

"It's all good, ya damn fools!"

Dudley shook his head in disgust and disappeared from the wharf's edge. There wouldn't be much of a wait. They knew Dudley'd been there for an hour or so already—making coffee; laying out gloves, bands, and cans of oil; and bailing up bait to have ready for the morning rush.

Sure enough, without warning, a bushel tub full of redfish came plummeting down, fetching up hard on its tackle line inches from the washboard.

"Come on, get into gear down there! I ain't got all day!" raved the voice from above. Another blossom of tobacco goo exploded on top of the rounded bait tub.

"I hate it when he does that," said Ross as he swung the tub over the bait box and upended it.

The performance was repeated with each bushel—the kamikaze fall, a blast of verbal abuse from Dudley, a dump, and the empty tub would disappear back up over the wharf. With the last one, Dudley peered out over the edge again. "You got 'nuff?"

"Yeah, dandy!" Ross yelled.

"Good! Get the hell away from the dock!" Dudley yelled and vanished from sight.

Eddie smoothly backed away from the wharf, then gunned the *Mr. Kelp* around in a tight circle and headed through the harbor.

Ross had his head down and was baiting bags wide open.

They made the outer harbor buoy and swung to run down through the islands.

In few more minutes, Ross knew, the day would officially begin.

He baited along steadily—grabbing a solid handful of herring cuttings that would fill each bag with one try—drawing up, tying off, reaching for the next one. Ross could make good time.

Eddie stretched, yawned, took a good look out the pilot window and then started back aft. He stopped alongside of Ross. Eddie looked as if he'd just noticed him for the first time.

"How's that stuff look?" he asked Ross.

"Handsome." Ross squinted through a wisp of cigarette smoke. "Gonna be a good chance, ain't it?"

"Yeah, dandy . . . just dandy," answered Eddie.

The day had begun.

Chapter 8

Willard Builds
a Boat

*Willard Bumsfurd was a one-time visitor to
Bearin's back in 1989. Lord only knows what he
might be doing now.*
I almost felt sorry for him. Almost.

≈

The money had come from toilet paper. Not that it
was actually *made* out of toilet paper, you understand.
The Bumsfurd family fortune had come from the
success of its paper goods empire, the crown jewel of
which was Sincere Bathroom Tissue ("You can believe
in us, we're Sincere").

So I guess you could say that the money Willard
Bumsfurd III had at his disposal was the fruit of the
seed his grandfather had planted—which had blossomed into a very popular toilet paper.

Now there's nothing wrong with that at all. It
wouldn't be a bad thing that Willard took a chunk of
the money and had a fishing boat built—except for the
fact that Willard, just plain and simple, shouldn't have
tried to go fishing. But facts like that hadn't stopped
him before.

Take, for instance, the fact that Willard wasn't all

that good of a driver out on the regular highway. That didn't stop him from buying a stable of three Grand Prix racing cars. Smashing up two of them before he even got out onto the race course really wasn't that much of a damper, either. He just sort of got bored with auto racing after a while and forgot about it.

Things went about the same way for cliff diving, lion taming, brain surgery, falconry, hang gliding, mercenary work, art collecting, rock climbing, laser dentistry, steeplechase riding, tattooing, professional gambling, and being an astronaut. The flame of an idea would burn brightly in Willard's head and then die out after a short while, replaced by another interest of even greater intensity.

Willard had two problems, basically. One was that his money-to-brains ratio was way out of sync. The second was that his forefathers were a tough act to follow.

The Bumsfurd men had always been flamboyant, rough-and-rugged types, famous in the early days for their "roll up your sleeves and do it" attitude.

Willard's grandfather was known for his surprise visits to the lumber camps where the trees were cut that eventually ended up as Sincere Bathroom Tissue. He'd grab an axe and take to the forest, setting a pace that even the best of the woodsmen found hard to keep up with.

The rough-and-ready-businessman torch was passed on to the next generation, resulting in Willard's dad being asked to throw out the first pitch on opening day for major-league ball games and having a TV miniseries loosely fashioned after his life.

As Willard came into manhood, he found himself faced with a major legacy to lug around, plenty of money, and not one living clue as to how the money was made. And he didn't *want* to know. About all that Willard wanted was to be regarded as smart, rich, and—more than anything—tough.

So it was that in his search for the perfect role in life to play, Willard got it in his head that he wanted to be a fisherman. The thought hit him one afternoon as he was sprawled out on the couch in a full-dress NASA space suit, watching video tapes of moon missions, sozzling Kool-Aid, and munching on gourmet popcorn. Willard wiped his buttery fingers on the front of his astronaut outfit as he watched one of the old Apollo capsules splash down.

The pickup by the Navy was a routine one and the aircraft carrier with the space crew aboard was shown returning to harbor. Willard, frankly, was starting to get a little bored with the whole thing and was just getting up to turn off the VCR when he saw it. A handsome little Eastern rig dragger chugged in by the massive Navy ship—dwarfed by the giant, but somehow looking powerful and, well, *tough* just the same.

Willard dropped his empty popcorn bowl on the floor and stared at the screen, his orange Kool-Aid-ringed mouth hanging open.

In his mind, the fishermen were definitely the stars of the show. The astronauts looked sort of pale and shaken compared to the crew of the dragger, swaggering around the deck, coiling up lines.

Willard took quick and immediate action.

Within seconds, he wriggled out of his space suit and was out the door, on his way to have a fishing boat built. He had no idea what you actually *did* with a docking line, but he would get some—the best that money could buy.

He would make his mark in the fishing world, Willard decided, as he roared off down the street in his Corvette, dressed only in the underwear he'd worn under the space suit.

≈

It took a number of attempts before Willard found a designer and builder who would help him fulfill his dreams. The simple fact he didn't have the least bit of an idea as to what sort of boat he wanted or what he wanted to fish for did turn out to be a major stumbling block.

This resulted in Willard's being dismissed as a flake and thrown out of the first three offices he barged into, the initial one while still in his underwear.

Even after purchasing a new wool sweater, jeans, a full set of oilclothes and boots, Willard's luck was no better. Plus, the temperature out on the street was in the mid-80s and he was dripping with sweat, bordering on having a convulsion with all that gear on.

Things were looking pretty bleak when Willard was suddenly struck with an idea. He double-parked the Corvette in front of a newsstand and clomped up to the vendor, demanding the latest copy of any fishing publication. Shoving a wad of sweat-soaked dollars into the man's shirt pocket, Willard grabbed the paper offered to him and raced clumsily back to the car.

Quickly he tore through the pages until he found what he was looking for. There on the center spread was a photo of a handsome fishing boat looking something like the one he'd seen in the NASA video. Close enough. It was identified in the caption as a longliner, which meant nothing to Willard except that the big pile of balloons on deck looked kind of neat.

Fortuna was really smiling on him now, as on the same page as the boat photo was an ad for "FARNSWORTH BOAT BUILDERS—We design and build, you pay and leave."

Within minutes, Willard was standing in the Farnsworth office flapping his arms excitedly and pointing at the picture of the boat. Old Man Farnsworth was grinning around a mouthful of cigar and rubbing his hands together.

They were a perfect match.

≈

Actually, when it was all said and done, Mr. Farnsworth probably wished that Willard Bumsfurd had never come lathering into his office. Farnsworth was a firm believer in the fact that a fool and his money are soon parted and that somebody should be in charge of such things. Over the years, he had successfully done business with a series of fools with money.

Willard, however, was another story.

Willard didn't have a living clue as to how his boat was to be put together, but that didn't stop him from spending the next several months camped out at the Farnsworth yard (he was even charged rent on the space where he laid his sleeping bag), and offering opinions and advice constantly during his waking hours.

Farnsworth, for fear of driving off the crazy golden-egg-laying goose, had to adopt a grin-and-bear-it attitude with Willard. He gave strict instructions throughout the yard: don't argue with the insane man with the money. The result was a constant series of reworkings of the basic vessel layout.

Farnsworth began to get a little nervous after a while. He detected that Willard was getting frustrated with things—possibly to the point of going off on another tangent and forgetting the whole project.

Out of desperation, Farnsworth came up with a brilliant idea. He set Willard up in a far corner of the yard with a mountain of sheet metal, some blueprints, and a piece of welder's chalk. After strict instructions on the basics of the cutting torch, Farnsworth left Willard alone with the idea that this was a way for him to be involved, to be a part of the whole creative process. Willard could actually cut out the forms and pieces that went into his boat.

"There you go, skipper," said Farnsworth. "You get any new ideas, no problem. Just keep cutting, however you see fit. We'll take care of the rest."

This tickled Willard to no end. If only his grandfather could see him! This was not the bumbling airhead playboy Willard—no way. This was *Captain* Willard, King of the North Atlantic, creating his own boat with his own hands! This made him very happy.

And every few hours, Farnsworth would send a forklift over to pick up Willard's latest work. The lift would lug off the jagged, odd-shaped pieces of metal with their proud creator looking on. Once out of Willard's sight, the whole mess was dumped into an old quarry hole at the opposite end of the yard. Everything went smoothly.

≈

Finally, after many long months (during which Farnsworth almost went crazy himself trying to keep Willard content), the boat was completed.

The day of the launching was a handsome one: sunny, cool—a perfect fall day.

But poor Willard. His family took this new adventure no more seriously than they did his previous dozen or so. There wasn't a single one of them who had any interest in the launching festivities. This, of course, bothered Willard greatly, but he was determined not to let it ruin the moment.

He showed up that morning once again in a full set of oilgear. "Moby Dick" had been the subject of recent bedtime reading and had been a great inspiration to him. In fact, Willard had taken to wearing an eye patch the last few days.

Fortunately, there hadn't been time enough for him to have a leg removed before the launching.

Willard had insisted on busting the champagne over the bow himself, at which point he would scurry aboard for the ride down the ways.

"Aye, Matey," Willard said to himself as he got a grip on the bottle. Then, screaming "THAR SHE BLOWS!" at the top of his lungs, Willard swung with all his might, missing the boat completely, losing his balance in the process, and toppling down into the muddy shadows below the cradle.

Farnsworth and crew raced to Willard's rescue. They found the King of the North Atlantic dazed and slathered with mud, stivvering around beneath the boat.

"Did it break? Did the bottle break on the bow?" Willard moaned. "It's bad luck if it didn't!"

"Sure, sure, Cap," Farnsworth lied reassuringly. "It was a beautiful moment. Now, let's get you aboard!"

"Aye, Matey," Willard replied weakly as they half-dragged him up the ladder. He was carried into the pilot house where Farnsworth propped him up in the captain's chair. This made Willard feel a little better and he straightened his muddy eye patch around on his head.

At that moment, the boat began to rumble beneath their feet as the cradle started down the railway.

All hell broke loose.

Willard, recharged by the excitement of the moment, leaped to his feet and lunged at the controls. In a matter of seconds, he somehow managed to:

A.) get the main engine started;

B.) yank the transmission into reverse; and

C.) haul the throttle wide-open.

The boat, once afloat on its own, leapt clear of the cradle. It cut a crazy backwards arc around to the rock pile beside Farnsworth's boatshed while Willard stood in the pilot house screaming "FULL SPEED AHEAD!"

Within seconds it was all over. The boat fetched up hard and solid, ripping a large gash in its bilges. It immediately laid over and filled. The yard crew jumped clear, swimming to shore with Farnsworth in the lead, yelling "I can't stand it! I quit! I'M ALL DONE!"

Willard in the meantime, was standing on the side of the hull that was now facing skyward, slowly pulling off his oilclothes, a strange grin spreading across his face. He was watching an antique biplane pass overhead.

"Ohhhhhhhhh . . . " Willard said dreamily. "Now *that's* nice."

Chapter 9

Eddie & Ross:
The Lobster Car

I don't remember right now, but I'm guessing the winter of 1990 must've been cold enough to inspire this ice-laden Eddie and Ross story at the time.

The "carring" of lobsters (storing them in a large wooden float sectioned off into pens) by individual lobstermen used to be a popular practice. Guys would take a chance on hitting a nice winter market with lobsters they'd put in the car that had been caught during a much cheaper price period. Of course, there was a gamble involved, too—and you could easily be out a good chunk of your year's work if there was a mishap with the lobster car or the market went soft on you.

A note of clarification: hog rings are used to fasten the panels of a wire lobster trap together. I didn't want someone from North Dakota thinking we dealt in jewelry for barnyard animals here in Maine.

A disclaimer: I don't know how well Eddie's idea would work in real life. Don't try this at home, kids.

≈

48

The radio had lived a good life. It had spent many years on Eddie's nightstand as a clock radio, rousing him to go to haul thousands of times. When the time-keeping part of it let go, Eddie found the radio a spot in his workshop, where it kept him and his sternman Ross company as they worked on gear.

On this particularly frigid winter morning, the radio was spewing out the Beach Boys' "Surfing USA" when a hammer came whizzing through the air and crashed into it, goring the speaker. The whole mess tottered for a moment, then fell off its perch above the workbench and landed facedown on the floor of the shop.

Ross, from his berth in the corner where he'd been lacing heads into Eddie's new wire traps, stopped in mid-knot and stared at the smoking wreckage, which was now making bad squealing noises. Ross watched as Eddie slowly strode over to his victim, drew back his foot, and kicked the radio the length of the shop with its cord trailing along behind it.

There was a good minute of silence during which Ross was pretty well convinced that the inhuman cold spell they were suffering through had finally driven Eddie over the edge. Ross held his breath, waiting for Eddie to snap and come after him next.

"This is good," Ross thought. "He'll prob'ly hog-ring me to death . . . closed-casket stuff for sure."

Eddie, though, seemed to be content to blow off his rage in a good rave. Pointing out the frosted window alongside the workbench, he began.

"Surfin'? Surfin'? It's 10 friggin' degrees below zero; the wind's blowin' 20 or 30 miles an hour; the snow's halfway to the roof; we ain't been to haul since I don't know when and some idiot's got the friggin' gall to get on the radio and sing about SURFIN'? What the hell's goin' on here? Has the whole world gone crazy?"

"Now comes the part about the carred stuff,"

thought Ross, lighting up a Viceroy while keeping one eye on Eddie.

"And on top of it all," continued Eddie, "we've got a car chock full of lobsters without a friggin' home sitting out there in the harbor!"

He reached over, etched a peephole in the coating of frost on the windowpane with his thumbnail, and peered out.

"Worst cold snap in I don't know how many years," Eddie went on. "We couldn't take them lobsters out if there WAS a decent market—which there ain't—and them fools on the radio wanna go SURFIN'?"

He spun around and looked at Ross, who blew out a charge of smoke and shrugged, knowing that Eddie's raves never required a definite answer.

The assaulted radio had come to rest against a pile of bricks that Eddie had gotten for free when a local contractor tore down an old schoolhouse nearby.

Eddie walked over to the bricks. "I think the friggin' bears got the right idea," he said in a calmer voice. "Oughta hibernate right through this mess—get up in the spring an' go to haul."

Ross watched as Eddie bent to pry the hammer clear of the radio's insides. He had just wrapped his hand around the handle when he stopped and stared at the bricks. Ross had seen that look on Eddie's face before: the wheels were turning.

Eddie straightened up and kept staring at the bricks for another minute or so. Then he walked back to the window and with the top of a can of spray paint, scraped the pane completely clear of frost. The view out over the harbor was pretty bleak—and looked awfully, awfully cold.

It was still quite early in the season. Until the last few days, the water in the cove had been warm enough and the wind blew so fiercely that only the shore bore any amount of ice. But the savage, record-busting freeze was gaining ground all too quickly. With a calm spell promised for that night, an iced-in harbor seemed inevitable. As of that hour, a trip off to Eddie's boat and lobster car in his outboard would be possible—but it would probably be the last one for a while.

Eddie took a deep breath and let it ease back out slowly. He rubbed his chin, then his cheek, working up to a good swipe through his hair that knocked his hat onto the floor. Eddie ignored the hat and just kept staring out at the harbor. If Ross hadn't gone into a bad coughing fit at that point, Eddie might have stood there forever. But Ross' gagging brought him around.

"Come on, chum, get your gear on," Eddie said as he bent to pick up his hat. "We're gonna get ready to hibernate."

≈

For a number of years, Eddie used a skiff that his father had built as a tender for his lobster boat. But the old rowboat was getting shaky, and when the opportunity came during the past summer to buy a fairly beamy outboard boat with a decent motor from one of the seining outfits, Eddie was tickled. "It'll be handy for a lot a stuff," he said to Ross at the time of it. "You could even take the family on a Sunday picnic now and then."

This day was no Sunday picnic.

Bundled in every piece of clothing that they could possibly get around them, Eddie and Ross were lathering out through the frozen harbor in the outboard, loaded down with bricks and a few empty crates.

It was no easy passage. Without question, one more good overnight freeze would take care of things in good shape.

The action repeated itself many times; with the men

rocking from side to side in sync with each other, the boat would ride up onto the ice and plunge through with a dull "shwump." A number of times, the ice was simply too heavy in places, big solid junks of whiteness that the outboard would fetch up on. Ross would push off with an oar while Eddie backed the motor down, being careful not to drive the prop into the ice cakes in their wake.

The wind was bitter, cutting the men's breath short and wearing them down quickly. At one point, Ross felt his pockets for a Viceroy, but figured he'd better hold off until they made the lobster car.

"Friggin' smokin'," Eddie said, wheezing. "Why dontcha find some other nasty habit?"

"Yeah, I oughta," answered Ross, rocking the boat in time with Eddie. He paused to turn and poke Eddie in the belly with the butt of the oar. "Maybe jelly donuts, huh?"

"Shut up and rock," Eddie growled.

Just as it seemed that they plain wouldn't make it, the ice eased up a bit and the going became a little easier. Eddie brought the boat up alongside of the lobster car and Ross got out and made the painter fast.

The men paused for a minute to get their breath, then went to work. The top of the car had a thick coating of ice which they went at with a maul and a hatchet.

"You want to pry open the doors and take a look?" asked Ross.

Eddie paused with the maul and shook his head. "Nope. What's in there's in there. Last time I checked, they was pretty peaceful and hadn't been feeding. That's all I wanta know." He went back to pounding.

They cleared spaces the size of a crate on the four corners of the lobster car, then midway along each side. Ross fetched the crates from the boat and slid them to

Eddie, who, armed with a charge of 10-penny nails, began fastening them to the top of the car. Once that was done, they began filling the crates with bricks, spreading the weight evenly around the car.

When the first charge of bricks was used up, Eddie and Ross climbed aboard the boat and headed back to shore.

Their path from the first passage had filled back in some, but it was still a lot easier going. Once back to the dock, the men loaded the rest of the bricks from Eddie's pickup into the outboard. Then they headed back off.

Eddie gazed out to where his lobster boat, Mr. Kelp, sat on its mooring. He cleared his throat and then turned to face Ross.

"I ain't worried about the Kelp—everything's drained, and when the ice starts to go, we could always get aboard somehow and get her started if the moorin' starts to drag." Eddie pointed to the lobster car. "I remember the Old Man tellin' about cars comin' apart in the ice, or goin' ashore when the ice left—helluva mess."

They were alongside the lobster car again now, and began loading the crates once more. The top of the car began to wash as Ross passed the bricks to Eddie, who spread them out amongst the crates.

Before long, the car was listing in good shape to whatever side that Eddie was standing, dipping him almost knee deep on his last crossing. That was enough. Eddie swung aboard as Ross undid the painter.

The car was slow to even up this time, and was still under the surface when it did.

Eddie worked the boat along to one end and Ross cautiously placed a few more bricks into the nearest crates, which were just breaking water. The car held steady for a minute or so, then the close end began to settle. Quickly, they guided the boat around to the lighter crates and Ross loaded in some bricks, wanting the car to go down as evenly as possible.

When it finally happened, it happened quickly.

There was no drum roll, bugle call or siren—one moment the lobster car sat there, wallowing beneath the surface, then it was gone. Sunk.

Eddie let the outboard idle in a circle around the hole left in the ice. Staring down into the water, he waved his hand and said, "See ya later, guys . . . We'll send a diver down when the coast's clear."

Eddie swung the boat around and headed for shore. Ross hunkered down in the bow out of the wind and wondered if they'd done the right thing.

Of course, he reasoned, the only option was to have Eddie go insane, so there was actually no question: it was done and it was good.

Ross cocked his head to listen. It was hard to tell over the wind and the noise from the outboard, but it sure sounded like Eddie was singing "Surfing USA".

He didn't dare to turn around.

Chapter 10

Eddie & Ross:
Alewives

Does anyone stay up all night going after alewives for lobster bait anymore? No? Well . . . you don't know what you're missing.

Oh—and the whole thing with the crate at the end? It could happen. Trust me—it could happen.

≈

It was spring, when an alewife's fancy turns to swimming upstream in its annual spawning ritual.

Ross rebraced his knees against the dashboard of Eddie's speeding pickup and struggled to get a Viceroy fired up.

"This is my friggin' life," he said to himself, coming clear of the seat as Eddie took a fairly rough frost heave at 50 miles an hour. "If I ain't gettin' the tar beat outta me on the boat, then I'm starin' right into the jaws of death aboard this truck!"

Ross turned to Eddie, who was humped over the wheel—a solid mass of concentration and nerves, white knuckled and unblinking—and opened his mouth to lodge a complaint about the ride he was getting. At that moment, Eddie took a hellishly bad rut at just three times the speed he should have and the whole truck came off the tar, big time. Ross' head rammed into the ceiling of the cab and then he collapsed against the door, dazed.

Eddie's attention flipped for a second to the rearview mirror. "Damn!" he exploded. "We lost a crate!"

Eddie reached over and slapped Ross on the arm. "Hey, quit dozin'!" he snapped. "Your cigarette's burnin' a hole through your vest. Look in your mirror and see if you can see that crate."

His brain screaming in pain, Ross thumped at the butt searing his breast pocket, burning his palm in the process. Following Eddie's finger, which was jabbing wildly towards the passenger-side mirror, Ross squinted his eyes and could just make out one of their empty alewife crates going end-over-end into the dust cloud behind them. As the crate disappeared, first one, then two trucks came into sight, gaining slightly on Eddie until they fetched up bad on that same rut. Ross' head hurt too much to watch any further.

"Looked like that crate was still in one piece. It went hallahoopin' into the puckerbrush," he said to Eddie. "You want to go back and get it?"

Eddie shot him a look of total disbelief. "ARE YOU CRAZY?" he yelled. "WE'LL LOSE OUR PLACE IN LINE AT THE BROOK!"

Ross clamped his hands to the sides of his skull to keep it from coming apart.

Alewives, he decided right then and there, should come with a warning label on the sides of them. "Bad craziness."

Actually, the way things had been going, Eddie and Ross wouldn't miss the lost crate, as they still had a couple aboard. They, along with half the other lobstermen in the county, had spent the last five nights at the alewife brook. Three times they came home with only a single crate for their efforts, and the other two times they returned empty handed.

The few alewives that they had been able to lay hands to proved their value. A change of taste looked pretty good on a one-night set—and if you were one of the lucky ones with alewives on, well . . . it didn't hurt.

Unfortunately, there weren't enough alewives to go around. The town bailed them up on a first-come, first-served basis. Each of the five nights that Eddie and Ross had been at the brook, they had been within a half-dozen trucks in line of success or failure. The night before, in fact, the truck in front of them had slapped the cover closed on a slack half-crate of alewives just as the guy in charge of the trap hollered, "That's it fer tonight, boys!" leaving Eddie and Ross weary, bleary-eyed, and empty handed.

This had left Eddie in a very bitter frame of mind all the next day down the bay. Ross avoided him the best he could aboard the 38' Mr. Kelp.

As far as the rest of the lobster fleet was concerned, everybody was watching how long everybody else stayed out. There wasn't much radio talk, and by midafternoon a good part of the boats were working their way back up the bay.

At three o'clock, Eddie turned to Ross and snapped, "That's it, we're headed in."

Everything was a full-throttle tear from then on: a mad race into the wharf, a scurry to get the boat unloaded and on the hook—even a hipboot-clad dash through the parking lot to Eddie's truck. Melvin Thompkins, who had nosed by the Mr. Kelp just as they came into the cove, made the mistake of slowing his pickup down for the stop sign at the end of Main Street. Eddie blew out around him with Ross still struggling to get his door closed.

This was serious stuff.

≈

There were two ways to get to the alewife brook—
a two-lane gravel secondary road that branched off
from the highway, and a much shorter (but also much
rougher) logging path which ended on a bluff overlooking the fish trap.

There was no doubt in Ross' thumping head which
route Eddie would take.

The logging path split off at the entrance to the
gravel road, which they were rapidly approaching.
Actually, to Ross, it really didn't matter which way
Eddie intended to go, as they were rolling much too
fast to make the turn.

The handwritten "ALEWIVES" sign flashed by.
Thirty yards remained to the sharp left hander leading
to the brook.

Ross cleared his throat. "I'd really like to say somethin'," he began, but was cut short as Eddie made his
move.

Stumping on the emergency brake, Eddie open-
palmed the steering wheel hard down to the left. The
truck swung crazily around, the centrifugal force pin-
ning Ross against his door. One complete loop carried
them deep into the entrance of the brook road, whipping up a tornado of gravel dust in their wake.

Eddie let the pickup spin one more time, snapping
the emergency brake release at just the right moment
while pumping the gas pedal. The truck started up
on two wheels, threatening to tip over, then slammed
down on all fours and rocketed down the mouth of the
logging path.

From Ross' vantage point, his face mashed up
against the passenger-side window, the view in the
mirror was amazing. The dust cloud behind them
looked like something out of the Wizard of Oz. It
would take a couple minutes for the trucks that had
been tailing them to even find the entrance.

Ross got himself propped up and was about to ask Eddie where he'd learned to do that when they struck the roots and stumps.

WHAM! WHAM! WHAM! WHAM! WHAM! WHAM! WHAM! WHAM! WHAM! WHAM!

The undercarriage of Eddie's truck hammered out unmercifully, punctuated by savage leaps into the air when they'd crest a bad stump.

They were rapidly approaching the bluff that over-looked the fish trap. Ross wasn't sure just how high the drop was, but knew he didn't want to watch. Arms now braced against the dash, Ross closed his eyes just as the truck launched into the air. The engine raced crazily as the tires spun freely. Ross was about to crack one eyelid open, convinced that Eddie had somehow overshot the target and was going to smash them into the side of the moon, when they touched down. Hard.

This time Ross actually lost consciousness when he slammed into the overhead, landing in a heap on the floorboards with his face jammed into a heater duct. He had no idea how long he'd been out when Eddie shook him awake.

"Well, I'm glad SOMEBODY got some rest," Eddie said as Ross struggled to lift his skull above his shoulders.

"Ooooooooooooooohhhh," Ross moaned, "Are we dead?" Then, remembering what he'd gone through all this for, he asked, "What about the alewives?"

"Got 'em already," said Eddie matter-of-factly, "while you was snoozin'. Damn good thing we took the short cut or we wouldn't have got any. One crate again, but it's better'n nothin'."

Eddie opened up his door and slid out from behind the wheel. "Here." he said to Ross, "you drive on the way back. IF you can stay awake, that is."

Ross sighed and then eased gently across the seat.

"Yeah, no problem," he said weakly. "I'm all rested up."

≈

Compared to the run to the brook, the drive back to the wharf was pretty uneventful. The worst part for Ross was the bad explosions and cymbal crashes inside of his head.

Eddie had always been pretty intense, and once struck with an idea, would fasten onto it solid. But this alewife experience was about the worst Ross had ever seen him. Sitting on the passenger side now, Eddie looked peaceful and calm—strangely so.

"Dr. Jekyll and Mr. Alewife," said Ross.

"Whatcha say?" asked Eddie, leaning to turn down the radio. A country station had been playing, but didn't sound all that great—the speakers in the doors of the cab had gotten dislodged during one of their savage landings and were rattling badly.

"Nothin', just talkin' to myself," Ross replied. He really didn't feel like heavy conversation. "What do you want to do with these things tonight?"

Eddie thought for a minute. "I guess I'd just as soon bring the boat into the wharf and load them aboard while we're rollin'. We'll just leave the Kelp tied up to the float tonight. Then in the mornin' we can just jump aboard and go."

"Sounds good," agreed Ross. They were only going to get a couple hours' sleep, anyway—he'd just as soon know that the precious alewives were aboard.

"Hey, Ross?" asked Eddie. "You feelin' okay? I wasn't goin' ta say anything, but you been actin' kinda strange tonight."

Ross had started to yawn, but the pain in his head cut it short. "I feel great," he said. "Just great."

≈

They were at the wharf by midnight.

After helping get the crate out of the back of the truck, Eddie went off in the punt to get the Mr. Kelp.

Ross remained on the wharf, leaning against the bait shed, too beat to even smoke. The welts on his head had swelled so badly that his hat wouldn't fit, and his brain was chock full of badly out-of-tune bells.

Eddie idled the boat into place beneath the hoist and cleared a spot for the crate just aft of the baitbox.

"OK!" he hollered up to Ross.

Ross peeked out over the edge of the wharf at the Mr. Kelp waiting below. They were in the throes of a full moon low-drainer tide, and the view of the long drop made him dizzy. Ross stepped back, took the tackle line for the hoist in his hands and took a strain.

No go. The crate was rounded up in good shape—a capacity crowd.

Ross took a turn around one of his gloves, then bore down on the rope. The crate lifted slightly and Ross nudged it out with the toe of his boot. He was holding his breath with the strain, touching off a bad fireworks display behind his eyes.

"Come on, come on," hollered Eddie from below as the crate bobbled on the edge of the wharf, the very end of it fetched up on a nail.

"Hold yer water," said Ross, and he gave the crate a kick. Out it swung, with an alewife or two sliding off and dropping onto the dock of the Mr. Kelp waiting below.

"Are you gonna throw 'em down one at a time or are you gonna send that friggin' crate down here?" bellowed Eddie.

Ross never heard a word. His throbbing head was forgotten in a flood of horror as he watched one of the crate's beckets—a sunburnt chunk of poly—slowly explode.

"Poof" went one strand, unlaying itself a few turns.

"Poof" went a second strand, whipping around the standing part.

Ross stared at the remaining piece, unable to think, breathe, or move.

"Poof" went the last strand, and the crate swung down, fetching up hard on its one good becket. A charge of alewives rained down on Eddie, who was too dumbfounded to even shield himself with his arms.

Ross was frozen, watching as the end of the crate— badly splintered from the beating it had gotten in the back of the truck—slowly pulled itself apart.

"Let it down!" screamed Eddie from below, "Let it DOWN! LET IT DOWN DOWN DOWN DOWN DOWN DOWN DOWN —"

The end pulled out of the crate with a sickening creak and the load of alewives disappeared from Ross' line of vision. There was a heartbeat of silence followed by a nasty sounding crash and a splash.

Ross fainted.

≈

"Sea Dog—you on here, Bob?"

"Sea Dog back—go ahead, Ronnie."

"Yeah, uh, is Eddie out? I ain't seen or heard him all day."

"Well, I don't know, Ronnie . . . when I left this mornin', the Kelp *was tied up alongside Eddie's wharf. I was thinkin' he musta had somethin' in the wheel."*

"Why's that?"

"Well, Eddie was just sorta standin' there, starin' down inta the water. Never moved the whole time I see him. Never waved or nothin'."

"Huh. Well, hard ta tell with Eddie. Okay, just wonderin'. See ya later, Bob."

"Yep—see ya later. Sea Dog out."

Chapter 11

Josh & Dot: Wedding Day

Ah, yes. June of 1990 seemed to be a good time for an old bear and his one true love to make things official. There'd been some demons for Josh to wrestle along the way (the reference to the broken leg), but he'd finally admitted a few things to himself.

By the way—if you're not familiar with the song "Hands On The Wheel", then you need to do something about that.

≈

"At a time when the world seems to be spinning
Hopelessly out of control,
There's deceivers and believers
And old in-betweeners
That seem to have no place to go."

Right up until the moment he mouthed the words "I do," standing before the local minister in Dottie Nickerson's living room, Josh Bollard never doubted for a second that marrying Dot was the best thing he had ever done in his fifty-odd years of living.

And the odd flash of fear that struck him in the gut as he made his pledge didn't really have as much to do with Dottie as it did with Josh himself. Every stupid mistake he'd ever made poked at him right then and said, "Hey, great—now you can let somebody *else* down besides yourself."

All of a sudden it was very hot and hard to breathe and those fears were burrowing right into Josh and he wished he was somewhere—*anywhere*—else but here, because he'd just end up frigging up again somehow and it would be better if he was out on a boat—*any* boat—because then he'd be in his own world and he was good at that and if he had a drink—just *one* drink—maybe that would make it better and it had been a *long* time since he'd had a drink, because the last time he'd had a drink was . . . was . . .

Was the last time he'd frigged up. And the last time he'd frigged up, Josh had frigged up bad, with a broken leg to show for it. And by doing all that—by digging into a head and heart full of questions—Josh had found the answer that put him in front of this preacher in Dottie Nickerson's living room.

For all that sharing your life with somebody asked of you, it could give a lot in return. And Josh knew that was what he wanted and needed.

It took just a few seconds for all those thoughts to run their course, for the rumbling fears to be washed away by a wave of comforting realization.

And by the time it had passed, Josh Bollard was a married man.

> *"It's the same old song.*
> *It's right and it's wrong*
> *It's the way that I feel about you*
> *And with no place to hide. I looked deep inside*
> *And I found myself in you.*
>
> *"And I looked to the stars, and I tried all the bars*
> *And I'd nearly gone up in smoke*

> *Now my hands on the wheel of something that's real*
> *And I feel like I'm going home. "*

The local VFW hall was chock full, waiting for the bride and groom. Josh had insisted on nothing more than an open invitation to all their friends in the local paper ("No fancy invites," he'd said. "Most of the folks I know, they don't dare go to the mailbox this time of year if fishin's slack."), and that had been enough.

Grub was stacked on tables that ran the length of one wall. A good haul of spring lobsters had given their lives in the name of finger rolls and a damn good tow was represented by the kettles of chowder sitting on warming plates.

Darryl Owsley stood on the front steps of the hall and sipped at a cup of Myers rum with a splash of water in it. "This is a good thing," he was saying to Sparky Hanson, who stood on the step below him. "Them's two of the nicest people I know."

"Hard to believe, though, ain't it?" said Sparky, who'd cut short an offshore lobster trip on his *Nicola* to be in in time for the wedding. "It didn't seem like Josh was ever goin' to get married." He wiped a trace of beer foam from his beard. "He never acted like he cared about that stuff."

Darryl caught sight of Dottie and Josh rounding the bend at the foot of the hill leading up to the VFW hall. They were walking hand in hand, with Dottie's four-year-old grandson Billy clutching Josh's other mitt.

"I don't think," said Darryl with a smile, "that he ever gave himself a chance before now."

> *"In the shade of an oak down by the river*
> *Sits an old man and a boy*

> *Setting sails, spinning tales, and fishing for*
>   *whale*
> *With a lady that they both enjoy. "*

The afternoon was full of grins and handshakes and slaps on the back. The bleakness of the past winter was truly forgotten—and even though spring wasn't looking all that good so far, well, there was still time for things to straighten out.

It seemed like the marriage of Dottie and Josh made a spark that fired the hearts and souls of everyone who came to the VFW hall that afternoon. There was no other way to explain the feeling than to call it hope—and the reminder that things don't always have to have a sad ending to be real.

It was just prior to the last waltz of the evening when Josh was prodded into getting up on the bandstand to say a few words. And although he didn't have a clue as to what he was going to say as the crowd cheered him, the words came easy once he began to speak.

"I gotta tell ya—and this is the honest truth—this is the happiest day of my life, right here.

"And I'll tell ya somethin' else—I'm the luckiest guy in this whole world. I'm lucky 'cause I got so many friends and I'm lucky 'cause I'm marryin' my best friend of all."

The explosion of applause from the crowd made any further talking impossible, which was fine with Josh as his joy was making his eyes shiny and his throat tight.

As the band eased into "Hands On The Wheel," the one special song that Josh and Dottie had asked to be played during the reception, Dottie came forward and stepped into the old bear's arms. He rubbed the back of one paw across his eyes, then whispered into Dot's ear, "I guess this is the last dance, Dot."

She smiled as he held her and they began a slow circle around the dance floor. "Well, then let's dance backwards, Josh . . . they say that way it'll last forever."

One way or the other, they both knew it would.

> *"It's the same damn tune as the man in the moon*
> *It's the way that I feel about you*
> *And with no place to hide, I looked in your eyes*
> *And I found myself in you.*
>
> *"And I looked to the stars and I tried all the bars*
> *And I've nearly gone up in smoke*
> *Now my hands on the wheel of something that's*
> *   real*
> *And I feel like I'm going home."*

"Hands On The Wheel" was written and recorded by Willie Nelson, from the album Red Headed Stranger.

Chapter 12

The Amazing Grace: One for Abe

This was the last of the Amazing Grace stories—and a good way to say good-bye to those folks, I thought. What was in that tobacco can? You tell me . . .

≈

It was the first time any of the men had been in the boatshed since old Abe had passed away. In fact, none of them had entered the building since they all (including Abe) had put the *Amazing Grace* to bed the previous fall after a successful boat racing campaign. And they wouldn't have been there now if it hadn't been for the attorney's phone call.

Each of the crew—Philmore, the packrat wheeler-dealer; Walter, the wrench man; fiery Lester Junior, the *Amazing Grace*'s pilot; and grumbly Burt, the unofficial "coach"—had plenty of time, sweat, and love invested in the *Grace*. But Abe was the original owner of the hull, and without him, it didn't seem to be right to be thinking of the lobster boat races. Nobody had made an official "throw in the towel" speech—but none was needed. In the men's hearts, they had all decided: the *Amazing Grace*'s racing days were over and done with.

The boat sat in the coolness of the shed, looking handsome. To anyone who didn't know the *Amazing Grace,* it took a close inspection to realize that her sleek 40' hull was wooden and not fiberglass, she was so smooth. And the men had been lovingly thorough in readying the *Grace* for her winter's nap, both mechanically and cosmetically. She sat in fighting trim, needing only a few days in the water to swell her seams.

One by one, the men looked at the *Grace,* then turned away, choosing to stare at the overhead rafters or their shoes. Burt found his attention drawn to Abe's pile of chewing tobacco cans in the far corner of the shed. "Must be a thousand of 'em," he said to himself. "That'd be just about a year's worth for Abe."

Burt grinned, shook his head, and sighed deeply. He turned to the attorney who'd been waiting for them in the boatshed.

"Well, Mr. Attorney," Burt said, "whatcha see is whatcha get. This is the whole of us. Now how about lettin' us in on why you called this little meetin'?"

Burt grabbed a cigar out of his jacket pocket and chomped down on it.

The attorney grinned at Burt and shrugged his shoulders. "Fair enough, Mr. Woodward. We may as well get to the point.

"My name, as you may or may not know, is Michael Brown." There was a quiet round of raised eyebrows and cocked heads amongst the men.

"That's right, Abe Brown was my uncle. I remember when he first came to our office to have a will drawn up, he said I was probably the closest thing he knew of to a lawyer he could trust."

The mood was eased somewhat as the *Amazing Grace*'s crew exchanged looks.

"Sure sounds like Abe," said Walter.

"Yeah," agreed Lester Junior, "I can see him standin' there a'tuggin' on his ball cap an' lookin' for a place to spit."

"You must be Abe's sister's boy. I remember him mentionin' you," added Philmore.

"Look, I'm pleased ta meet ya and all," said Burt. "And any relation of Abe's is the finest kind with me. But Abe's been gone for months now—way back 'round the first of the year. I know whatever will readin' there was to do was done before now. So, what's this all about?"

Michael Brown nodded. "You're right, Mr. Woodward. Uncle Abe's estate has been taken care of, distributed equally among his three children. But, there was an added clause—with two provisions. One, this meeting today wouldn't have taken place if Abe's children hadn't agreed to what I am about to tell you. And second, once I had permission from the heirs to proceed, I had written orders from Uncle Abe: 'The meeting will be held one month before the Wentwell Island Boat Races.' So, here we are."

"This has somethin' ta do with the *Grace*, don't it?" said Burt, pointing his now sodden cigar toward the sleek hull they were sitting beside. "Well, I tell ya: I don't want no part of this. We were a team, but Abe and his boat were the makin's of it all . . . that's *Abe's* boat and *Abe's* gone. Case closed."

He got to his feet and headed for the door.

"Mr. Woodward, if you truly were a friend of my uncle's, you'll listen to what he had to say."

Michael Brown's tone was sharp and his words caught Burt by surprise, stopping him in midstride. The attorney was now holding a document in his hands.

"What I have here is a letter written to you all by my uncle months before he passed away. At that point, he knew his health was deteriorating and —"

"Wait right there," said Bert. "You mean Abe knew he was gonna go *months* before he did? Like—when we put the *Grace* to bed last fall?"

"Apparently so," said Michael Brown. "And he wrote this letter to the four of you at that time. Please wait until I finish before asking any questions."

Burt rubbed his jowls for a moment, then sat down on a sawhorse. "I'm all ears, sonny."

≈

Michael Brown cleared his throat and began to read as the men before him listened silently.

"I guess my main reason for writing this," Abe's letter began, "is because you are my friends. And when I say that, I'm talking about the boat that you're sitting beside, too. The *Grace* is maybe my best friend of all.

"What we've done with the *Amazing Grace* has made me very proud these last few years. And I'd like to go out of this world thinking that everything isn't going to fly all to pieces if I'm not around to watch over you birds. Now, I've lived a fair number of years more than any of you, and that's probably one of the reasons why I know more, so listen.

"There isn't a one of us that's going to make the world stop turning when he leaves it. Life goes on. I know that, and I hope you're smart enough to know that, too. What we've started with the *Amazing Grace* has no reason to end with my not being around.

"My nephew Mike has the authority to read this only if the rest of the family agrees. Well, I guess they must have, or you wouldn't be hearing these words. That means there's no reason not to do what I'm asking.

"The *Amazing Grace* is yours, as long as you want

to race her. The boathouse goes with her, along with the extra gear and spare parts that Philmore has got stashed away around here. There's even an account down at the bank with some money in it—not much, but it'll cover your expenses. The only thing I ask is this: When you're done with the *Grace*, and you're done as a team, burn her. I'm serious. Don't let her sit on the bank and fall apart or sell her to some fool that's going to abuse her. The boathouse and the land it's on is yours to do with as you want.

"That's it. That's the deal. All I've got left to say is, you guys were never quitters while I was alive. Now's no time to start.

"I'll see you all on the other side. Don't rush getting there—I've got plenty to do in the meantime.

"Good luck, Abe."

≈

It was a good minute after Michael Brown finished Abe's letter before any of the men moved, spoke, or even blinked. And, in turn, it seemed that all their gazes ended up falling on Burt sitting on the sawhorse.

Burt's attention, in turn, was fastened on the pile of snuff cans in the corner and had been all during the reading of the letter.

He finally coughed, cleared his throat, shook himself all over, and turned to face the rest of the crew.

"Sure sounded like Abe, didn't it?"

Philmore, Walter, and Lester Jr. all remained motionless.

"You know, you guys could go ahead without me," Burt said. "I don't know if . . . if . . . well, I just don't know." He shrugged his shoulders and bowed his head.

The crew continued to watch him silently.

It was Michael Brown who finally spoke up, clear and strong.

"I think you'd be letting Abe down if you didn't try."

Slowly, Burt looked up from his feet and over at the *Amazing Grace*. He made a swipe across his eyes with his sleeve, then began slowly nodding his head.

"Yeah, sonny . . . maybe you're right. I guess we owe him that much." Burt dug through his pocket, finally coming up with a wooden match. He fired up his cigar, drawing deeply and blowing out great billows of smoke.

"Well . . . anybody know how the tides are next week?"

≈

Walter spent the next day hovering over his lathe, fine tuning the *Grace*'s propeller. His method was a little old fashioned, but effective. He would freewheel the prop on the lathe, letting it spin until it stopped. If one blade seemed to be the heavy one for a couple of spins in a row, Walter would take a grinder to it. Then he would spin the wheel again, watching for anything other than perfect balance.

Some of his concoctions in the past had been a little weird looking, but they always made for a smooth ride. This year's prop had been found by Philmore at a local machine shop, dust covered and forgotten. Walter took one look at it and told the men to haul the previous season's wheel off and put it on the shelf—this one was truly a weapon to behold.

Philmore readied his secret copper paint, laced with powdered graphite, which he always insisted on applying himself.

"You've got to move the brush right." he maintained. "You get a streak here and there, and a thick spot or two—hell, you might as well be towin' an anchor!"

He performed his duties shortly before the launching.

Lester Junior and Burt spent the *Amazing Grace*'s first night in the water aboard, watching her bilges and making sure the pump took care of what weepage her seams allowed. The winters in Abe's boathouse always seemed to agree with the *Grace*, and it never took long for her to swell to.

It was a handsome night, too good to sleep through. The moon lit up the cove fiercely, cutting a beam across the water that seemed to be angled right at the *Amazing Grace*.

Burt was standing at the wheel gazing out of the pilot house window, when his elbow nudged something tucked alongside the compass box. He picked up the little canister, realizing immediately what it was: a can of Abe's chewing tobacco.

"We'll keep ya right here by the wheel, ol' buddy," he half whispered, sliding the snuff can back in its hiding place.

Burt was still standing by the wheel when the sun came up.

≈

Walter was a sucker for a fast banjo breakdown and could happily spend the rest of his natural life listening to Lester Flatt and Earl Scruggs picking and flailing away. But if he was going to admit to his favorite song of all, it would be the roar of the *Grace*'s engine when the big Buick was tuned right on the mark.

It took a solid two weeks of fiddling and diddling before Walter got the music the way he wanted it. He finally pronounced the *Grace* ready to race late one afternoon after watching Lester Junior put her through her paces up and down the reach.

Lester Junior's eyes were snapping and his face was split into a wide grin as he idled the *Grace* back into the float where the rest of the crew stood.

"Keeeerist!" he hollered, his red hair standing

almost straight on end. "We got us a friggin' water rocket this year!"

"Well . . . she does sound pretty," offered Walter. "I guess she's about as good as she's gonna get."

"Good? Hell, she's *perfect*," answered Lester Junior. "I'd like to know what could ever get by us."

At that point, none of the men believed that anything could get by the *Grace*. Their confidence remained in place right up until race day morning.

The Wentwell Island races were traditionally the first of the summer circuit, and had been the debut of many a new model hull or engine over the years. So nobody had a living clue as to what was going on when the tractor trailer bearing the Billfold Oldsmobile entry pulled up and backed down the public landing.

It was no secret that J. Edward Billfold harbored hard feelings towards the *Amazing Grace* and her crew. His attempt to buy his way to the "World's Fastest Lobster Boat" crown the previous season by offering to finance a major repowering of the *Grace* had been spurned by Abe and the boys. Billfold was left an ugly and bitter man, chock full of thoughts of revenge.

Red, white, and blue stripes were gelcoated into the hull of the Billfold boat, from stem to stern, with "BILLFOLD OLDSMOBILE—THE AMERI-CAN WAY" emblazoned down the sides. A solid half dozen figures in matching jumpsuits ("Them California guys that Billfold hired last year" snorted Walter) swarmed over the engine box, pausing only long enough to look up when some of the entourage on the shore touched off a small cannon as the racer slid into the water.

"The friggin' circus is in town," said Burt. He turned away from the activity, patting down his pockets, looking for a cigar. There was none to be found— not even a stray one in any of the lockers down below or tucked away in a corner on the bulkhead. He saw Abe's tobacco can though, which made him smile.

"Today's the day, old buddy," he said quietly, and slid the tin back into its place by the compass box.

DAWOOO   DAWOOO   DAWOOO *DAWAAAAAHHHHHHHHHHHHH!*

The hybrid Olds aboard the Billfold entry rolled over three times, then exploded into a savage bellow. The crew aboard the *Grace*, as well as any unprepared onlookers on the shore, were frozen in place. The powerplant sounded something like an enraged, rabid animal trying to clear its throat in preparation for ripping somebody's head off. There was a minute or two of tinkering by the jumpsuited figures, then one of the crew took the wheel and punched the throttle. The results were scary.

Many people considered the Grace to be like a race horse when at speed—smooth and graceful. In comparison, the Billfold boat was vicious and nasty, slatting wildly and appearing to be just barely under control.

"If I had a dog that acted that mean, I'd have it put to sleep," offered Philmore. "It *does* go though, don't it?"

Lester Junior's head snapped around to face Philmore. "You have to be able to steer a friggin' straight line if you're going to go racin'. They can't hardly keep that mess between the shores of the reach! That ain't even a boat, anyway—it's a wedge of plastic with an engine bolted to it."

Burt rubbed his forehead and shook himself, as if to ward off a chill. "You wanta be keeping an eye on that wedge," he said.

≈

As it was, the men didn't have much of a wait for the big showdown with the Billfold entry in the "World's Fastest Lobster Boat" grand finale. There was a bank of fog hanging off outside and everyone was aware of it, keeping the delay between classes to a minimum.

Lester Junior, of course, would be at the wheel of the *Grace*, and it was decided that Burt should make the run with him while Philmore and Walter stayed shoreside.

The pace boat circled around the racers, like a border collie nippong at their heels to get them into an orderly line. Whether by intention or not, the Billfold entry ended up tucked on the *Grace*'s port side. Burt allowed himself one glance at the wildly colored beast—and looked right into the smirking face of J. Edward Billfold himself, strapped to the bulkhead of his racer, alongside the pilot.

It was like staring a chubby conger eel right in the eye. Burt shivered and immediately turned the other way. He rammed his hands down into his jacket pockets, desperately needing a cigar—and realized that he'd been so caught up in watching the Billfold boat rip around that he'd forgotten to get any more.

"Awww, hell," Butt said, and was just about to ask Lester Junior if they couldn't dart into the wharf and grab a couple cigars when they began to pick up speed. The pace boat was satisfied with the line-up and was coaxing the pack to a running start. Lester Junior's forehead was suddenly heavily beaded with sweat as he attempted to keep an eye on both the starter and the Billfold boat.

The starter's flag chopped the air and throttles were pinned a fraction of a second later. Burt looked to port and saw the wildly-bucking Billfold boat make a definite veer towards the *Grace*.

"LOOOOOOKOWWWWWWWT!" Burt screamed at Lester Junior, who had his hands full. The *Grace* couldn't afford to swing to starboard to escape the attack, as she would just be cutting off the boat on her other side. There was no alternative—Lester Junior yanked back sharply on the throttle, allowing the Billfold boat to scoot across their bow. Accident or not, the incident gave J. Edward quite an edge—and there were no apologies on his leering face.

It seemed that no one else had noticed the near-collision, as the pace boat had swung off and dropped away. The race was on.

"Dammitdammitdammit!" Lester Junior pounded his fist on the bulkhead as the *Grace* leaped ahead, desperately trying to make up lost ground. (He wouldn't realize that he'd broken two bones in his hand until later that day.)

It didn't take long for the two leaders to pull away from the rest of the pack—and despite her poor start, the *Amazing Grace* was slowly but surely gaining on the wildly-thrashing Billfold boat. But Burt could see the finish line markers up ahead and it was obvious—the *Grace* was going to run out of racecourse long before she could ever catch up.

Tears were welling up in Burt's eyes as he dug frantically in his jacket one more time—oh, for a cigar! Burt didn't dare to even look at Lester Junior for fear of cracking altogether. He was aware of a buzzing at his elbow and glanced down to see Abe's tobacco can, which had worked its way clear of the cubbyhole.

He grabbed the canister, looking again at the rapidly approaching finish line. No way could they catch Billfold in time.

Burt ran his thumbnail around the lid on the tobacco can, thinking that a pinch of snuff would be better than nothing at all. "I'm so damn sorry, Abe, but . . . we're gonna lose," Burt said, his words swallowed in the engine's roar. Then he popped the top off the can.

After it was all said and done, Walter and Philmore

would accuse Lester Junior of sandbagging; of holding back on the power until the tail end of the race for effect. And the press coverage would say what an exciting finish it was, with a show of confident strength by the reigning champ in the final seconds.

Those who were shoreside could say what they wanted to. Although Lester Junior and Burt never acknowledged it to anyone else, the fact was that neither of them was even on his feet when the *Grace* blew out by the Billfold entry.

When Burt popped the top off Abe's snuff can, the *Amazing Grace* literally leaped clear of the water her full length, throwing the two men into the platform. Lester Junior was back up first, grabbing the wheel and expecting to find the *Grace* cutting a crazy arc across the channel. He was shocked to find that they were tracking as straight as a die, and the miraculous burst of speed was propelling them out by their challenger.

"YEEEEHAWWWWWWWWW!" Lester Junior yelled, as Burt shakily got to his feet. He caught one last glimpse of J. Edward's face pressed up against the windshield, full of shock and disbelief as the *Amazing Grace* pulled away. Then they were across the finish line, and the tears were flowing freely down Burt's cheeks as he crushed Lester Junior in a massive hug.

≈

It was late evening and completely still on the water, finally. Burt had offered to put the *Grace* on her mooring by himself, and was now sitting quietly on the trunkhouse after slipping on the pennant.

The day's excitement had left everybody drained, and Burt's voice sounded pretty weak when he began to speak.

"Abe, I don't know how you did it, but I know it was you that got us out of that mess today. Now, I know what you was sayin' about tryin' and all—but sometime we're gonna *hafta* lose. I just hope it's to somebody that *deserves* to win, ya know? Anyhow, I'm willin' to keep all of this goin' fer awhile—and maybe next time you won't hafta bail us out, eh?"

There was a sudden "splat" on the trunkhouse behind Burt, and he automatically looked to the sky for the offending gull. The sky was empty, however, and Burt turned to see what had made the noise.

There was a line of tobacco juice along the top of the trunkhouse, just as if it had been spit from the open pilothouse window.

Burt grinned and shook his head, hauling a cigar from his breast pocket which was now crammed full of them.

"You know something, Abe?" he addressed the sky. "That's a nasty habit ya got there."

Chapter 13

Eddie & Ross:
The Sun Jelly

For Dick Bridges. And if you want to know why, ask my brother Stevie.

≈

It was hot. Wicked hot.

Even down the bay, the air just hung there in front of you as you pushed your way through it—heavy, humid, and just plain too frigging hot.

"Dog days," thought Ross to himself as he stood at the bait box aboard the Mr. Kelp, sweat creeping down the furrows in his forehead. "Why call 'em 'dog days'?" he wondered. "It ain't like it's special weather for dogs—they suffer as much as anybody else . . . ought to look that up in the kids' encyclopedias."

For one fleeting instant, Ross almost considered asking Eddie, the owner of the Mr. Kelp, if he had a clue as to why they called these miserable spells "dog days," but he caught himself. Eddie would normally be fit for conversation at this hour of the morning, but on days as hot as this, you were better off giving him as wide a berth as the 38' lobster boat allowed. Some days, it might be close to mid-afternoon before Eddie would speak. And it never ceased to amaze Ross that Eddie always acted as if he'd just noticed that Ross was aboard the boat with him, even though they'd probably been together for a good 11 or 12 hours at that point.

The sweat overflowed the bottom furrow on Ross' forehead and ran down the bridge of his nose, where it became really annoying. He flicked one glove clear and grabbed a couple of sheets of paper towel off the roll hanging from the overhead of the pilothouse, grinding the wad into his face. While he had the glove off, Ross figured he might as well fire up a Viceroy, which he did smoothly one-handed.

They'd been running between strings and were now approaching the first buoy of the next batch. Eddie throttled back and gaffed; Ross scooped and tucked one more handful of bait into a bag and then turned to the rail to break the first trap of the pair aboard.

"Woah!" Ross started, surprised to see Patrick Bailey and the Irish Mist right along side of them. Patrick appeared to be just starting his string, too, which for the last couple weeks had matched Eddie's gear just about buoy for buoy right along this strip of bottom known by the locals as "Noah's Rip."

Patrick's sternman caught Ross' eye and they exchanged waves, then Ross bent back to the rail. The head trap of the pair could be seen a few fathom down coming up, coming up, coming up—and as it broke water, Eddie eased up on the hauler handle slightly as Ross grabbed onto the becket with one hand and flipped the bight up over the davit with the other. The trap was landed, Eddie leaned back on the hauler, and Ross whipped the door open and dug in.

Lobsters—counters, they looked like, at least three of them and a fourth to be measured. Eddie landed his trap in the meantime and was matching Ross' flurry. Crabs, too; bitch crabs, ugly as they come—pick, sling, pick, sling, pick, sling, and as Ross pitched the last one, he reached behind him with one hand and grabbed the waiting bait needle.

Eddie was back on the throttle, winding the Kelp around in a tight circle to catch that same deep gouge in the "Rip" that they'd set this pair into last time. Ross slid a bag onto the string of his trap, then slid sideways to bait Eddie's tailer. Once done, he slapped Eddie's door shut, then his own. Eddie eyed the sounder for the word—right . . . there! Over went Eddie's, then Ross' trap, and as the warp snaked out over the stern, Ross turned to the plugging box, blowing another bead of sweat off the tip of his nose.

Out of the corner of his eye, Ross noted that they'd gotten their pair hauled and set back quicker than Patrick and his man, but once they began running, the Irish Mist was quicker through the water than the Mr. Kelp and was already slowing to grab their next buoy in the string.

Ross tried to catch the edge of his t-shirt sleeve, with a pass across his brow. This was bad hot—still, thick air that just draped itself on you. Eddie yarned back on the throttle and went for the gaff just as Ross finished banding.

"Six counters out of that pair?" Eddie asked as Ross turned to the rail, uttering his first words of the day. This almost scared Ross, who'd been watching Patrick's sternman. Ross could see from here that the kid had hove the bait needle off to one side—he'd lose time digging for it once the traps were picked.

"Seven," answered Ross. "That small one went the measure, too."

Eddie nodded just as the head trap made for the surface. Ross wound his trap aboard, flipping the warp up over the block as he blinked away sweat. With a quick glance as he tossed a crab, Ross could see that this was where they had it on Patrick—the

Irish Mist's sternman was just getting his door open as Eddie broke their second trap onto the rail. With a little dash of professional pride, Ross jumped to tackle Eddie's trap, too. Back on the throttle, wheel spun down and the doors slapped shut just as the sounder showed the edge they wanted; Eddie and Ross were on the mark.

Ross slatted a glove clear and made a quick grab for another Viceroy, noting that the Irish Mist was just slipping their head trap over the side, but gaining rapidly on them. This had blossomed into a serious challenge, without a word or gesture from either boat. You always put your head down and went at it when another boat was close—this buoy-to-buoy stuff was a matter of honor.

Eddie yanked the throttle back once again as he wrestled with the straps of his oilpants. He'd peeled off his shirt and hove it into a corner.

Gaff, into the hauler—sheaves whining as the top rope bit in.

"Five that time," reported Ross as he jumped to the rail.

"Give 'em hell," replied Eddie.

By the time they'd set the next pair back, they'd carved out a definite lead on Patrick. Ross was fired up, feeling good and on the mark; eight counters out of that pair—they'd struck.

Snap! Ross fumbled a band, not getting quite all the way onto the tips of the bander, and managed to snap himself a good one right in the eye. Keeerist, that smarted! "Dub!" he snapped at himself, blinking back tears as he turned to the rail.

"How many?" asked Eddie.

"Seven," said Ross, rubbing at his eye the best he could with a dry spot on his forearm.

"How many?" repeated Eddie, not looking up.

"Seven!" yelled Ross. This was good—he'd managed to grind a dollop of bait juice into his eye, too.

The hauler was whining, the tone deepening as the first trap got closer to the surface. The Irish Mist had just made their next buoy and their wake slapped off the side of the Mr. Kelp.

The water ran freely from Ross' eye, but he didn't want to turn away from the rail.

He tried to stare down over the side; the trap should be . . . should be . . . should be—there it was, but— "NOOO!" Ross yelled, leaping back. This made Eddie jump, momentarily letting go of the hauler handle.

"WHAT -" he began, but his words were lost as the trap exploded clear of the water, wrapped in a massive red jellyfish. Eddie made a lurch for the control, but it was too late; the trap crashed wide open into the block, and a sheet of stinging sun jelly slime splashed onto the two men.

Patrick's sternman told the story half a dozen times that evening as he waited for his check at the wharf.

"Yeah, Eddie an' Ross thought they was smart, but they don't know how to pace themselves. We blew by 'em after a while—they just gave up. The heat got em."

"The heat got 'em?" someone would ask each time.

"Oh yeah. Last I saw 'em, they was hove to, dousing themselves with the deck hose and buckets of water. They looked right feverish. Patrick said it looked like Eddie was in one of his moods, 'cause every now and then he'd try to hit Ross with the gaff."

Chapter 14

Trading Whiskers for Scallop Drags

Written in early 1991, this column was a little vignette from the scalloping years—and another thank-you to Pa.

For the record, the beard thing hasn't gotten any better with age. Just greyer.

≈

I can't grow a beard.

According to Pa, there's a good charge of Native American blood in our heritage on his side of the family, and that's just not good fuel for whiskers.

Anyhow, the fact that I can't grow a decent beard doesn't bother me, but it doesn't seem right that I should have to frig around with shaving on top of that.

It should be an option. Maybe you want to wear a beard sometime, but not right now—shave in the meantime, stop when you want whiskers. But for men like me who look like they're waiting for the wine truck to unload at the corner market whenever they try to grow a beard, there's no need of it. The whisker roots that are there serve no purpose, other than making you run the risk of slicing big chunks of your face off every day you shave.

There were a few times when I was younger that I tried to grow a beard—times when I refused to acknowledge the fact that my face was just not meant to have fur on it.

It was just about this time of year, in fact—11, maybe 12 years ago—when I took the pursuit of facial hair as far as I ever have.

My brother had taken his family on a vacation (down to Texas, as I remember, where he fell in with a bunch of guitar pickers who all looked like Hoyt Axton—but that's another story), and I took the 44' *Shirley & Freeman* scalloping around home here for a little while.

It was Pa who convinced my brother that rigging the boat over winters and towing in the bays was a sensible alternative to trying to squeeze in trips offshore to tend the lobster gear. As able as the 44' Stanley was, Crowell Basin was a hard place to be on a steady basis in the middle of the winter.

And, inevitably, it was Pa who would have the answer to a problem when were dragging—maybe a gumped-up sort of solution at times, but he helped us out of a number of scrapes.

When I was 20 years old, I was renting a place of my own (if you're ever in Stonington, it's the little house across the street from the funeral parlor—which made it keen about parking spaces if you had a big gang over), and was chock full of independence of all sorts.

Along with my duties as temporary captain, I took on the added responsibility of growing a beard. This, I reasoned, was the perfect time: head down, busy, no time for socializing; my brother was gone (sparing me great mockery about the early wino stages of the beard); and it just seemed like the thing to do.

The *Shirley & Freeman* (named for our mother and Gramp Robbins, two people my brother Stevie always said were the major influences on him growing up) was a very forgiving boat. She handled super and lifted like a champ, never offering to give you a scare, even side-to in a chop with 15' of rock drags full chock to the jaws with trash hanging over the side. There are plenty of boats you couldn't do that sort of stuff with, but the old 44' Stanley used us well.

As good of a work boat as she was, the *Shirley & Freeman* had no magical abilities; you still had to find the scallops on your own. So we spent the time while my brother was away trying to eke out a day's pay; me with my mind on running the boat and my face trying its best to be bearded.

What whiskers decided to sprout were very red, and made odd patterns around my cheeks and chin (the right side of my face featured a splotch of hair that strongly resembled Elvis' profile in his later years). To most folks, I must have looked like the government had been performing experiments on my head—but me, I could only see the oncoming of true manhood in the mirror. The hair on my scalp had already begun to turn gray at that point . . . I was going to look *some frigging wise* once I had a real beard on my face, too.

In the end, however, the fate of the beard was decided for me. What I mean is, I *did* shave it off myself, but it was a sacrifice of sorts.

We'd been towing down off the west shore of Heron Island one morning with a small dollop of success. It was sandy bottom that you could scoot right along over, and we were getting mostly sponges with some old dinner-plate-sized scallops tucked in amongst them. I was letting our circle work slowly to the east'ard in towards the shore and what looked on the paper machine to be harder bottom.

"BAWUMP . . . WUMP" came the message up the towing wire—we'd scuffed the edge of a rock pile. Sure enough, there was a whisker of a black mark on the sounder, which disappeared as we swung away towards the deeper water.

We hauled back and the drags looked a little sweeter; it was certainly worth making the circle again—maybe even give that hard spot another nudge.

Tied up, out and over. The drags were run forward on the fall, unhooked, and swung in the water as the boat turned. Watching, watching, watching . . . slacking the brake off to let the head bale disappear at the right moment on the proper angle . . . letting the wire feed out till the wob of paper towel I'd stuck on the drum as a marker appeared.

I remember that I was right where I wanted to be when we set out. And I remember that I did a little "nub math" in my head as we began our circle: "We got 'x' number of nubs that time and we towed for 'x' number of minutes, so if we stay here till 'x' o'clock and everything doesn't go all to pieces, maybe we can end up with 'x number of gallons." And I remember glancing up at the paper machine and seeing the beginning of a black sliver just as the wire went "WUMP" behind me—then it was awfully quiet.

I knew even before I turned around what had happened—and sure enough, the towing wire was hanging limp in the block: we'd parted off the drags.

I let a bellow out of me and Joe Champ (I am not making this up: a guy named Joe Champ was going with me—that was his real name, and he was the finest kind of a guy to have aboard) threw the marker that we always had ready in the stern over the side.

I felt like puking as we sailed back up the bay. I wasn't sure just what I was going to do—a diver would be great if one was handy; towing grappling hooks would be the other option. Either way, I knew life was going to be very, very grim until I got that gear back up off the bottom. I beat the heel of my fist bluish-black on the bulkhead on the way in.

I'll spare you the gut-knotting details of that afternoon, except to say that there *was* a diver handy when we got in, but he couldn't see a frigging thing by the time we got him back down on the site. The tide had begun to run hard and everything we'd stirred up that morning was now swirling and going of it. It was time to head back in and regroup—to lay hands to a set of hooks and plan for the next day.

There was something I wanted aboard even more than the hooks, though: Pa. He had the knack and, more importantly, the *patience* for that sort of thing. After explaining to him on the phone what had happened, Pa agreed to run down the bay with me the next morning and see what we could do.

"Weather don't sound the best," he said, just before hanging up.

"Yup," I mumbled.

Never mind the weather, I figured, I have single-handedly pooched the operation.

I spent the night on my own couch. The few times I began to drift off to sleep, a big recorder stylus, etching out a solid black mark, would chase me over top of a rock pile. The fact that the bushes outside were beginning to stir with wind and scratch against the house didn't help.

If the weather could just hold off . . . if we could get the drags back . . . I'd . . . I'd . . . I'd *shave*.

That was it: "Please let me get the drags back," I said to a crack in the ceiling, "and I'll shave my face."

I know it doesn't sound like much now, but you had to have been there. Deals struck in the middle of the night between a desperate boy and the powers that be are chock full of solemn resolve that should never be questioned.

I sat on the couch and waited for morning.

There was wind with the sun's coming, enough so that a lot of the boats didn't bother to leave their moorings. Pa had every right in the world to tell me that it was probably too nasty to strike out in the first place. Drags don't often grapple back the way they went out—and you want to have a half-decent chance when you're laying there with a 15' head bale with seven two-and-a-half footers hanging upside down over the side.

But Pa never said a word. He met me at the shipyard. We walked down to the float, got aboard the outboard, and chugged off to the *Shirley & Freeman* in silence.

There wasn't much said on the way down the bay, either. At one point, Pa stuck his head through the corner of the canvas that we had to close in the wheelhouse and took a peek at the weather. He wasn't long in buttoning it back up again, and stood just off to one side of me by the wheel, dripping with water from a sea we'd broken over us. I ignored him. He never made a sound - just peeled off a handful of paper towels after awhile and wiped his face.

The sun was just coming up about the time we reached the marker. Hauling around with the bow into the chop, we hove the hooks over the side and ran them out.

The next few hours were pretty uneventful. My guts made more of a rumble than we got from the wire. We made enough frigging circles to strike oil on those marks.

We hit all points of the compass around the marker buoy that Joe Champ had scaled over the side. There wasn't a bite—not an offer of anything. It was breezing up a little bit more all the time, just to add to the desperation I already felt.

I'm not sure what time it was when somebody gave us a shout from shoreside on the VHF: most everybody was on the mooring—were we going to be much longer? I glanced over at Pa, who never batted an eye. Sitting here writing this, I know that he would have hung to it with me for as long as I wanted to stay. But with the wind coming on and the tide starting to run, there wasn't much more sense in hanging to it that day. I was feeling pretty low.

"Won't be much longer," I said, then hung up the mike.

There wasn't anything specific running through my head as I made the last circle of the day, just a lot of black thoughts. I could claim great wisdom and strategic steering; the truth is, I wasn't aware of how close I was to the marker when the Old Man said, "Look out or you're gonna run that buoy down."

Sure enough, I'd let her sort of sag around on the wire a little bit and our swing was a lot shallower than it should have been. I had the marker coming right up—and awful close.

Just about that time, we fetched up. "Keep a strain," was about the only thing Pa said as I swung to haul back while trying not to get the marker in the wheel.

The hooks were heavy. We had to be into the drags.

I remember giving Pa the wheel and scurrying to get some good-sized rope for tying things off. I remember silently thanking Joe Champ for tossing the marker when he did. I *don't* remember breathing.

I stood looking over the side and staring down into the water, waiting. When there finally was a shape coming up out of the depths that I could recognize, I thought at first we'd towed into a train wreck. It looked like a mess.

Just before breaking the surface, though, something took a flip and everything shifted. I thought for a second that the whole works had parted off, but then realized just what we had—the hooks had sifted into the *last row* of rings before the clubs on the *very last drag* on one end of the bale. I leaned out over the rail to get a rope into things as the hooks broke water. I knew we had the whole works upside down and cock-eyed, which wasn't the best way to have them *but we had them.*

It was just plain too choppy to do anything right then, so after tying off the mess half a dozen different ways, we limped up the Marshall shore into the lee of Ringtown Island. There, by stoppering off, heisting, and overending, we eventually got the drags righted up and aboard. I ran down and grabbed the marker and we headed for home.

There's no sense in telling you how I felt as we steamed back up the bay—needless to say, I was one relieved pup. About the only thing Pa said was that I should take the next day and overend the wire on the drum—even though it looked okay to the eye, it was when you unlaid it and bent the individual strands that you could see how brittle it really was. Then he went below and made a cup of tea.

Anyhow, that night I kept my promise. Armed with a fistful of "Good News" shavers, I went at my face, taking it down to the bare skin for the first time in weeks (and below the surface in a couple places).

The rest of the time I took the boat that season had its high and lows. More often than not, it was a set of marks from Pa that made the high spots.

Regardless, the remainder of that winter I never went more than two days in a row without shaving.

Chapter 15

These Hands are the Hands of a Stupe

A reflective moment on my own numbness from back in the summer of '91. I was 33 by then—much older and wiser. Yep.

≈

If I had a dollar for every time in my life that I made my mouth go when I should have just shut up and listened, I'd be a rich man.

I probably *am* better about such things than I used to be, but big deal. I'm into my 30s now; I think my mind is already beginning to go (well, I *guess* it is . . . wait—what was the question?); and I'm not always sure what the rest of me is going to do at any given moment.

I suppose I should just be thankful that most of the foolishness I've managed to put myself (and those around me) through over the years hasn't done too much damage and let it go at that.

I guess my hands are the best reminder I have of what can happen when you don't want to listen to anybody except yourself.

I don't have much to look at for hands—even though they've softened up awfully since coming ashore, they ain't very pretty.

The fingers on my left hand sort of fold in under each other in the shape of an E7 chord on the guitar, which makes it great unless you want to change keys—then you've got to work at it. I can't really make a decent fist (not that I ever have much call for throwing punches). But when I do, there's a scar running from the knuckle of my ring finger pretty near to my wrist.

The back of my right hand has no scar, but there is a fair-sized hump running up to the base of my pinkie.

I could say to you that these knurls, twists, and scars represent great turning points in my life: lessons learned, moments of drama and courage, blah blah blah, and all that. But no.

All my hands really represent is that when I was 20 years old, I was a stupe.

I had, for a long time, a very bad habit of questioning just about every living thing that my brother would say to me. That, of course, isn't unusual or earth shattering—perfectly normal sets of brothers all over the world have their problems at times, I suppose—but my brother was also my *captain* for many years, too.

As I've explained before, from my earliest days of trying to develop some sort of a work ethic, it was my brother Stevie who really taught me *how* to work. If you looked in the dictionary under "driver," there'd no doubt be a picture of my brother; and being part of his efforts enabled an uncoordinated mess of baby fat (me) to buy school clothes and such when I was a kid by going lobstering and working in the shop on lobster gear for him.

There was nothing easy about my brother's method of teaching. Over the years, as the operation expanded from the two of us working out of an open outboard to a 55-footer with a full crew of four or five guys, I began to notice that the way things were explained to me was sometimes pretty intense compared to the way they were said to the rest of the crew.

That can be easily explained: my brother cared only that I became the best that he knew how to make me—he was trying to make me *be* something—but that's a hard thing to realize when you're standing in the stern of a boat and the guy up by the wheel is screeching at you. Ah well . . . I lived. And truth be known, probably if it hadn't been for some of that screeching, I might *not* have lived, so that's that.

But, back to my hands.

By the time I was 20, we'd moved offshore with lobster gear in the 44' Stanley that my brother had. It seemed like we had hip-hopped all over the Gulf of Maine for months without doing much more than burn up a lot of fuel before we landed on Cashes Ledge. (Here's to ol' old Clyde Conary—he stood by us in the beginning, and was our market for a long time when we first began getting a few off outside.) Looking back, Cashes Ledge was about like finding a piece of driftwood to latch onto when you can't hardly swim any longer. That summer on Cashes was pretty work at times—there was a little bit of money made and some recharging of courage.

Fishing trap trawls was new to us: triples off on the winter grounds was the most we'd ever got into before, so there was a lot to learn about handling gear. The way the old *Shirley & Freeman* was set up with her stern deck (one fuel tank was tucked under that with four others under the platform), all the gear was set over the side. There were no open-transom lobster boats in Stonington, ME back then.

I could make this sound just as sugar sweet as I

want to, but if the truth be known, I bet my brother and I argued about two out of every three things we did. I had a little bit of confidence in myself by this time—and what's worse, when I didn't have confidence, I had a lot of mouth. Feathers flew fairly often, but we got by.

By late in the summer, Cashes was starting to get crowded. It had been a nice visit, but it was time to leave. We began to lug gear to the east'ard, Stevie having an eye on the deep water in Crowell Basin (remember, this was a few years before the World Court put the fence up).

I honestly can't remember how or why it worked out that way, but when we left on the trip to haul some of the first gear we'd shifted to the east'ard, Pa happened to go with us—just him, me and Stevie.

I know now that a million and one things were going through Stevie's head: there were no guarantees as to what we might find for fishing in the deep water—and that was assuming the gear was still there. Me, I just knew that Pa was aboard and I was going to show him that I knew my stuff.

Now, one of the things you learn about setting trawls (usually the hard way) is that once the ground-line is running out, you need to get the next trap on the rail and ready to set. You can run your mouth all you want, but when it's time for that trap to go over, it's going over. There's no arguing the point.

I used to (once I'd learned the right way to do it) take some pride in making sure that each trap I set off the side went over flat. Every now and then as I'd swing a trap off the platform and up onto the rail, the sill would catch a bight of rope. I'd always reach out and clear the corner of the trap, although my brother would usually holler back, "Let it go! Let it go!"

I'd yell back at him, "I got it! I got it!", and get the

trap cleared just as the rope was coming tight.

My brother would always tell me, "You can't hold that trawl back—when the trap comes tight, it's got to go over and you want to have your hands clear."

Yeah, well, maybe, I figured—but I had done it *my* way and it had worked.

You can see what's coming, can't you?

We hauled back the first of that deep-water gear and knew right then and there that we'd been blessed. The lobsters were there—as good fishing as we'd seen up till that point; the kind of moment that makes you want to howl because it just as easily could have been an outright broker of a trip.

There was a lot of hooting and hollering between the two of us—Pa just grinned a little and put the bands to them.

When it came time to set back, we were fierce— this, for once, seemed like a reward of sorts for having tried. All I had in my head was that I was going to make every trap that I set count.

We were probably halfway through setting back when it happened. I swung a trap up off the platform and onto the rail, kitty-cornering it a little to get my angle right. There was a second or two pause, and then I noticed that there was a loop of rope caught around the outboard end of the sill on the bottom of the trap.

I yanked the trap back a ways and made a swipe at the rope.

"Get clear! Let it go!" Stevie yelled.

"I got it!" I hollered back, although I was still fumbling with the trap.

"Get the hell out of there!" he bellowed.

"I got it! I got it!" I screeched back at him, now sort of off balance.

Just about that time, a snarl came in the groundline

and everything drew up tight all to once. A clump of traps slid aft towards me along with a goodly-sized ball of rope. Stevie had the engine in reverse by then and was backing down as fast as he could, but there was still plenty of headway. Things were happening awfully quick.

I was in the middle of it all, glomming around and still muttering, "I got it."

Thump.

The standing part of the groundline drew tight and whipped the trap I was half-draped over up into the air. I had a mess of rope around my feet, but caught myself with both hands on the toe rail and kept my balance. The bad part of it was that the trap I'd been messing with did a somersault as the rope snapped off the end of the sill. It smashed back down on the rail before it flipped overboard.

My hands were under that trap when it hit the rail.

That's the best that I remember things. I know that I didn't even realize at first what had happened. All I knew was my left hand didn't work very well and within a very short time I was pretty useless on deck. Pa and Stevie finished off the gear we had left to haul that trip while I put the ice to my hand.

I did manage to stand the wheelwatch on the way in, which gave me time to sit and mentally kick myself for a few hours.

There's not much else to say about it all except it was my own damn fault. I frigged things up in good shape. As it turned out, my left hand was stove to a scrump and needed to be pinned up. My right, I guess, had only a cracked bone. I didn't even know I'd done any-thing to it at the time although within a month or so I pulled another stupid trick and finished *it* off, too.

Well, there was a lesson to be learned out of that, although I guess I really didn't see it till a long time after.

Maybe if I'd just shut up and listened, my hands would look (and work) a lot better than they do, if nothing else.

But you know what?

Not once has my brother Stevie ever said to me. "I told you so."

Not once.

Chapter 16

Josh Bollard
Casts Off

And then it was December of 1991 and Josh Bollard was gone. I took some grief for this, but it didn't happen out of malice toward Josh on my part—I liked the ol' bear, too. It just happened.

A note about the song: I really don't know anything else about Garth Brooks or his music (except he always wore a big hat). But "The Dance" is quite a piece of work.

≈

*Looking back on the memories of
The dance we shared 'neath the stars above
For a moment, all the world was right
How was I to know that you'd ever say good-bye?*

Josh Bollard's only written instructions were easy enough to follow: "When I pass along, don't spend three days sitting in a funeral parlor with nobody knowing what to say or do and wishing they were somewhere else.

"I want to be cremated. And I don't want to be buried in the ground. Who knows—the piece of land where you end up might belong to *anybody* a hundred years from now, but hopefully the sea will always belong to all of us.

"Have it be a decent day—don't do it in the middle of a pouring rainstorm or a snow squall, there's no need of it—and row my ashes out until the church steeple lines up with the spiling on the sou'west corner of the town dock and Smitty's Ledge is just peeking out by the eastern bluff of Big Stocking.

"Then let me go—and make damn sure that you're not downwind of me!"

You could hear him laughing as he wrote those words.

"Those marks were always good for the first trap once you'd let the mooring go. That would be a dandy place to launch."

Those words were written on a piece of undated, yellow legal tablet. The paper had been folded twice and tucked into a small manila envelope that was placed on top of the handful of documents he kept in a metal box on a shelf in the cellar stairway.

The cancer that had taken him had come quickly. If such a disease can be referred to as being merciful, then you could call his that. There was no long period of slow failure or drawn-out suffering. It seemed like one day he was chock full of life, laughing and a'going of it; then he was sick; then he was gone.

> *And now I'm glad I didn't know*
> *The way it all would end, the way it all would go*
> *Our lives are better left to chance*
> *I could have missed the pain*
> *But I'd have had to miss the dance . . .*

Apart from his written instructions, there was another part to the day that his ashes were to be spread: the music.

The men he had shared a thousand and one tunes with over the years had come to see him off. They stood at the head of the mowed field that gradually sloped down to the shore where his skiff lay on a pulley line. Two guitars, a mandolin, a fiddle, a harmonica; the sounds from these instruments over the years had made him laugh, had made him cry. They were part of who he was and it was right for them to be there.

None of the musicians spoke, none even looked at each other.

The fiddler drew on a long note, sweet and sad, and the rest followed.

They began to walk down to the shore as they played.

His widow sat in the stern of his skiff, her eyes closed, listening to the music. A very good friend of her husband's, a man he'd gone to sea with, had worked hard alongside of, and had stayed up on many a late night watch to talk with, was there to row her off on the marks. He untied the rolling hitch from the pulley line, tossed the painter aboard the skiff, and with one foot digging into the sand, pushed them off.

The men on the beach played on as the skiff cut easily through the water. There were tears, but the music never faltered.

> *Holding you I held everything*
> *For a moment wasn't I a king?*
> *But if I'd only known how the king would fall*
> *Hey, who's to say? You know*
> *I might have changed it all . . .*

The man who'd been rowing now brought his oars clear of the water. It was funny how the music had gone out of earshot just as they made the intended marks.

The widow squinted through the tears that were clustered in her eyes. She could imagine him saying, "Double-check your marks before you set." She could *hear* him saying it.

Yes, this was right. The white peak of the steeple of the town's church was perfectly centered over the sou'west corner spiling of the big pier . . . and you could just catch the ragged outline of Smitty's Ledge showing past the high barren bluff on the northern side of Big Stocking Island.

They were where they were supposed to be. These were the marks that her husband had directed them to.

Dottie Bollard leaned forward and took in her hands the brass urn that she had requested her husband's ashes be put in. Then she rose to her feet.

What little bit of wind there was was out of the nor'west, which was good. As she slowly poured him free of the urn, the slight puffs of air carried his ashes seaward . . . Josh Bollard was heading offshore for the last time.

She closed her eyes and could see him, stomping his foot as he laughed—and laughing till he cried. Then *she* was crying and knew she'd better sit down.

"I love you, Josh Bollard, you old bear," she whispered.

They began to head back to the beach.

The music ended as it had begun, with a lonely wail of the fiddle. Then it was quiet, except for the sound of the oars rolling in the oarlocks.

The musicians stood there until Dottie was ashore, then walked behind her up across the field.

As her feet struck the gravel of the roadside, she turned and looked out over the waters where her husband now rested.

The wind now gusted on hard from the nor'west.

It was a fine breeze to head off on.

And now I'm glad I didn't know
The way it all would end, the way it all would go
Our lives are better left to chance
I could've missed the pain
But I'd have had to miss the dance

"The Dance" was written by Tony Arata; recorded by Garth Brooks.

Chapter 17

Eddie & Ross:
Rock Day

Ballast rocks. A leftover from days of wooden lobster traps that needed extra weight to sink them when they were dry.

And remember, if anyone tries to tell you "a rock is a friggin' rock," well, don't believe them.

≈

It was the first day of April, and that meant only one thing to Ross as he sat on the stern of the Mr. Kelp eyeing the towline of the rowboat trailing behind—it was Rock Day.

He realized that to a good part of the rest of the world, today wasn't Rock Day. It was April Fool's Day, but April Fool's hadn't meant that much to Ross for years and years.

Having spent most of his adult life going sternman for his brother-in-law Eddie, Ross had barely enough time for the major holidays, like Thanksgiving and Christmas, let alone stuff like Groundhog Day and April Fool's.

Not that Eddie Pluggs wasn't a good man with a joke, thought Ross as he glanced up at the man himself, braced off at the wheel with his face stuck out the pilothouse window. Then Ross tried to remember the last time he'd heard Eddie say something funny (intentionally), but couldn't seem to come up with much of anything.

Anyhow, it was Rock Day.

Eddie Pluggs was one of the few lobstermen in the area to still have any wooden gear. In fact, Eddie's total gang was about half wood, half wire—with the wire pots seeing the offshore winter duty while the wooden stuff was brought in to the shop for a going-over. Eddie had some good-fishing wire gear, but he was bound and determined that there were places up inside that you had to have wooden traps for if you were going to catch anything.

"The lobsters there'd never take you serious if you set a wire pot on bottom alongside of them," he would say, pointing to this little crack or that little nubble on the chart. "It's a respect thing."

Every year on the first of April, weather and tide permitting, Eddie and Ross would make the sojourn down the bay to one of the coves on an outer island. From there, they'd anchor off the Mr. Kelp and row ashore. Working in a circle around the beached skiff, the men would get several loads of ballast rocks to use setting the dry wooden gear.

Years before, Eddie had made a conscious effort to save his rocks from spring to spring. But for some reason, they'd always come up way short when it came time to set. There were the borrowed rocks from Eddie's stash that never quite got returned; there were the ones used by the local kids to dive bomb their wooden play boats in serious summertime war games; and there were the rocks that had been gathered up by tourists (Honest," said Eddie more than once, "I bet I got two ton of ballast rocks on coffee tables and mantles all over the Midwest!").

So, after a while, Eddie and Ross gave up trying to

save their rocks and simply hove them overboard when they hauled back the wooden gear for the first time. From then on, Rock Day was an annual ritual; a sign of spring if there ever was one.

This was a fine Rock Day, as Rock Days go: sunny; cool, but not cold; hardly a breath of wind. The weather sounded good for the next few days, too. They would be doing some serious trap setting, Ross expected.

Eddie cut back on the throttle as they eased into the cove on the sou'west side of Black Diamond Island. Ross took up the slack in the towline, guiding the rowboat up alongside the Mr. Kelp as Eddie hove to.

Over the side went the anchor. Once satisfied that it had bit hold, the Kelp's diesel was shut down and the men headed ashore.

"I wouldn't have believed it if I hadn't seen it myself," said Eddie as he pulled on the oars. "Harmon Jr. took a load of gear out this morning. He never sets 'til after we do. He wouldn't know where to set if he didn't have our buoys to follow!"

Ross knew that this was one of Eddie's pet peeves: Harmon Jr. was perpetually hanging around Eddie's strings; he'd never bother a trap, but he was a wicked annoyance.

"Well, I don't know," said Ross, trying to think of a bright spot. "Maybe he's got a big mechanic bill to pay off. He's been tied up at the shipyard now for a week or more with engine trouble. I ain't got a clue what was wrong with her."

Ross knew that engine problems for Harmon Jr. would probably ease Eddie's wrath some. Every now and then, Harmon's Miss Molly would jog up behind the Mr. Kelp; Eddie'd pretend that he didn't know Harmon Jr. was behind him and keep laying on the throttle. Ross would see the Miss Molly climbing out of the water at the same time—and before you knew it, the two boats were racing wide-open all the way to the mooring without a nod, a glance, or a word between Eddie and Harmon Jr. The Mr. Kelp could hold off Harmon Jr.'s charge, but it was always a close race.

Eddie slowly shook his head and dug in even harder with his oars. Through gritted teeth, he grunted between strokes,

"Harmon-"

Splash!

"Jr.-"

Splash!

"is-"

Splash!

"a-"

Splash!

"pain-"

Splash!

"in-"

Splash!

"the-"

WUMP!

The bow of Eddie's skiff drove up onto the beach at that point, defusing the mood. The men climbed out and went to work, gathering ballast rocks by the armfuls and loading them into the rowboat.

Eddie liked his ballast rocks fairly flat, Ross knew, with no sharp edges. One time, years ago, he'd heard someone say to Eddie, "A rock is a friggin' rock." Uh-huh. That was good for a 5-minute Eddie tangent about good rocks and bad rocks and stupes who'd never know the difference if they lived to be a hundred. Since then, Ross had always paid attention to the ballast rocks he gathered to avoid any outbursts from Eddie.

They made a number of trips out to the Mr. Kelp

and back, working along as they most normally did, with hardly a word between them. Ross was used to it, not letting Eddie's prolonged silences bother him anymore than his occasional raves did. Finally, a simple "Good 'nuff" from Eddie signaled that they were done.

With the load aboard and the rowboat trailing behind, Eddie and Ross headed back up the bay for home. They were just up by the sheer bluff face of an island known as the Fiddler's Chin when out from the other side appeared Harmon Jr. and the Miss Molly.

Harmon had apparently set his load of gear that morning, grabbed another batch, and set them also. Now he was steaming in, straightening up back aft with a peek over the bow every now and then.

Ross saw Eddie tense up like a pointer on the scent. Eddie wasn't going to frig around racing Harmon Jr., was he? No way—not with a load of rocks on, plus the skiff on a towline behind them.

Sure enough, though, Eddie was laying on the throttle, trying to get out ahead of the converging Miss Molly before Harmon Jr. realized what was going on. A moment or two went by, and then Harmon Jr. glanced over and spotted the Mr. Kelp. Ross could swear Harmon was grinning wickedly as he strode up to his own steering station and gave the throttle a nudge.

The poor old Mr. Kelp wasn't up to full potential, by any means. Ross held his breath as the Miss Molly ever so slowly began creeping up on them. Eddie, refusing to acknowledge the presence of Harmon Jr. with so much as a glance, purposely looked over his opposite shoulder at the distant horizon, pretending to be searching the sky for clouds. Then he slowly turned his head a little further and stared at the big pile of rocks in the platform.

Ross thought he knew what Eddie might be thinking, but he didn't really expect that Eddie would actually say it until he did:

"Throw 'em overboard."

Ross figured that he wasn't hearing Eddie right, because even though Harmon Jr. was slowly edging by them, it wasn't anything to get wound up over and Eddie'd have a good excuse for getting beat and only a crazy person would even suggest . . .

"THROW 'EM OVERBOARD! THROW THEM FRIGGIN' ROCKS OVERBOARD!" yelled Eddie, and Ross, ever the faithful, unquestioning sternman, scrambled across the platform to the pile of rocks.

Balanced off in a crouch, Ross began dinging rocks over the side, glancing now and then to check on the whereabouts of the Miss Molly. Harmon Jr. was only a couple of gaff lengths off their starboard rail, casually leaning against the bulkhead while eating an apple out of his lunch pail.

Eddie, meanwhile, had his head stuck out the pilot house window, refusing to even glance over at the Miss Molly.

Ross paused in his rock tossing, questioning Eddie's sanity for a moment. Maybe he ought to just try to reason with Eddie and talk him out of . . .

"THROW THEM DAMN ROCKS OVERBOARD!" bellowed Eddie over his shoulder, and Ross went back to work.

A steady stream of ballast rocks flew over the rail of the Mr. Kelp as the two boats raced up the bay side by side. After a few wild minutes of knuckle-busting pitching and tossing, Ross paused to get his breath and survey the situation.

There wasn't hardly a scale basket of rocks left in the

platform—not enough to make a difference, but the Miss Molly was still holding them even without any trouble. Of course, they were towing the skiff, thought Ross, although Eddie wouldn't . . .

"CUT THE SKIFF CLEAR!" Eddie hollered at that moment. But before Ross could even get to his feet, an awful thing happened.

Harmon Jr. slung the apple core he'd been gnawing on, taking Eddie in the back of the head with it. Then he reached over and, with great grace and flair, pushed the throttle of the Miss Molly out of sight. The boat launched half of its length out of the water, settling off on a slick-sailing plane and going like she'd never gone before.

Within seconds, the Miss Molly had blown out by the Mr. Kelp. Within a minute or so, it was hard to read the name on the stern. Ross stood dumbly with his mouth hanging open in disbelief. Eddie, meanwhile, was slowly easing back on the throttle, staring at the apple core that had ricocheted off his head onto the bulkhead.

Ross sort of snapped back into focus, thinking that Eddie was now going to flip out and he would have to try to tie him up and take the boat in with Eddie laying on the platform, kicking and frothing.

Eddie, however, seemed to lose his steam altogether. With the Mr. Kelp now cut back to an easy jog, Eddie took out his sheath knife, speared the apple core off the bulkhead, and flicked it over the side. Then, tucking his knife away, he slowly walked back to where Ross stood and said casually, "Guess Harmon Jr. musta repowered when he was tied up, huh?"

Ross, taken totally off guard, nodded his head. "Uh huh."

"Goes good, don't she?" said Eddie.

"Uh huh," answered Ross.

"Well," said Eddie after a moment or two, "maybe we'll get us a load of rocks tomorrow."

Then he went back up by the wheel and Ross went back in the stern to light up a Viceroy. As he got older, Ross decided, things had a way of getting stranger. And Rock Day, for him, had sure lost its zing.

Chapter 18

Jeremy's Row Boat

Written in late 1992, this column celebrated my son Jeremy's introduction to the art of rowing a boat.

There are many miracles with children. One is the way that one day the sun comes up and they're able to do something that they couldn't the day before.

I suppose one could say that later in life the process reverses itself.

≈

It'll be three years this Christmas since the kids' grandfather on their mother's side (who all of our kids call "Buff") built my son Jeremy's row boat.

A handsome little flat-bottomed 8' skiff, she was just right for a young fellow to explore a cove with.

For the first few months, the row boat remained right in the corner of our dining room. Jeremy, who was 3 at the time, was tickled to death with that arrangement. Over and over again, he'd set the wire trap he'd also received from Granny and Buff in the shoals behind the couch, then climb back aboard of his row boat and haul the warp in by hand.

Jeremy's imagination was fairly realistic. Sometimes he'd have great hauls; other times he'd do "pretty good." Then there were the nights when you tucked him in and he'd tell you that he hadn't been able to catch hardly anything at all. "But I'll do better tomorrow." It was a fine life.

When the snow melted, the row boat made its way out onto the lawn. And by the time summer had struck, we had her overboard.

We didn't get a lot of chances to go down to the shore that first summer. But we *did* have a new pair of Jeremy-sized oars and a couple of opportunities to try them. The boy was now 4 years old; he tried rowing a time or two, but it was a little more than he was ready for. The novelty of just riding aboard his *own boat* was enough for Jeremy . . . there'd be plenty of time for rowing next summer.

Well, there wasn't. The summer of '91 saw Jeremy and I together a lot—at the boat races, sea trials for launchings, or truck driving. But we never got down to the shore to even wet the bottom of his boat.

"Next summer will be different," I said to myself. "We'll launch her early and Jeremy will be rowing wide open by the 4th of July."

Yeah, right.

I will remember the summer of '92 as one of accidents and illnesses on both sides of our family. There was a lot of stuff to try to tend to all the way around . . . and Jeremy's row boat sat idle until fairly late in the season.

We finally got her overboard about the middle of August—freshly painted and ready to go.

We eased her down the beach and got aboard. I offered Jeremy the oars. We talked for a spell about how the blades should be angled and what they actually do when they cut into the water. Then, Jeremy took a pull . . . and almost fell into the bottom of the boat when one of his oars popped out of its oarlock.

He got resettled and tried again. One oar dipped—

the other skittered across the surface without biting
in at all. I leaned over him, guiding him through the
process: "You dip 'em and pullll—long, slow strokes
are better than short, choppy ones. See how you're
really just makin' a circle with your oars? Dig in and
pullll . . . lean into it and pullll . . ."

But each time I let Jeremy go on his own, he'd get
crossed up; the more mistakes he made, the more
frustrated he got. The tears showed in the bottoms of
his eyes.

"I can't do it," he said.

"Cryin' won't do any good," I told him. He just
shook his head and looked down at his boots. "You
can't give up," I said.

He looked away from me, wiping away tears and
rubbing the rail of his boat. We drifted along and I
finally said that it was getting late and we might as
well go ashore. We'd try again.

A couple more weeks snuck by us before the next
chance came to grab the oars and head down to the
shore.

I was prepared for Jeremy to have a hard time of
it—what little bit I'd been able to show him had surely
been forgotten since the last attempt. We launched, I
rowed us out a little ways, and then he said, "Can I
have a turn?"

"She's all yours," I answered, pleased he had gumption enough to try.

I slid into the stern and Jeremy took over the pilot
seat. He eyed over his oars, angled them just so, fur-
rowed his brow, took a deep breath, leaned into it . . .
and pulllled. We scooted ahead. Jeremy never smiled,
never made a noise, just leaned into it again as he
dipped his oars and pulllled . . . we glided along.

I looked at him. "You been practicin' while I've been
workin'?"

"Nope," he said, keeping his rhythm going.

"You musta been thinking about rowin' since last time, huh?"

"A little," he grunted as he rowed us out of the cove. "I thought mostly about what you told me."

I dug into my brain quickly, but I couldn't come up with just what it was he was talking about. "What I said . . . when?"

And then he got me: "Last time when we were here—when you said you can't cry, you gotta try." He took another pull on the oars.

I do not know where the years will find us. Jeremy will always be my son, of course. I hope he will always be my friend, too.

At that moment, he was more than a 6-year-old boy rowing his dad around a quiet cove on the coast of Maine. He was my captain, quietly teaching me a lesson about life.

Chapter 19

Eddie & Ross:
Reel Trouble

My brother Stevie and I did our share of early-morning rope work on Main Street in Stonington, ME years ago, but there were never any horror shows involving ice cream trucks or randy octogenarians.

I didn't say there were never any horror shows—they just didn't involve ice cream trucks or randy octogenarians.

≈

"Volume—that's the way to go," said Eddie Pluggs, hunched over the wheel of his pickup truck.

It was 1:30 in the morning and Eddie, along with his sternman Ross, were on the way home after making a flying road trip in pursuit of a wicked buy on pot warp.

After a number of stops, their search had finally borne fruit. Tucked away in the back of Happy Mel's Discount Cordage Warehouse ("You're **Bound** For Glory With Happy Mel's!") were a couple of big, staving reels of $^3/_8$" poly, just the thing for the lengtheners Eddie and Ross needed to make up for moving gear off onto the deeper bottom.

Eddie had never bought reels of rope before: each of these jumbo rascals was the equivalent of a dozen of the coils he'd normally get—but the price was right, once Eddie and Happy Mel had worked on each other a little.

"What's wrong with it?" Eddie asked Happy Mel as he pointed to the two reels sitting in the shadows of the warehouse.

"Not a thing, not a blessed thing," said Happy Mel as he fluttered around the reels, making swipes at the dust that covered them with a big pea green hanky that matched the leisure suit he was wearing.

"How come it's just sittin' here, then?" asked Eddie.

"The color," replied Mel, as he snapped on a light, revealing the warp's odd, sort of powder-blue, tint. "It was a special order for a customer a while back and at the last minute, he went on to a greater reward."

"Ohhh . . ." said Ross, shaking his head. "That's too bad. What did he die of?"

"Die? He didn't die," said Happy Mel, giving Ross a strange look. "He made a career change and went to Nashville."

"Nashville?" Ross shot a glance at Eddie to see if he was following the story, but Eddie appeared to be in the middle of some serious mental ciphering.

"This rope is almost what you'd call a collector's item," said Happy Mel, patting the cheek of one of the big reels. "It was nearly the property of Yodeling Lonesome Hobo Smith, King of the Cowboy Six-Stringed Bass Guitar!"

"Who?" Ross asked.

But before Happy Mel could reply, Eddie announced that he'd take the reels: "Two for the price of one."

This diverted Happy Mel's attention from Ross (although he did seem peeved that the mention of

Yodeling Lonesome Hobo Smith's name didn't carry more clout). "Two for—you must be joking!"

"Nope," Eddie said. "I know and you know that if I don't lug this stuff outta here today, it'll lay in this warehouse 'til the friggin' rats eat it up. I mean, I ain't the superstitious sort, so blue rope don't bother me—but I know I never seen rope that was that color blue. That's just too weird, Mel—you gotcha a couple of dust catchers there. In fact, you oughta be payin' me and Ross for luggin' it off."

From there, Happy Mel got serious and made several counter offers. Eddie stood tough, to the point of heading for the door, claiming it was senseless to talk with this man any longer. Happy Mel herded him back, with an arm around Eddie's shoulders, describing in hushed tones the absolute bottom price he could sell the rope for and what it meant for the Happy Mel profit margin for 1992.

Ross stood there the whole time, uncomfortable with the high-powered dickering that was going on and trying to remember if he'd ever seen Yodeling Lonesome Hobo Smith on "Hee Haw."

After what seemed like hours of haggling, a deal was finally struck, cash was passed, and the walloping big reels were loaded into the back of Eddie's pickup with the help of Happy Mel's forklift.

"I like you boys," Happy Mel confided through the driver's side window of the cab as Eddie gunned the engine and prepared to pull away. "It's been a pleasure—an absolute pleasure. How long a drive do you have now to get home?"

"I don't know what kinda time we'll make—prob'ly three or four hours," said Eddie, trying to maneuver around Happy Mel without running over his shoes.

"Wait just a moment," said Happy Mel as he disappeared into his office. He was back within seconds with a rectangular object that he tossed in through the window of the truck. "Happy trails!" he called as Eddie made his getaway.

Happy Mel's gift had landed in Ross' lap. He looked down, studying the label on the shrink-wrapped package which announced that this was "The Finest Collection Known To Man Of What Could Someday Be The Greatest Hits Of Yodeling Lonesome Hobo Smith, The King Of the Cowboy Six-Stringed Bass Guitar."

If that wasn't rare enough, the collection was on an 8-track tape. Ross pondered for a minute, deciding that the last time he'd even seen an 8-track player was maybe in 1979, which sort of made you wonder about just how long Happy Mel'd been sitting on that rope, but, who was he to ruin the mood?

Eddie was happy, cranking away at the wheel and fanning the old pickup through the gears with one eye on the mirror, watching his great buys gently rocking in the back of the truck. Eddie began his chant of victory, softly repeating every minute or so, "Volume—that's the way to go."

≈

With an elegant-sounding weather report coming over the truck radio—perfect for lugging loads of gear off outside—Eddie had things pretty well figured by 2:15 in the morning when they arrived at the wharf.

They would pull an all-nighter, cutting up the new blue lengthener warps and loading them on to Eddie's lobster boat, the Mr. Kelp. With luck, by the time the sun was coming up, they'd be down the bay taking on their first string of traps to shift off outside.

"There's a trick to everything," said Eddie as he and Ross wrestled one of the reels around in the back of the pickup. Eddie had found a rugged length of iron pipe under the bench in his shop that would serve as an axle for the reels to turn on, straddling the sides of the pickup body.

After lashing the ends of the pipe down, Eddie gave the free end of rope leading off the reel a tug. Slowly, the big spool turned. "Ha!" said Eddie under his breath.

"Now," he said, turning to face a yawning Ross, "all you've got to do is run this end up there to the end of the driveway—that's our mark for 40-fathom lengtheners, right? No measurin', no nothin'—just run 'em off to length and cut 'em. Piece a' cake."

Ross nodded, took the end of the rope, and started up the sloping driveway that led from Eddie's wharf to the main drag. It took a little more muscle than what he expected to get the big reel turning.

"Hold on," said Eddie. He sprinted back into the shop, quickly reappearing with a can of grease. He globbed some around the iron pipe where the reel revolved on it.

"Now try it," Eddie said. The rope paid out a lot easier, and Ross started up the driveway again.

"Whoa, hey. Hold on a second," hollered Eddie. He ran up to where Ross was standing and took the end of the warp from him. "I'll hold this end down here while you sorta work the rope up towards the road. Just let it render as you walk and we'll end up with a big 'u'—two lengtheners instead a' one! Twice as fast! Ha!"

Ross nodded silently. Whatever Eddie wanted to do was fine with him. He gave the big reel a tug to get it rolling and then started off up the driveway one more time, paying out the rope through his hands as he went.

When Ross made the tarred street at the mouth of the driveway, he realized that he was in a little bit of a frig. Normally, they'd try to cut new rope with a cutter gun, but they couldn't really make use of one with this arrangement. No matter, though—he could always tape up the rope and just cut it with a knife. Of course, he had neither tape or knife with him, so he'd have to drop his loop and jog down to the shop.

As soon as Ross let go of the rope, it took off down the hill, quickly rolling up into little spirals, seeking its own shape after having spent years coiled up on the reel.

"What's goin' on?" demanded Eddie, squinting into the glare of the streetlight at the top of the hill. "You okay up there?"

"Yep," called Ross as he scampered after the retreating rope, humped over and trying to grab hold of one of the spirals. Ross finally snatched it up after taking a header into the driveway.

"Look at yerself," scolded Eddie as Ross slowly rose to his feet, trying to brush the gravel out of his bloodied knees. "Use yer friggin' head, Ross. You don't see me rollin' aroun' in the dirt—I tied my end off."

Eddie gestured back to the pickup, where the end of the rope was secured around the rear bumper. "See? No fumblin'—just common sense."

≈

"Now," Eddie continued as Ross started back up the driveway, "you ain't really got anything to tie to up there. Tell you what: run out a little extra and lash onto Ol' Rooster's bumper across the road."

Ross nodded, taking notice for the first time of the "Munster's Ice Cream" truck parked in the widow Rawleigh's driveway on the far side of Main Street. The Munster folks hadn't been able to sell much of their ice cream and other "fresh frozen de-lites" until Herman "Old Rooster" Harris had taken over the route.

Of course, it was to be noted that Herman's customers were, almost to a one, widows and divorced women ranging from 65 to 85 years old (he himself was somewhere in his 80s), and what was, by rights, an eight-hour circle through town usually took Old Rooster two days (and nights) to complete. Facts were facts, though: the Munster people were delighted that regardless of whatever else he had going on, Herman Harris was setting the ice cream world on fire (so to speak) with his sales of ice cream in the area—mostly "Old Fashioned Vanilla."

By the looks of things, Old Rooster was making an overnight sales call at the home of Esther Rawleigh. His truck sat with the reefer unit chugging away as Ross made the powder blue poly fast to the bumper.

He still needed his knife and roll of tape, so Ross started back down over the hill. "You know somethin', Ross?" Eddie said as he approached the pickup. "Someday when I start gettin' lamed up, I oughta just sit and write all this stuff down. Sorta like a handbook for the smart lobsterman."

Eddie looked up at the stars as he untied the end of the rope from his bumper and knotted it, "Yep. 'How I Done It' by Eddie Pluggs. And then maybe, a VCR tape, or —"

Eddie never finished the sentence. The quiet darkness was punctured by the roar of a diesel engine. "Who's that?" Eddie asked, spinning around to check the boats in the harbor. It was too early for any of the other boys to be leaving the mooring.

The sound of the gunning engine wasn't coming from below, however—it was coming from above. Esther Rawleigh's driveway, as a matter of fact, realized Ross with horror. Old Rooster Harris was letting his rig roll out onto Main Street before he turned on his headlights, unaware of the rope fastened to its hind end.

"Oh noooooo!" Eddie began to holler as he started up the driveway with Ross right behind him. "ROOSTER! Wait! No-no-no-no-nooooo!"

The yells went unheard as the Munster's Ice Cream truck tore off up the road, and the big reel of rope in Eddie's pickup began to pay out at an ever-increasing speed.

"HIT THE DIRT!" Eddie yelled as the 3/8" poly whistled up by them. Both men flung themselves into the frost-covered tall grass off to the side, watching in helpless horror as the big spool of rope emptied itself before their eyes. Every now and then, there'd be a little jerk as Rooster's tow line fetched up on a mailbox or maybe a garbage can, but things kept right on happening.

Trying to think of some bright spot to talk about, Ross cleared his throat and said, "Well, looks like pretty strong stuff, anyways." Eddie's head snapped around and he was just about to draw off and punch Ross square in the nose when the reel emptied itself.

SHWOOOSH! The bitter end of the rope pulled clear of the reel and went firing off up the driveway.

"Come on," hollered Eddie as he ran to the cab of the truck. "We gotta follow that rope! Hopefully, Rooster'll be makin' another stop somewhere right off quick!"

Ross leapt into the seat just a heartbeat behind Eddie, slamming the door shut as the pickup slid around in a crazy backwards arc. As they took off up the gravel driveway with the truck spinning its tires and slewing wildly from side to side, Ross realized that they hadn't secured the other reel of rope—in fact, they hadn't even closed the tailgate.

Ross turned to Eddie just as the second reel, sitting on its side all free and clear, began to roll out of the bed of the pickup. Eddie hit the brakes, but it was too late; the big reel hit the ground flying and proceeded to head for the wharf. Staring wide-eyed out the back window of the pickup's cab, the two men watched as the jumbo spool of powder blue rope shot out across the wharf and rolled off the far end.

There was a moment or two of silence followed by a large crash, rather than a splash. Ross looked quizzically at Eddie, who simply replied in a weak voice, "The outboard. It got the outboard, too."

Then they were in motion again, roaring clear of the mouth of the driveway with the tires screeching as they skidded sideways on the tarred street.

"We ain't lost yet," said Eddie as he rammed the straining gearbox into second.

Off they screamed into the night, watching the end of the blue rope dance in the path of their headlights. Eddie wrestled the steering wheel like a crazy man, while Ross braced off with his knees against the dashboard.

He couldn't help but wonder if, at the age of 80-something years old, he too would be in the mood for love at three o'clock in the morning.

Again.

Chapter 20

Jackie Grant
Of Munjoy Hill

Here's one written after revisiting the offshore grounds between Christmas and New Years in 1993.

I haven't seen ol' Jackie Grant for years, but I hope this finds him well.

≈

I have never met any prizefighters.

I'd like to, though. I'd like to ask them about putting your head down and going for it.

I'd ask them what kicks in in the final round when their eyes are so swollen that they can't hardly see, and their head feels like it's been pounded pretty well clear of their neck, and their arms and legs are just extensions of the pain that most people call a body—but they still haul their arse up off the stool in the corner when the bell rings and put their head down and go for it.

I have never met any prizefighters, but I have known some wicked drivers in my lifetime, fisher-men who have a pretty good idea of what that prizefighter thinks when the bell rings; guys like

*Junior Bray, George Sawyer, Lawson and Melvin
Bridges, Benny Beal, and my brother Stevie.*

*You can add Jackie Grant of Munjoy Hill in
Portland, ME to that list.*

They don't come any tougher.

For quite a while now, I've been telling folks, "I came
ashore from fishing a couple of years ago."

Well, that's a lie. It's not meant to be a lie, but after
seven years of being ashore, at some point you have
to come to terms with the fact that you "came ashore
from fishing seven years ago."

Two years on the wharf ('86, '87) plus five years
('88-'92) here at the paper. Seven years.

In that time, my family has been born, grown up,
and grown older.

My job here keeps me close to the boats, for which
I am thankful, but it's still a lot different way of life
than I used to know.

I learned how to work in the stern of my brother's
boats over the years—from the old days aboard his 37'
Campobello boat *Stevie III*; to his beloved 44' Stanley,
Shirley & Freeman, that we first went offshore in; and
then in his present boat, the rugged 54' *Stacie Vea* that
Eddie Gamage built back in '81.

I learned how to work aboard some able boats with
one of the best captains that anyone could sail with.
For that, I am thankful, as well—and I guess I never
want to get too far away from it.

The recent realization that it had been seven years
since my last trip pretty well sealed the deal. I told
my brother that if there were an empty bunk between
Christmas and New Year's, I'd like to sail with him.

Well, there was and I did.

Wayne Grindle, who fishes out of home here, usually sums up any hard situation by simply shrugging his shoulders and saying, "You gotta be tough."

From what I've seen of Jackie Grant of Munjoy Hill, he lives by the same motto.

Talking to him, you realize he's covered a lot of territory in his lifetime, both on the land and on the water. His 52-year-old hands look like they've been around the world. They've broke traps over the rail, cut fish, dug a billion worms out of the mud flats—and knocked a few dozen teeth out of heads that he felt had it coming to them at the time.

Jackie Grant has done some hard duty, some by his own choice, and some as it was dealt him. The loss of both a son and a daughter to illness a couple of years ago would have sent many spiralling off into the dark side, from which most don't return. Jackie Grant says just enough about it so you get an idea of the love, the loss, and the hurt.

But when the bell rang, just like that prize-fighter, he got off the stool and onto his feet to go another round.

It was as good of a crew as I ever sailed with. My brother will always be the one person who I have complete and utter trust in when it comes to running a boat. That's the way it is; there's none better as far is I'm concerned.

His son, Stevie III, was a kid in his midteens the last time I sailed with him during the summer of '85. He is now the mate, a man with responsibilities and experience who knows his job. When the going got tough earlier in the year, just the two of them made a few trips, my nephew and my brother. Sometimes you do what you have to do. They did it.

And then there's Jackie Grant.

> *The weather box spoke of some wind, circling the compass a couple of times over the next two or three days. My brother Stevie reached over the table and snapped it off with a grunt. There was a moment or two of silence, and then Jackie Grant of Munjoy Hill spoke up: "Well, Cap, if we go, it might not be too good . . . but you know what? We can do it."*
>
> *Time to get up off the stool and go another round.*

Maybe the hardest part of the whole trip for me was the mental wind-up before we left. Back through the years, that was always there to be dealt with, along with the wind-down when you got in.

The hours just before we left, I was wound tighter than a 10-day clock. The turning point came on the way out when I jotted my first entry in seven years in the watch log. Then it started to feel all right.

> *Down in the bait hold on the second day of the trip, ramming redfish into bags, Jackie Grant of Munjoy Hill said, "The way they got it, anybody that ever runs for president had better be right perfect. If they ever did anything in their life at all, it's a mark against them. I don't know . . . some stuff you gotta do if you're ever going to learn anything—that's just the way it is.*
>
> *"Me," he said with a grin, "I'll never be president."*

It went okay. We had a little bit of weather with an occasional fairly flat spell. There were a few lobsters and there were no bad horror-show snarls. We pulled, we tugged, we laughed when we felt like it, and we raved when it seemed to help. I kept poking my face full of wintergreen Beechnut chewing tobacco, surprised that I wasn't seasick. My nephew amazed me with his slick handling of the hauling station. Jackie finished the trip with his foot in a plastic bag inside his leaking boot.

We headed home on New Year's Eve with a fair nor'west breeze just about on the bow. During my watch, I saw Mt. Desert Rock for the first time in seven years. "How you doin'?" I said, braced off in the wheelhouse chair.

When all was said and done and the boat was on the hook, we drove down to the co-op to fetch our sea bags we'd left on the dock. Jackie Grant of Munjoy Hill still had a good three-hour drive before the trip would be over for him. It was New Year's Day and when he got home, he would park his car, kiss his wife, and go down the street to have a drink. I shook his hand and said, "I'm some tickled I got to sail with you."

"Damn right," said Jackie Grant. "That was a good one."

That tickled me even more.

Chapter 21

Bradford the Cook

*1994 began with the loss of one of the most
unforgettable characters I've ever known. Seldom
do my brother and I get together without a Bradford story being told. I imagine it'll always be that
way.*

≈

I loved Bradford, our old cook.

Bradford's full name was Bradford Henry Weed,
and he was 72 years old when he died on Feb. 7. He
was my sister-in-law Brucine's uncle, but that really
doesn't describe what Bradford meant to me.

He went cook with us fairly steadily from the late
'70s into the early '80s when we were offshore lobstering with the 44' *Shirley & Freeman* and, from time to
time, on the 54' *Stacie Vea* once she went overboard in
1981. But saying that doesn't really tell much of the
story, either.

Bradford lived for the ocean. He pulled a 3-year
stint in the Navy (1942-45) and went from there into
the Merchant Marine. Brad put thousands of miles of
a lot of oceans and seas under his feet, returning home
to Little Deer Isle, ME for good in 1971. He was our
very own frigging Popeye come to life, bent nose, pipe,
and all.

I have an early memory of Bradford, probably from about the time that he had come home off the ships. My brother Stevie and I were in the shop working on gear, and Brad had driven down the island to Stonington for a visit. I can see him crossing the street, dressed in a set of khakis and wrestling with a pipeful of Edgeworth tobacco. Bradford had a way of walking, knees slightly bent, as if he were bracing for the next old roller—or a punch.

In through the door he came; and although I really can't remember what he said that day, I know just how he said it. Bradford's tone of voice and delivery were a lot like those of the actor Burgess Meredith (you know, the guy who played Mick in the Rocky movies): a half growl with heavy emphasis on every third or fourth word and a barking chuckle that was usually directed at himself as much as anyone or anything else.

I listened to his stories: places that were only dots on the globe to me; hard weather, hard duty, and the occasional mate that needed a good thumping to get his head on straight; missed ships, missed buses, missed trains, missed rickshaws. Bradford never made himself out to be a hero or anything—his attempts to portray himself as a victim of circumstance were done with a grin and a wink.

I listened while I worked on traps. Years later, Bradford would compliment me on that, saying, "I watched ya, Bri . . . you never laid your hammer down. You're a good worker." And that meant a lot to me.

Brad was an occasional visitor to the shop over the next few years while he kept himself busy lobstering up inside with a small wooden boat he'd bought. And then came the offshore years.

Once we were making regular lobstering trips in '77, there were a number of folks who went to "see what it was like," or just to get away from some land-bound situation, or maybe to fill in during the months when I'd managed to stave up both hands or churn a hole through my guts.

And somehow, out of the shuffle of crew that had come and gone, it evolved into a core group of Stevie and I, another man to help work the deck, and Bradford - who had officially become the cook.

There were a lot of cooks who passed through our galley, each memorable in his own way. But there was only one Bradford. I can say this now because we *always* said it to him then: to be honest and true about it, Bradford wasn't much of a cook.

Many a trip went by when the only thing we'd have to eat for several days would be Hydrox cookies and chewing gum, along with your choice of lukewarm instant coffee, Coca-Cola, or Ballantine Ale. Weather was a problem at times, and there's no question that the stove had its share of bad spells, too. The thing was, Bradford always seemed content to sum things up with a shake of his head, saying, "The damn elements are against us, Bri . . . the damn elements," while offering up some cookies in a damp paper towel, grinning around that ever-present pipe.

Oh, there were some pretty meals that he served up ("glass plate suppers," he called them—it was a great piece of promotion). But the truth is, after three days without eating a decent meal, anything would look good.

So why did we take Bradford?

Because he made you smile, he made you grin, he made you laugh 'til you felt like you were going to puke. He was there for the best of it; he was there through some of the worst of it, too. And he basically was oblivious to it all. He talked about the boat like it was a full-fledged ship, with its ongoing battle between "the ordinaries" and "the bridge."

Stevie will tell you: though he could have strangled Bradford out of sheer frustration at times, it was Brad's humor that kept him going, as well. And by the mid-'80s, when Bradford finally gave in to the fact that even an occasional trip took too much out of him, we knew things would never be the same.

Bradford fought a lot of his own battles over the years (some literally) and left a winner, as far as I'm concerned. He went peacefully, in his sleep.

You were carved from tough stock, Brad. We're going to miss you something fierce.

Chapter 22

Riding it Out

This one was written in 1994—a tough year. With thanks to Junior Bray: you've been an inspiration in more ways than you'll ever know, Cap.

≈

The process, although Eddie Pluggs never knew to call it that by name, was what his grandfather used to think of as "riding it out."

Over the years, Eddie'd heard the same phrase used in dozens of offshore heavy weather stories, where the teller described the conditions as being so bad that "all we could do was just hold on and ride 'er out."

The storms that Eddie's grandfather was talking about weathering, though, weren't the kind generated by Mother Nature; they were storms of the soul.

Actually, it was sort of ironic. Eddie and his long-departed grandfather had never talked about the feeling of waking up from a fitful sleep with a head full of thoughts that couldn't be shaken . . . in fact, Eddie once realized, his grandfather never spoke to him of weaknesses, only strengths.

But the two of them, separated by a generation of Pluggs in between, handled their night demons (call them worries, concerns, or a "spell of nerves") in the exact same fashion.

Of course, Eddie'd never sat in Gramp Pluggs' kitchen at midnight (or one or two o'clock in the morning) when he was dealing with a situation by "riding it out."

The general categories of the problems were ageless; only the specifics had changed with the generations. Eddie's life as a bachelor had saved him from some of the problems his grandfather had known—but loneliness has its own dead weight that sometimes hangs awfully heavy by itself.

Most times, burdens could be put to rest at night and sleep came easy to a tired fisherman. But every now and then, there was the load on the mind that couldn't be shrugged off. If restlessness was replaced by sleep, then came the dreams, which were usually worse. Then there'd be a period of half asleep-half awake thoughts, where the dreams and the real problems churned around and got bigger.

That was when Gramp Pluggs would haul himself clear of the bed (sometimes dressing fully, sometimes staying right in his nightclothes) and head out to the kitchen where his chair was.

That same chair sat in the kitchen of Eddie's trailer. He'd never asked his grandfather where he'd gotten it; it was assumed that it was fairly old—and it was a fact that it was built very rugged. It was built out of some kind of exotic hardwood—the name of which Eddie'd forgotten and always suspected his grandfather of making up, anyway.

The back was high, high enough so that even a tall person could comfortably rest his head against it. The arms, thick and solid, still bore the marks of Gramp Pluggs' years of head knitting: little black marks where he'd snuffed out a few million pieces of burning twine. The seat, which needed no cushion, was worn to fit the contours of the Pluggs family rear end (or lack of it), which had been passed down through the generations. The legs were heavy enough to bear the biggest of burdens, leading down to their curved feet. And the feet were the most important feature, for this was a rocking chair; the finest kind of a rocking chair.

Gramp Pluggs would settle into his berth and begin to "ride it out." There were times when an hour or so of the chair would bring some chunk of thought that led to enough inner peace to allow sleep to wash over him. And there were other times when the problems couldn't be shook, but they had to work awful hard to keep pace with Gramp Pluggs and his chair.

On the hardest of the nights, Eddie's grandfather hauled the chair right over in front of the kitchen door and yarned it wide open. He then sat, rocking fiercely, sometimes with the wood stove roaring fiercely while a cold wind blew in through the open door and whipped around him.

No handbook on coping with stress or any licensed therapist on record had offered up Gramp Pluggs' method as an approved procedure for dealing with worries, concerns, or a "spell of nerves." But there are a lot of things that don't need a stamp, badge, ribbon, or document to prove their value.

And so it was true that even on the longest nights, when no answer came, Eddie's grandfather would still have "ridden it out"; ready to go to work as the sun came up, with his courage intact.

The chair became Eddie's with his grandfather's passing, but there were no written instructions that came with it—or whispered message telling him of its powers. No, the knowledge that the chair was the place to be when Eddie couldn't sleep just *was*.

Of course, it goes without saying that if Gramp

Pluggs, or his grandson—or any one of us—never had worries, concerns, or a "spell of nerves" to contend with, it would be a fine thing.

But in this life as we all know it, whether or not he realized where it came from, Eddie Pluggs was very lucky to have a place where he could "ride it out."

Chapter 23

He Just Quietly Guides Me Along

And then came 1995 and we lost Pa.

≈

My father, Stephen Harold Robbins Sr., passed away this past May and I miss him something fierce.

There was a time, as I'm supposing everybody goes through, that I was easily aggravated with my father because I felt that Pa just didn't get it.

I had to grow older to come to appreciate him for the treasure that he was. Unfortunately, Pa grew older, too. But he never lost his humor, he never forgot how to tell a story, and he never forgot how to listen, either . . . and that's very important, because as I sit here, I know that Pa knew exactly how I felt about him— because I told him, and he listened. I guess I'm lucky.

By the time I was old enough to work—really work—Pa and my Uncle James were all done with their years of herring seining. My brother Stevie, 14 years older than me, was right in the thick of some of the best and worst of it. Me, I was just a chubby little guy peering over the rail of a sardine carrier watching the fish flip around in the pocket after a shutoff. Other than that, seining for me wasn't much more than the occasional Saturday morning spent bailing dories.

But, there were a couple times when I was little that Pa took me on what seemed like the greatest of all adventures: just me and him, staying aboard the seiner *Lucky Star*, moored in whatever cove they were tending with the stop-twine outfit.

Looking back, I know now that those were undoubtedly times when the herring weren't exactly jumping right out of the water—chances are, Pa probably could've taken the night off without feeling like he missed the big shutoff. But we were there, me and him.

Marm had already fed us supper, but we ate again aboard the seiner, because, well, that's what you did. Nothing tastes quite like a macaroni-and-cheese loaf sandwich (slathered with mustard—the fo'c'sle style of French's that nobody ever quite tightens the lid down on, so it has that rind of deeper-yellow crust around the rim) on Wonder Bread. Wind that into you with a slab of rat cheese that has been loosely wrapped in butcher paper, sweaty from the heat, and a lukewarm bottle of ginger ale that has been hanging over the side of the seiner in a sack, and you've got it all. It'd really make you wonder, as you wiped the mustard from the corners of your mouth, what the poor and unfortunate kids of the world were eating.

I remember rolling into one of the upper bunks (a lower one wasn't half as thrilling), burrowing into a sleeping bag, and waiting for the best part.

I'd be awake when Pa's feet hit the fo'c'sle floor. Without a lot of talking, we'd go topside and ease down aboard of the big workhorse outboard—the yawl boat, Pa called it—and once he'd started the motor for me, we'd cast off.

I didn't know a whole lot about what was going on, except that you had to be quiet. The old Evinrude was never run above a dead idle for this part; I was on the tiller and Pa was up in the bow.

He'd have the "feeler stick," the long pole that was used to feel if there were any fish—and if there were, how big a body of them there was. It may sound primitive to some, but I've been told more than once that "Old man Steve could tell you how many you had within a couple hogshead with his stick," so I guess it did the job.

Around the cove we'd idle. I'd focus all of my attention on Pa's silhouette up in the bow; when he wanted me to bear one way or the other, he'd simply lean his shoulders to that side. All I had to do was keep still and pay attention; Pa would guide me along.

We never found any fish the few times I went with Pa. But that wasn't the point, as far as I was concerned.

And you know, now that I think about it, I wonder if Pa didn't feel the same way.

Through the years, I'd look at this person or that person, usually some hard driver, and say to myself, "I'd like to be like him—he's making things happen." But recently, I've realized that all the bulls in the world could never be as much of an influence on me as Pa.

There's only so much you can smash your way through. The personal gales and squalls I've seen over the last couple years weren't thwarted one bit by letting myself get wound up . . . the key to survival seems to be patience.

And nobody had any more patience when it was needed than our father. At the worst of the sickness—and during the upset days following his death—if I'd ask myself, "What would Pa do? How would he want me to handle this?" then I could get along.

And it has worked since. I quote from him, I bet, every day. It might be something that makes a lot of sense; or it may be something foolish—and even that in itself is worth quite a lot, as life without laughter wouldn't be much at all, now, would it?

So, even though he's gone, Pa will never really leave me. As I meander along, he's right up there in the bow. And when I need him to, he just quietly leans one way or the other and guides me along.

Chapter 24

Buff's Damfino

Originally written in 1996, this one's for Granny & Buff.

≈

Gardner is a good friend of mine.

Gardner used to be my father-in-law. He'll always be Jess, Jeremy and Cassie's grandfather (or their "Buff," as they refer to him). And regardless of anything else, he and his wife, Cheryl, are just plain good people . . . divorce doesn't change that, no matter which side of the family folks are on.

Gard is clever at a lot of things (which makes him ideal Buff material), from basic bicycle maintenance to boat building.

Over the years, he has built a number of boats for folks—including Jeremy's one-of-a-kind rowing skiff, an able little craft if ever there was one. Gard has managed to maintain his allegiance to wood except for a couple of exceptions where friendship and respect for the people involved, allowed a fiberglass hull to be slid into his shop for finishing.

Of course, if you were to ask him, Gard would refer to himself as a lobsterman before he would a boat builder, as that's how he's spent the best part of his years. Since 1974, Gard's been working out of a 32-footer that he designed and built for himself.

Probably about 10 years or so ago, Gard began to talk about building another boat of his own. "One more ought to do me," he'd say.

The "what if" sort of conversations were good fodder for us over cups of tea now and then. What would he do different from his faithful 32-footer? What would he go with for power? For a prop?

And, of course: what would he do with his old boat? "Keep her 'til I figured out which one I liked the best," Gard would answer.

The talk gradually transformed into some cedar planking and noble-looking oak, then some sweeping lines on a sheet of paper. And about four years ago, work began in earnest—whenever Gard wasn't busy doing something else, that is.

"Whatcha gonna name her?" visitors to the shop would ask.

"Damn if I know," Gard would answer. He wasn't kidding.

The hull of Gard's new 35-footer was just beginning to take shape about the time I left the neighborhood with most of my belongings in the back seat of the car. We promised each other that when the time came, though, we'd get together and go for a sail.

Two years later, we did.

Gard's new boat made me smile just to look at her. The overhead came just about right—room enough so I wouldn't knock myself out if I went to haul with him, just like we used to joke about.

Gard fired her up and made a few passes while I took some pictures. I jumped aboard and he told me, "Take her and see what you think."

And standing at the wheel on that early May day, watching the pretty water out behind her, I guess I wanted to hug him.

But we don't do that, me and Buff. We just grinned a lot.

Chapter 25

Young Eddie: Ending the Season

For all the young members of the outboard-powered mosquito fleets; past, present, and—one hopes—future.

≈

It was November of 1970, Eddie Pluggs was 12 years old, and he had just brought in his last load of gear for the year.

Between lack of time (cussed school sure got in the way of tending a string of lobster traps), lack of boat (it was starting to get blowy and snotty on a regular basis), and lack of lobsters (at least within range of Eddie's 13' skiff and his faithful 18-hp Oftenrude), the season was over. Eddie'd taken advantage of a pretty decent Saturday to bring in his gang of gear—all 25 singles—and was now just circling out in the harbor, washing down his skiff and getting ready to haul her up.

Eddie was a little put out over getting skunked on his last haul of the year, although he'd rationalized things by figuring that Gramp Pluggs would've made him bring his gear in anyhow—and it would've felt far worse to be loading on traps if you were getting a pound to a trap.

147

Tugging on the visor of his low-riding ball cap (even back then, most of Eddie Pluggs' face was obscured by his hat), Eddie swung the skiff around and headed for shore. The strong gas smell he'd tried to ignore all day seemed to be getting worse, and Eddie was just about to slack back the throttle and pull the cover off the motor when he realized he was in a mess.

Eddie's 18-hp Oftenrude was spouting flames.

On that same November day in 1970, Jasper Jacobs was celebrating his 50th year of service as foreman at the Sprigg Brothers' dock.

After those 50 years of watching highliners and dubs experiencing everything from record landings to complete and utter brokers, 73-year-old Jasper Jacobs was as qualified as anyone around when it came to judging if a young person had what it took to make it on the water.

More than once, he'd looked out over the harbor, squinting at the little ball of foam steaming along that was Eddie's 13' skiff and said, "That Pluggs kid is a real ball of fire. He's gonna go places."

On that particular day, it appeared that Jasper's words (or some of them, anyway) had taken quite literal shape. It was hard to tell where Eddie was going, but the ball of fire part was pretty damn obvious to Jasper, even without his glasses.

Jasper had just about seen it all—good and bad—but the sight of Eddie's skiff ripping into the harbor with a fireball roaring off the back end of it just froze him in his boots. The only thing he could think of was the Pluggs kid, who was always messing with stuff to get his skiff to go a little faster, had somehow rigged up a rocket to its transom. And to top it off, the rocket boat had suddenly taken a tack to starboard and was heading directly for the lobster car where Jasper was standing.

A big wob of Beechnut chewing tobacco caught in Jasper's windpipe as he attempted to bellow out a warning. Gagging for air, he staggered one . . . two . . . three steps backwards, tripped, and landed arse-first in an open lobster crate. The shock of the landing dislodged the Beechnut, along with a string of curses that turned the air above Jasper's head a foul shade of blue.

Young Eddie Pluggs was oblivious to Jasper's troubles, as he had his hands pretty well full with a blazing outboard. The heat from the fire had gotten so intense that Eddie knew he was going to have to abandon the tiller. Quickly scanning the harbor, Eddie decided that the lobster car at Sprigg Brothers was the closest solid point. He aimed the skiff for the target and headed for the bow.

Fortunately, for weeks Eddie had been ignoring how hard his motor steered, thinking he'd grease it over the winter when he didn't have anything better to do. So now the roaring, blazing Oftenrude held a rock-steady course, and the skiff bore down on the lobster car.

As the gap closed, Eddie kept glancing over his shoulder at the flaming motor, amazed that it was still running (and actually sounding like it had gained a couple of turns, if anything).

With about a hundred feet to go, Eddie realized that getting to the car wasn't the problem—crashing into it was a *very* likely possibility, however. He braced for the impact.

About two boat lengths away, the poor old Oftenrude suddenly sputtered, backfired, and died. The skiff fell off plane just as the stem fetched up on the lobster car, sending Eddie in a graceful arc through the air. He landed in Jasper Jacobs' lap, knocking the wind out of both of them.

The skiff's transom, now engulfed in flames, completely ripped clear of the hull, motor and all, and disappeared beneath the harbor's surface in a sizzling cloud of smoke and steam.

The now stern-less skiff slowly slid back down off the car and settled in the water.

Moments went by without a word, and then Jasper Jacobs cleared his throat and asked, "Did ya get all your gear up?"

"Yeah . . . I just brought the last of it in," replied Eddie, sounding dazed.

"Good timin' kid," said Jasper. "Ya got good timin'."

Chapter 26

Ol' Sarge

Give them flowers while they can still smell them.

Once in a while, I've gotten it right. I wrote this piece in late 1996, towards the end of our buddy Emery Herrick's long battle with cancer. He had a chance to read it, for which I was thankful.

A few weeks later, though, I was reading it myself—at Emery's funeral. The simple act of changing "is" to "was" is sometimes a very hard thing to do. (I've left the original text alone here.)

When his wife Judy and the daughters—Amy, Lori, and Jan—asked me to be a part of the service, I was honored . . . and then kind of worried.

"It's got swear words in it," I told the Herricks.

"So did he," said Amy. "Don't change a thing."

I didn't.

I can't tell you much about that day except that about halfway through my reading I realized where I was: standing at the altar in a church for my friend's funeral—and the crowd was laughing at something I'd just read. With swear words in it.

I figured Emery would've liked that.

≈

His given name is Emery—Emery *H.*, as opposed to his father, who was Emery S., which is why nobody calls him "Junior." Some do call him "Sonny," though Pa always called him "Ol' Sarge." I think that's the best of all.

Emery was a Marine, you see, during the Korean War. I guess Pa figured that Emery will always be a Marine, although it has been years since he's worn a uniform. I don't pretend to know all that it means to be a Marine, but I do know that Emery is proud of his time in the corps. And I think that the experience probably had a lot to do with shaping Ol' Sarge into what he is: One tough son of a gun with plenty of heart.

Emery has been a friend to our family for a long time. And, for a while back in the late '70s and early '80s, he was even part of the crew when I was fishing with my brother, Stevie.

Ol' Sarge wasn't brought up in a fishing family; his people were blueberry growers. Of course, you can draw plenty of parallels between fishing and farming: Never try to figure what you make by the hour; do what needs to be done when it needs to be done; Mother Nature can spin you around and kick you in the butt whenever she feels like it; and your catch/crop is always at the mercy of the market.

So when Emery took a step back from the fields for a little while and went offshore lobstering and inshore scalloping with us, he more than made up for what he lacked in fishing experience with the kind of head-down-and-don't-look-up drive that'll get you through the toughest of situations. If you can imagine the Energizer rabbit chain-smoking Lucky Strikes, working like a wild man, and breaking into unbelievable gales of curses and raves every now and again, then that's Ol' Sarge. I don't care what the deal was—

he'd always keep on going . . . and going . . . and going . . . and going.

I remember the first trap on the first trawl on the first day of the first trip that Ol' Sarge made with us offshore. We were fishing wooden four-footers back then, with the bottoms of the end traps loaded with cement—a good 200-plus pounds to wrestle around the deck. We picked and baited the first cement-ballasted trap, and then Emery took off with it, sliding it down the rail in preparation to drop one end on the platform and stack it over on the far side of the deck.

I was alongside my brother up by the hauler, bending to break the next trap in over the rail, when there was a crash back aft that didn't sound like your average trap landing on the fir platform. In fact, I swear you could hear a sickening crunch over the whine of the hauler. Sure enough, one look told the tale: Ol' Sarge had landed the cement-laden trap right square on the toe of his boot, which now ballooned out from underneath the dead weight like a Looney Tune cartoon character's foot.

We didn't even have time to say anything—Ol' Sarge just let loose with an explosion of curses that turned all the air within a good 50 feet of him a solid blue and swung the trap around, propelling it towards the far corner of the deck.

"How's your foot?" we asked as he scurried back to the hauling station, limping slightly.

"Great—never been better!" Emery snapped back, diving up to his armpits into the next trap on the rail.

We just sort of looked at each other and shrugged, but it became obvious as the day went on that something wasn't quite right with Ol' Sarge's foot.

Although he didn't slow up a bit, Emery took on the

gait of a hobbled penguin, sort of dragging that one boot along as he ripped around the deck.

We were running between trawls when my brother called Ol' Sarge up to the wheel, "You think you might've broke somethin'?" Stevie asked.

"Oh fer Chrissakes," Ol' Sarge said in a totally disgusted tone, flicking the ash off a Lucky and spitting over the rail. "Are you two fruits lookin' for an excuse to go the hell home? I thought we were out here to get somethin' done!"

My brother looked at Emery with the kind of look that you give somebody when you're halfway between patting them on the shoulder and punching them in the nose, and said, "Well, nobody cares about your damn foot, anyways—shut up and get back aft."

Ol' Sarge let a blast of curses out of him, grinned, snuck a wink at me, and wobbled back aft. When he finally did let us get a look at his foot (a couple of days and many trawls later), his big toe looked like an eggplant that had gone bad. Sure, it was broken—but we'd gotten the trip in, and that was what counted to Ol' Sarge.

I don't get the time (or make the time, I guess) to see Emery much these days. But I think he reads my ramblings and I wanted to tell him: don't think for a minute that I'm not thinking of you, Ol' Sarge.

You're not only a good friend, you're one tough Leatherneck.

Chapter 27

Captain Brown

Ask my brother Stevie about who the inspirations were for our going offshore lobstering back in the 70s and I'm pretty sure what he'll tell you: Benny Beal of Jonesport, ME and Bob Brown of Marblehead, MA.

We were fortunate to be able to count two of our heroes as friends, too.

This was written in January of 1998.

≈

Exactly 10 years ago, I'd just returned from the first trade show I'd ever attended for *Commercial Fisheries News*, the Massachusetts Lobstermen's Association (MLA) annual weekend in Hyannis, MA.

That trip was the first time I'd been on Cape Cod since 1979 when I had sailed on the *Sea Fever* and the *Sea Holly* out of Harwichport. Bob Brown of Marblehead, MA, one of the pioneers of the offshore lobstering industry in New England, owned those boats. 1979 was a year during which I left home for the first time; worked with a crew of strangers for the first time; made some mistakes—and grew up a bit.

I have just returned from this year's MLA show. A lot happened over the weekend, but I guess what I'll always remember is being in the middle of setup for the trade show when I heard the news: Bob Brown had died from injuries suffered in a fall from a ladder at the State Fish Pier in Gloucester.

This was the man who proved with his own hands, back, and money back in the '60s that you could catch a lobster on the southern side of Georges. If the state of Maine looked to Benny Beal back then as a brave man with a vision for going off to the canyons, Massachusetts could claim one of its own as the inspiration: Bob Brown.

And with the success of those early years came the stories that spawned the legend: Brown landing great trips with boats that had been pounded by savage weather and crews that had been worked beyond the point of exhaustion. When the boats were ready to go back, so was Brown. And if the crew wasn't, well, he replaced them and kept going. He penciled marks on the chart where nobody had business being in boats that size—or bigger, even. "Suicide Brown" they called him. If his approach could be argued with, his success couldn't. He was the first highliner in a newborn industry: offshore lobstering.

My brother Stevie was one of the ones inspired enough by Bob Brown stories to head offshore in the mid-70s. Ironically enough, Bob bought a house on Deer Isle about the time that we first struck off. And it was Bob's friendship and advice that helped us along, especially in the first few years of trying to make it all work.

As I mentioned earlier, I sailed with Bob (and his son Peter, a great skipper in his own right) later on during a time when Stevie and I needed to have some space between us. I eventually returned to my berth at my brother's side, but not unaffected by the experience of working for Bob. There was an intensity to him that could make you uncomfortable, but there was also a strength that you had to admire.

His operation expanded as the years went by. Bob had bigger boats built; boats that not only went off to the shelf, but chugged up to the Grand Banks in search of swordfish, as well. Shoreside management of the business took up more and more of his time. A lobster pound on Vinalhaven, ME was added. Bob ran his business with his usual drive and hands-on involvement. But he never looked like himself in the cab of a truck. He was meant to be at the helm of a boat.

Recently Bob had returned to the water, back in the wheelhouse and enjoying himself. "This is where I'm the happiest," he'd confided to a friend over the cellular phone just a few days before his accident. I was glad to hear that.

There's a Bob Brown story that's been around for years and years. Whether it's actually true makes no odds—it's believable.

Back in the early days when Bob first blazed a trail offshore that others would later follow, it wasn't uncommon for him to return to port with a pilothouse window or two cleaned out, lost to whatever gale of wind he'd butted heads with that trip. Those empty window frames helped to build the legend of "Suicide Brown."

"You wouldn't catch me out there" was the phrase most commonly used. "He's crazy" was another.

That kind of talk didn't bother Bob Brown—in fact, it suited him just fine. The threat of a good pounding by the elements kept the peekers and the chasers away. They wanted no part of the ocean that Brown was battling on a regular basis.

The story that I heard from time to time was that if Bob went for a spell without losing a window to the elements, he'd sometimes pop one out with a hammer just before he got into port. The wharf would buzz accordingly when he arrived: "Brown got another beating last trip." "Yeah, well, you wouldn't catch me out there."

As I say, I don't know if Bob actually ever did that, but I could imagine him, hammer in hand, giving the crowd on the dock something to think about.

They say that mariners leaving this world cross the bar at the helm of big, beautiful vessels, arriving in their final ports with their holds overflowing.

And I bet Bob Brown showed up with a deckload, scuppers just awash—and a pilothouse window or two missing.

Just to give them something to think about.

Chapter 28

Monroe's Tow

*This column, written in April of 1998, intro-
duced Monroe Sinclair. The best thing about
having Monroe around was that he made Eddie
Pluggs look sane.*

*You may notice that by that point in time,
Eddie's boat changed from the Mr. Kelp to the
Black Crow. It's a long story. But then again,
aren't they all?*

≈

Eddie Pluggs squatted in front of his pickup and
peered beneath the front axle, noting the lack of day-
light between it and the mud it was nestled in. He
slowly straightened up with a sigh. "I think I found the
only soft spot in the whole friggin' yard."

His loyal sternman/brother-in-law Ross had to
agree with him. Even with the lobster gear they'd
brought down to the shore unloaded off of Eddie's
pickup, it was just plain mired. And to make matters
worse, it was a Sunday, it was getting late in the day,
and it was starting to rain.

"Good timin', I call it," said Eddie, mostly to himself.

Ross almost made the mistake of agreeing with
him, but thought better of it. "We'll have to tow it
out," he said instead.

Eddie glanced around the empty, muddy parking lot at the head of the wharf. "With what?"

Ross was desperately trying to come up with an answer when a voice behind them said, "You could use the boat."

Startled, Eddie and Ross spun around to find Monroe Sinclair, dressed in his usual attire of battered cowboy hat, coveralls with "Smokey's Greater Shows" stenciled across the front, and galoshes.

"Hey," he grinned, tapping the brim of his cowboy hat and displaying a set of teeth that looked like the finish line flag at Daytona.

Most everybody in town liked Monroe, although there were some who felt he was a tad cross-threaded mentally. Many even referred to Monroe as the "village idiot," a title which he really wasn't offended by. In fact, Monroe felt it gave him a good reason to go to town meetings, just in case he should be called upon to give some sort of official village idiot report.

The fact of the matter was that Monroe had a wicked imagination and was prone to being easily distracted. Hours that could have been spent gainfully employed were filled with fantasies of being a U-boat commander or spent trying to play "Foggy Mountain Breakdown" on a two-stringed banjo retrieved from the town dump. Monroe could reel off names of constellations in the night sky and recite the cylinder firing order of every car American Motors ever made, but he didn't have a clue who the current president was or how to dial a telephone—all traits which, truth be known, Eddie Pluggs actually admired.

Ross could tell by the way Eddie was cocking his head that he was actually giving Monroe's suggestion some thought.

"I suppose," said Eddie, scratching his chin. "The only problem is, we don't have far to go and we'd

be hauling the truck towards the edge of the dock."
Eddie pointed to the big stones which made up the
face of the old wharf.

Monroe shook his head. "Naw, Eddie, not *that*
way. You run a rope from the truck—" he pointed to
a big oak further up the driveway—"back up around
that tree and *then* off to the boat. Remember that big
anchor line you've got down forward? You had it out
last summer when you were painting the boat."

Monroe was right—the big poly line in the forepeak
of the *Black Crow* was stout enough to do the job. And
even though Ross could hear faint warning bells in the
back of his head, he went along with the plan, duti-
fully following the orders given by his skipper.

So it was that Ross found himself standing in the
stern of the *Black Crow*, paying out the tow line while
keeping an eye on Monroe, who was sitting in Eddie's
truck, grinning like a . . . well . . . a madman, actually.

The line drew up tight and Ross waved for Eddie to
lay on the power, which he did. As the *Black Crow's*
diesel began to roar, Ross watched for a sign that
Eddie's truck was beginning to budge.

Nothing happened.

Eddie laid on a little more throttle.

The pickup wiggled a little, but it didn't appear that
the wheels turned at all.

Ross suddenly noticed that the truck's brake lights
were on—and it looked like Monroe was fumbling
with the radio, trying to tune in a station. "Hey!" Ross
hollered, waving his arms to get Monroe's attention.

Eddie throttled back, thinking something was
wrong. "What?" he yelled, throwing the *Black Crow*
out of gear and walking aft.

Suddenly the brake lights went out, the truck's
engine gunned a couple times, and it roared clear of

the muckhole—in reverse. Monroe, who had successfully dialed in a radio talk show concerning pets from outer space, had shifted into "R" instead of "1", and the rear wheels had suddenly found a place to bite onto.

"NOOOOOO!" yelled Eddie, scrambling to the *Black Crow's* controls. But it was too late. He was taken off his feet as the *Black Crow* was yanked stern-first towards shore.

The resulting misfortune made a heck of a picture on the front page of the local newspaper that week. Splashed across four columns was a big black and white aerial photo showing the *Black Crow* burrowed stern first, high and dry on the beach with a rope running humming tight from her transom to a tree up on the shore and back down to the front bumper of Eddie's pickup truck, which hung off the edge of the dock.

"Village Idiot Involved In Freak Accident" read the headline. Monroe carried the clipping around proudly in the headband of his cowboy hat for years afterwards.

Eddie Pluggs spent almost as long explaining who the headline was actually referring to.

And Ross denied all knowledge of the incident.

Chapter 29

Offshore Advice
for the
Capped & Gowned

A few years after this column was published in the July 1998 issue of CFN, I was approached by a teacher who told me she read it each June to her graduating class. I'm sure she's been institutionalized by now.

A side note: the "deckhand named Cronk" was my great friend, the late Ray Cronk. I used to sneak a shout-out to Ramie in my columns whenever I could. Sometimes it might be thinly disguised ("Crank", for instance), but it would give Ramie something to growl at me about (in the nicest of ways) when the paper hit the streets.

I miss him something fierce.

≈

[The following is a graduation speech that the author would have presented at one of the most prominent learning institutions in New England except for two reasons:

A.) He was real busy with other stuff; and

B.) They never asked him to.]

Greetings, graduates—present, past, and future.

Today marks the end of one long journey and the beginning of another. One logbook is full and it's time to start a new journal of your voyage through life. You've used up all the herring and it's time to switch to redfish. You've rowed far enough out so you can now drop your motor down and give it to her. Uhhhh, that's about all the analogies I can come up with for right now, but hang tight and I'll lay a few more on you later if they hit me.

Many of you know what your next step will be. Some of you, however, are unsure of that next step. And then there are some of you whose gowns fit so badly that you'll probably take a header into the gym floor when you attempt to take your next step. With you I share this thought, which has gotten me through many a situation: Heist up your skirt when you walk.

I myself remember trading my graduation gown for a barvel and loading traps on the boat soon after the ceremony marking the end of my high school years. (That was it for me. No, as surprising as it may seem, I did not go on to lead my class in the study of advanced brain surgery in medical school.) I knew for certain what my future was going to be and didn't think I needed a whole lot of advice from anyone on anything. Therefore, there was no reason to see, think, or even be aware of the rest of the world.

I see that same look in many of your eyes here today (at least the ones that are open). I see it not only in the eyes of the young and inexperienced, but in those of the older and (supposedly) wiser, as well.

What a bunch of stupes.

I didn't have a clue back then because I hadn't been alive long enough to know any differently and chose not to believe that anyone might know more than me.

And there are plenty of you sitting before me here today—older than I am, even (HA!)—who *still* don't allow yourselves a chance to feel, listen, and learn because you think you have all the answers (or don't want to know that you don't).

If we want to inspire the younger generations not to dig holes so deep for themselves that they can never grow out of them, then we must set an example ourselves.

And whether you take your inspiration from the words of Will Rogers or Jerry Garcia, it's all the same. It's the listening that counts.

Don't get me wrong; I'm not telling you that I have many, if *any*, answers. I'm only saying I feel fortunate I didn't bury myself so deep early on in my life that I couldn't see the sun these days. Or the moon.

So what am I telling you?

Nothing that you probably haven't already heard. It's the listening part that matters.

For example . . .

Sometimes you need to change the pace of things depending on whether you feel life's skipping along too quickly or you find yourself bogged down and loading your heart, mind, and soul up with crap.

Experiment: Shorten up your wire or let a little more out. Smaller circles might be the answer—or, in other cases, try longer tows. Keep a hand on the cable and you'll know whether you're digging or not by the vibes.

When faced with a large task, tackle the offshore portion first and work your way in. It's easier to keep your courage up if you're headed for a goal rather than an empty horizon.

If something falls off the bulkhead once, don't put it back in the same place.

If you're going to tie a knot, do it like you mean

it. This applies to rowboats as well as matters of the heart. A halfhearted knot will sooner or later result in something ending up grounded out on the rocks, all stove to pieces.

If all our mistakes carried as immediate results as peeing into the wind does, we'd probably smarten up a lot quicker.

Don't curse the zinc that has corroded away. It's only doing its job.

If you allow the deck to get slippery when it's calm, you're bound to fall when it gets rough.

If you think you're going to miss when you go to gaff, you will.

Don't eat a tuna sandwich without taking off at least one glove.

Now, whether you choose to take some of these words literally or sift them through on some higher plane, it really doesn't matter to me.

And I'm not telling you that any of these things will make your life better or easier to understand . . . I'm only saying that it wouldn't hurt for you to give things a little thought before you go any further. (That's not to say that you should worry about them—just ponder a little.)

So let us all leave this hall today heeding the words of a former deckhand named Cronk who, after taking a header face-first into a deckload of hake, yelled out, "Hey! Who put all these stupid fish here, anyway?"

Thank you.

Now wake up, heist up your skirts, and go forth.

Chapter 30

Down the Reach with Jess

I have the greatest kids in the world—I really do. Sometimes I wonder why they even speak to me, let alone acknowledge that we're related.

This was written back when I was living in the woods of Palermo, ME. With wild cows.

≈

Eggemoggin Reach runs between Deer Isle, ME, where I grew up, and the mainland. I used to cross the Reach all the time, driving the length of a big old green suspension bridge to do so.

These days, however, the average week finds me making the crossing only on Friday afternoons when I go down to the island to pick up my three kids who spend the weekend with me in Palermo. (Go ahead, ask the question: "Where the heck's Palermo?" "Halfway between Belfast and Augusta," I'll answer.) And, of course, there's the return trip to take them back to their mother's house on Sunday evening. So it goes.

I don't have many Reach memories from growing up. We lived in Stonington, on the southern end of the island, and Eggemoggin Reach might just as well have been on the other side of the world at that point in my life.

My sea time *on* the Reach has been pretty limited. Many winters ago we tried a few tows just below the bridge when we were scalloping with my brother Stevie's 44' *Shirley & Freeman*. I once took a ride on a speedboat down through, getting a good view of the underside of the big green monster. Did a few sea trials on the Reach. And I spent a super summer evening adrift on the reach with Spencer Lincoln and his little red Whaler—floating along with the motor shut down, pondering the great questions of life and boats. Neat stuff.

But there's one other run I made down through the Reach, the one that my oldest daughter, Jessica, usually reminds me of when we're crossing the bridge. "Wouldn't be much of a ride today, Dad," she'll say, winding a twist of beautiful red hair around her finger whilst pondering the water below with an old saltish eye. "There's not enough whitecaps."

Early spring of '96 it was. A Sunday right on the cusp of being nice if the sun came out. We'd moved to Brooklin from the head of Horseshoe Cove in Cape Rosier. *Almost* moved, that is. The 13' skiff that a bunch of Bass Harbor elves had helped build for my son, Jeremy, still lay nestled in the marsh grass in Cape Rosier and needed to be brought to Brooklin.

I suppose one could have laid hands to a trailer and brought the beamy one-of-a-kind skiff over the road, but the shortest (and much preferred) distance between the two points was down the reach. If I hit the morning tide right (with my brother's borrowed 15-hp Mariner bolted to the stern), it wouldn't take any time at all to rip down the Reach and make the beach by Brooklin Boat Yard.

Jeremy himself wasn't around that weekend, but my

oldest daughter Jessica was—and she was ready for a boat ride.

"You sure?" I asked.

"Come on, Dad," she said, swaggering like all good 12-year-old sailors do. "Let's go."

So we did.

All went well at first. With motor secured, we poked on out through Horseshoe Cove. Then the sky began to smear up a bit. Just as we made the swing off Seal Cove Boat Yard and were headed for the Reach itself, snowflakes—totally unexpected snowflakes— began to fall.

Jess, sitting up in the bow, caught a few on her tongue. "Is it supposed to snow?" she asked.

I shook my head.

"Oh, well," she shrugged. "We'll ignore it, then."

I opened up the throttle as we swung out into the Reach proper, thinking that speed would help the situation. No doubt it would have, but it seemed that Mom Nature was determined to prove that winter would be over when she was good and ready for it to be over. Within 10 minutes, the wind had hauled on in good shape and it was snowing hard enough so that we couldn't see the width of the Reach.

"The weather guy lied, Dad," Jess hollered.

"They always do," I called back.

As we got closer to the big green bridge, the tide began to run against the wind, quickly kicking up a short, steep chop—not the most ideal of conditions for a very wide-beamed skiff whose bottom could best be described as flaaaat.

It didn't take long for Jess to decide that the bow wasn't the place to be. Being Jess, though, she never complained.

"Poor Dad," she said, "the snow's freezing on your coveralls."

"I like it like that," I answered, trying to squint through the snowdrifts that were building up on my cheeks. "How are *you* doing?"

"Just ducky." said Jess, bouncing a good foot off of the seat as we fetched up hard on one.

There's not a lot more to tell. We jounced and thrashed our way down the Reach, eventually making Brooklin and the quiet cove below the house we were renting. We were both wet and cold, but Jess never complained.

"Jessie, I'm sorry," I said as we trudged up the trail from the shore.

"For what?" she said, peering out from beneath a snow-encrusted hood. "That was cool—wait'll Jeremy hears what he missed out on."

I love that kid.

Chapter 31

Three Wise Men & A Flying Sleigh

Note to all you aerodynamics experts out there: don't be writing me letters with long, detailed explanations of why this could never work in real life, okay? Just go with it. Sheesh . . . you must be a real blast to be around at Christmastime.

≈

The sun was setting on Christmas Eve. Anyone lucky enough to be hanging around the town dump at that moment would've been treated to the sight of the discarded tire mound brilliantly backlit by a fiery orange ball.

Monroe Sinclair, the incumbent candidate for the village idiot position, paused in the middle of his labors long enough to take in the view. "Gotta write a poem about that," he said to himself, taking out a ballpoint pen, hiking up one sleeve of his carnival worker's jumpsuit, and scribbling a note on his skin alongside dozens of others. Monroe's forearms were both covered with jottings, many faded by time (rather than by soap). "The day I wash these arms," he once told Roy Crank, the town constable, "there'll be more information lost than when the computers all crash on New Year's Day, 2000."

But now was not a time for poetry writing. It was Christmas Eve, the time of the year when magic runs rampant, when dreams become realities, and when one man's trash becomes another man's treasure. Or flying sleigh.

The town dump was closed this day, but Monroe had made his way in at sunrise that morning and been hard at work since. Now, with the sun rapidly sinking and his creation nearly finished, Monroe was keeping an ear up for the sound of Eddie Pluggs's pickup truck approaching, for without Eddie Pluggs, this dream would never become a reality—and as far as Monroe Sinclair was concerned, there would be no Christmas.

He was tightening the final bolt when he heard the rattle of Eddie's truck with a flatbed trailer in tow, heading up the dump driveway. Monroe's grin (at least the parts where there were teeth) spoke volumes.

He began dragging his creation toward the gate where Eddie was waiting.

≈

Eddie Pluggs's loyal sternman/brother-in-law Ross knew it was a foolish question to ask, but just for the record, Ross felt that he should say out loud the words "Are you sure this is a good idea?" Which he did.

Eddie Pluggs turned his attention away from the open pilothouse window as he steered his *Black Crow* out through the moorings. "Of course. It's Christmas," he simply said, then gave his low-riding cap a tug on the visor and peered out the window. Ross was about to point out that Eddie had made a lifelong career out of not getting too fussed up about Christmas, but then thought better of it. He sighed, turned, and walked back to the stern, where Monroe and his creation were balanced.

Monroe had constructed an ultralight version of Santa Claus's sleigh from various bits of scrap. Ross had to admit that it *did* sort of resemble a sleigh, if you overlooked the wings and tail rudder fashioned out of heavy-duty trash bags stretched over old lawnchair frames.

The sleigh was now lashed to the stern deck of Eddie's *Black Crow*. The plan was to get the *Crow* up to full speed outside the harbor, at which point Monroe and the sleigh would be launched, tethered to a towline. It was a perfect night: the moon was full, the wind was right, and the local schoolkids were gathered around a bonfire on the pitcher's mound on the ballfield singing Christmas carols. They would have an unobstructed view of the harbor.

"It don't get no better than this," said Monroe as he climbed aboard the sleigh. Ross just shook his head. Eddie hit the throttle.

The *Crow* climbed out on her bilges and the sleigh began to lift off the stern, gently straining at the bindings on her skids.

Eddie glanced over his shoulder at Monroe.

Monroe gave Ross a big thumbs up.

And Ross cut Monroe loose.

Wobbly, but steadily, the sleigh/glider began to rise. Ross could see that Monroe had his hands full with the various weird control handles he'd rigged up, but he appeared to still be smiling.

Even Eddie had a little grin on as he swung the *Black Crow* on a course for the head of the harbor with Monroe in tow, the full moon backlighting him for all the town to see. Headlights were already lined along the waterfront, where carloads of families pointed at the amazing sight in the sky.

Monroe then hit the button for a secret surprise that even Eddie and Ross didn't know about, touching off a CO_2 cartridge that inflated a string of reindeer from the bow of the sleigh. (Actually, they were three patched-up rubber swimming pool rings with giraffe heads and a lifesize latex doll named "Lola Luv" that Monroe had found on the dump, but there hadn't been much time to be picky.)

Horns sounded throughout the village as the *Black Crow* carved an arc in close to the town dock and headed back out.

"HOHOHOHOHOHOHOHO!" screamed a wildeyed Monroe Sinclair, waving at the crowd gathered below.

And Eddie Pluggs and Ross grinned at each other, totally caught up in the Christmas miracle in the sky above them.

Of course, they had no idea how they were going to get Monroe back down, but—hey—one miracle at a time.

Chapter 32

My Alfred
Osgood Boots

I began this search in 1999 and still haven't found them, just in case you were wondering.

I like the line about being over the 200-pound mark. Yeah—no kidding. And my boot size has increased to 14, as well. So it goes.

≈

I just thought of something: I wonder where my Alfred Osgood boots are?

Not my winter boots that I wear these days (although this past winter hasn't called for much boot-wearing).

And not my rubber boots that I wore the last time I made a trip offshore with my brother (which was a while ago).

I'm talking about my all-time favorite boots. They were perfect for everything from bait house to engine room, and, with the soles well-wiped and a pair of jeans with the seat fairly well intact, could be worn in most of your finer lower-level eating establishments. I bought them many years ago in a galaxy far away (or it might have been Portsmouth, NH).

It just came to me that I don't know where they ended up.

L.L. Bean-bought boots, they were. Stop right there, those of you who are about to turn on me about L.L. Bean. "Yuppie stuff" you might say. Well, there may be a fair slug of people wearing outdoor wear from Mr. Bean's who actually have no interest whatsoever in being outdoors, but that doesn't make it bad stuff.

Me, I like clothes from old L.L.'s because they fit me. At 6'4" or 5" (it changes daily depending on the weather) and well over the 200-pound mark (quite well over at times), I can't just grab your average shirt off the rack and have it cover up all of the parts it's supposed to. But Mr. Bean has a nice selection of things for the extraordinarily-shaped such as myself that just plain fit. It's as simple as that. Yuppies be damned.

(Here's an interesting historical side note: Do you know what actually did in the dinosaurs? They couldn't get clothes in their size. Eventually, the ones that weren't arrested for indecent exposure froze to death. Dinosaur skeletons have been found with scraps of polyester clinging to them, the poor beast's wrists hanging well below the cuffs of their sleeves and the bony cracks of their reptilian butts peeking over their waistbands. Share that with the crowd the next time you bring the tomalley dip to the MENSA meeting and watch the look of astonishment and wonder blossom on your listeners' faces.)

Anyhow, my boots were from Bean's—possibly purchased at an outlet store, but I'm not sure of that. I don't remember any fancy name for them; they were simple, short leather boots.

I'd seen Alfred Osgood of Vinalhaven, ME (one of the cleverest purse seiners to ever float a boat in the Gulf of Maine) wearing a pair of these boots and it inspired me to look for some of my own. Alfred's were well broken-in; easy to step into and just as easy to kick off. Just right.

I eventually found my own Alfred Osgood boots, mine needing to be size 13—and a good 13, at that. I remember that I immediately treated them to an oil change aboard the boat, managing to slather one of them in Delvac.

Shortly thereafter, I noticed that water tended to bead up a lot better on that particular boot. Even a 20-year-old rocket scientist like me could see the advantages of giving these fine leather boots a good coating of waterproofing treatment—or, in my case, more Delvac. In the years to come, those boots never lacked for some sort of salve, whether it came out of a grease gun or a pogey.

The soles were hard enough to withstand steady exposure to oils and goos of various chemistry, but still had enough give to be comfortable and provide good grip. Standing upright being the mother of invention, sometimes you end up having to make concessions in your choice of footwear when living and work-ing around the water. But my Alfred Osgood boots were perfect. Down over a soggy lobster car ramp or standing on the bow yarning up the mooring pennant, they'd hold their ground.

At night you could just step into them and stroll out onto the deck to perform that ancient ritual of the mariner: eyeing the weather whilst peeing over the rail. Flat calm or snotty conditions, my boots were appropriate right up to the worst of weather. More than once I timed a breaking sea wrong on deck and filled them, but after being dumped out and dried by the fo'c'sle stove, they were fine.

I don't know if dressing etiquette dictates that trou-sers should be worn over or tucked into Wellingtons, but I never bothered with it. I simply let my pants legs (usually jeans) wob up however they wanted to after I stepped into the boots. It worked for me.

Over the years, I remember I had to have my boots resoled once. And I almost think that one of them ended up needing a little cobbler work in the stitchings, too. Things are fuzzy after that, though. I must've still owned them when I first came ashore, but I can't remember wearing them much on dry land. They were just ugly enough and beat up enough to draw at least a comment a day . . . and I can't remember when the insults stopped.

Huh. Well, that's good, I guess. My mind isn't burdened by a tearful good-bye scene with my faithful boots headed for the dumpster. I guess somewhere along the way, I just plain lost them.

That's easy enough to believe. My hair turned white, too, and I was the last one to notice it.

Chapter 33

The Big
Bang Theory

I've never visited with Foy Brown out on North Haven without getting back on the ferry with at least one good dose of inspiration. I couldn't even tell you the original story Foy shared with me now, but here's what came out of my head sometime later.

≈

Monty may have been from away, but he was always welcome to haul up a stool at the bar with the locals, just as his 38' cruiser *Dixie Chicken* was always welcome to lay on her mooring snuggled amongst the town's lobster fleet.

And that was as good as it could get for Monty, for no matter if he decided to move to the little coastal village and live there (rather than just come for the summer) he'd still spend the rest of his life as "Monty; you know, that fella from away."

But Monty was cool with that, understood it, and completely signed onto it himself. After all, he "*was* from away, for Chrissakes," he didn't mind telling anybody who asked him. "It's a statement of fact," Monty'd say, "not a damn insult." Then he'd let out a hoot, followed by an infectious raspy laugh that can only come from years of Camels.

Then Monty would usually wave an arm in a sweeping gesture and say, "Hey—I got no complaints. Most people have to *die* to go to heaven . . . I get to spend my summers there." And then, if his audience seemed to appreciate his philosophy, Monty would buy them a cold one.

So it was that the locals had come to not only like Monty, but *respect* him as well. He knew enough to steer clear of gear; he never got in a working man's way around the co-op dock; and he was quick to offer a hand if it was something he could actually help with. (If not, he also knew enough to keep still and stay out of the way.)

Plus, he didn't take himself too seriously. If Monty dubbed up, everybody was going to know about it, because *Monty* told them. Didn't matter if it was during the summer months when the *Dixie Chicken* was in town to play or if it was during the rest of the year when Monty cruised the more southern waters— everything was potential fodder for a story. That first session of the season, when the *Dixie Chicken* arrived from her southern hiatus, was usually the best.

So it was that a well-tanned Monty was holding court in the bar with the newly-returned *Dixie Chicken* secure on her mooring. (One-Eyed Jack the barman had ordered extra cases of Corona and limes in expectation of Monty's arrival, as there would be a steady demand on such things with him in town.)

Monty had gotten to the point in his story where an attempt to maneuver the *Dixie Chicken* around in a Virginia gunkhole had resulted in a thumped propeller.

"No questions about it—my own fault, right?" he was saying, scanning the faces of his audience, who all nodded and sipped in unison. "And all I wanna do is get the prop pulled, get it straightened, get it back on, and get outta town, OK? I got too much goin' on to be layin' on the bank somewheres. So I ask the guy at the local marina, and he tells me he can't get me outta the water 'cause his lift is broke—BUT—he's got a diver buddy who can be there in no time, right?

"'Great,' I says, and before I know it this diver is under the boat, thumpin' away. He's down there for a while and then comes to the surface. 'Ain't gonna beat it offa there,' he says. 'What do we do now?' I ask. 'We'll *blow* it off,' he says."

The crowd all shook their heads and made negative-sounding noises.

"Yeah, tell me about it," said Monty. "But it isn't a minute or two later that the guy is lugging a box aboard marked 'EXPLOSIVES,' jumping over the side with something, and then climbing back aboard empty-handed and telling me 'Hold onto your hat.'

"He hasn't much more than said that and **BOOM!**—the whole boat leaps about a foot in the air and then splashes back down.

"I'm still trying to take it all in, right? The diver jumps over the side and comes right back up with the prop in hand. Just like it wasn't a big deal.

"He passes the prop up to me and then climbs aboard, grabs a towel and a beer, and sits on the stern. Doesn't say thing, right? So finally I says, 'Wow.' He shrugs. 'Wow,' I says again. The diver shrugs again and finally says, 'Well, it doesn't always go that way.'

"'Whatcha mean?' I ask him. He takes a long pull on his beer and says, 'Well, to tell ya the truth, I kinda overdid it on the first two boats I ever tried it on.'

"Now he's got my ears up, right? 'Why? What happened to the first two you did?' I ask him.

"'Sunk 'em,' he says and takes another long pull.

All of a sudden, I got the delayed sweats and shakes, right? And then I ask him, 'Just how many of these have you done?'"

At this point, One-Eyed Jack the barman grabbed his mop, knowing what was coming.

"'Well,' says the diver, 'this makes my *third*.'"

Mouthfuls of beer were spit down the fronts of shirts as the place exploded in gagging laughter. And the little brown man at the head of the bar was laughing the hardest of all.

No doubt about it, Monty was back in town.

Chapter 34

From The Sport's Desk

There was a string of years where the Maine Lobster Boat Races dominated my summers. Then I reformed. Kicked the habit. Pried that nitrous-fueled monkey right off my shoulders and never looked back.

I didn't become anti-racing, necessarily—I just reclaimed my summers.

For awhile, I didn't write a word about the races. Then I had the inspiration to make up a totally fictitious race report just for laughs.

It was bad enough in the beginning when people believed the foolishness I'd made up. After a few times, I realized that I couldn't come up with anything as crazy as what they were actually doing out on the race courses.

≈

SOUL'S HARBOR, ME—It's official: with a big thumbs-up from the Maine Lobster Boat Racing Oversight Committee and local town fathers, this Downeast port has not only been added to the 2000 season calendar, but will host the opening event, as well. Race organizer Myron Floren is playing his cards close to the vest at this hour on what surprises await those who make the Soul's Harbor contest.

The Sports Desk was able to wrangle one nugget out of Floren, however. Retired actor and three-time Academy Award nominee Belted Galloway will act as chairman for the event as well as race announcer.

"The only thing these races have lacked for years is a real sex symbol," said Floren. "With Mr. Galloway at the microphone, ladies will be swooning all over the course."

Galloway, who retired to this village shortly after the bombing of Hiroshima, was unavailable for comment as he was being fitted for a new truss and an eye patch, according to his press agent.

≈

KNOTS LANDING, ME—"Will he or won't he?" has been the question swarming around this mid-coast port all winter. The "he" in question, of course, is local resident Harmon Munson (who rocked the Maine Lobster Boat Race circuit last summer with the appearance of his controversial boat *Lil' Dumplin'*) and the issue in question has been whether Munson would race this season.

Munson's *Dumplin'* was certainly a crowd-pleaser last summer with its gas turbine engine and flashy profile, but the question asked by all was, "Is that *really* a lobster boat?" When one race official pressed the issue of what looked to be an airfoil on the *Lil' Dumplin's* hind quarters, Munson replied that his new vessel was actually a multipurpose boat.

"That ain't no airfoil—that's a gillnet setter," he explained.

The straw that broke the camel's back, however, was the accusation by another official that Munson's closed-cockpit speedster was, in fact, a poorly disguised *Miss Budweiser*, the famous record-setting unlimited hydroplane. When confronted with this charge (and a copy of *Powerboat* magazine which featured a shot of the *Miss Bud* on the cover—bearing a striking resemblance to Munson's entry), the accused skipper stormed down the wharf, hopped aboard his bright red craft, pulled on his full-face helmet, and slammed his cockpit canopy shut.

The impact apparently dislodged one of the pieces of cardboard duct-taped to the hull bearing the *Lil' Dumplin'* name. Those in attendance who had a clear view of the scene reported that the words *Miss Budweiser* could be seen once the cardboard fell away. Munson made a hasty departure before this could be confirmed, however, setting a new unofficial gillnetter class speed record of just over 200 mph in the process.

When contacted in early May by the Sports Desk, Munson said that he was "undecided" about racing this coming summer, as shedders seemed to be showing up early.

"Me and the *Dumplin's* gonna be busy getting lobster gear out," he said.

≈

ROCKY BULLWINKLE, ME—History could be in the making in this little coastal community as boat builder/performance fanatic Spiff Stinson is within a few weeks of launching his new contender for the title of "World's Fastest Lobster Boat." Stinson's as-yet-unnamed 28-footer is to be powered by 23 (yes, 23) 50-horsepower sailboat motors all connected by a series of universal joints and stub shafts. A quick pass at the calculator tallies up a total of 1,150 horses for Stinson's new entry, although he feels that there will be some power loss attributed to the spiral arrangement of the small 3-cylinder diesels around the 28-footer's deck.

"It's kind of a mess to look at," he told the Sports Desk, "but it might go like Ol' Glory. I just need to figure out where I'm going to stand."

Propeller experts had Stinson dialed into a 16" x 52" 3-blade with a mild cup for sea trials. "I just ain't sure about the cup," reported Stinson.

≈

MOXIE POINT, ME—A new method of solving the age-old question of whether a contestant in the Maine Lobster Boat Races is actually a "true fisherman" will be introduced this season, it was announced at a press conference here in late April.

All registrants will be taken into a room where an actual Maine lobster and a live Australian bush kangaroo will be tethered. Contestants will then have to identify which of the animals is a crustacean, with only their best two out of three answers counting.

"This should weed out the pack," said Soul's Harbor, ME's Belted Galloway (see opening item), who reportedly flunked the test himself.

Chapter 35

Bradford and
The Pillow
Case of Doom

*You met the one-and-only Bradford Weed in an
earlier chapter. This column was written several
years after his passing. Some folks might think that
speaking this way of the departed is disrespectful.
Trust me; Bradford would have loved it.*

≈

Christmas stirs various feelings in all of us. I have my
own stash of memories: great childhood Christmases;
wonderful holidays with my own kids; and way, way
in the back of my brain (the offshore part that sometimes crowds its way to the front), I remember how it
used to be when we'd be trying to pound in a couple
of offshore lobster trips just before Christmas to make
the holiday market.

I remember one trip in particular, back when it
was just my brother Stevie and me with our old cook,
Bradford. Bradford's gone now, but he'll never leave
us. If you could imagine an older version of Popeye
(pipe and all) with a voice like Tom Waits, then that
was Bradford. He couldn't really cook all that well; he

wasn't much on deck, either; and, at times, he'd annoy the living hell out of my brother.

But that was just Bradford—and we loved him.

So this one December evening, we were running off to the grounds after hurriedly loading the 44' *Shirley & Freeman* with grub and supplies. There had been a little problem when Bradford had accidentally dropped my brother's clean pillowcase overboard during the process, but Stevie hadn't seen it and I had faith that Bradford would get things taken care of.

The mood was tense as my brother scanned the weather channels for an updated forecast. Bradford was supposedly busy down in the fo'c'sle putting groceries away, while I stood in the corner of the darkened wheelhouse, listening to the weather with Stevie.

The next few minutes went something like this:

VHF: *And now, an urgent message for our mariner friends in the Gulf of Maine . . .*

BRADFORD *(head stuck up through the fo'c'sle doorway):* Hey! They had canned cream corn on sale— three cans for a dollar! What d'yer think of that?

STEVIE: Shut up!

BRADFORD: What?

STEVIE: Shut up! I'm tryin' to hear the weather!

BRADFORD: I'm just telling you that the creamed corn -

STEVIE: I don't want to hear it!

BRADFORD: Well, suit yourself -

STEVIE: **QUIET!**

VHF: *Yesterday's high temperature in Portland was -*

STEVIE: There—we missed the friggin' weather. Are you happy about your **STUPID CREAMED CORN?**

BRADFORD *(mumbling and fumbling with his pipe):* Ugly arse. . .

STEVIE: What?

BRADFORD: Nothing . . . nothing . . .

We steamed along for a few minutes in silence (except for Bradford making faint gurgling noises with his pipe). Then Stevie cleared his throat and spoke very slowly:

STEVIE: The weather should be coming around again in a second and I want to hear it—the cussed glass is starting to drop and I think they've changed that forecast.

BRADFORD: Nobody understands the elements that I have to deal with—

STEVIE: QUIET!

VHF: . . . *for the waters of the Gulf Of Maine and Georges Bank -*

BRADFORD: Oh, by the way—

STEVIE: HUSH!

BRADFORD: I've got bad news—

STEVIE: **SHUT UP!**

VHF: . . . *a very large, fast-moving low pressure system —*

BRADFORD: I couldn't get all butter; I had to get one pound of oleo, too.

STEVIE *(slamming the throttle back to idle and throwing the boat out of gear)*: I DON'T GIVE A DAMN ABOUT **THE OLEO, THE BUTTER,** THE FRIGGIN' **CREAMED CORN—NOTHIN'**! IN FACT, I DON'T CARE WHAT, WHEN, OR IF YOU COOK *AT ALL* THIS TRIP! (I could see Bradford perk up at *that* news.) I DON'T EVEN KNOW IF THERE'S GOING TO *BE* A TRIP! JUST SHUT UP! DO YOU UNDERSTAND? *JUST SHUT UP!*

BRADFORD *(tugging on my pants leg)*: See? Nobody cares.

STEVIE *(through gritted teeth)*: We're going to sit right here until that weather comes back around and **you**, Bradford, are going to keep your stupid face shut. And Brian, if he makes a single sound, *strangle* him.

We sat there for the next few minutes, drifting with the engine idling. I began to notice a slight smoky smell, but thought nothing of it, what with Bradford lighting a match every few seconds in an attempt to keep his pipe lit.

VHF: *And now, an urgent message for our mariner friends—*
STEVIE: Brian, gag him!
At this point, I could *really* smell smoke.
VHF: . . . *the Gulf of Maine and—*
BRADFORD *(peering down into the fo'c'sle)*: Uh. . . .
STEVIE: SILENCE!
(There was no doubt: something *was* burning.)
VHF: *A massive low centered over —*
BRADFORD: **FIRE!** *FIRE!*

Yep, there was a fire. Up through the doorway came Bradford with what looked like a flaming rag. It was, of course, Stevie's pillowcase that had gotten dunked while we were loading the boat. Bradford had draped it over the oven door to dry, but apparently had misjudged the process, not being all that familiar with the stove (even though he *was* the cook).

Bradford charged out past my brother in a shower of sparks and smoke and flung the flaming pillowcase over the side. Then he paused, caught his breath, tapped his pipe out against the toe rail, and made his way back down below past my brother, who stood stone-still by the wheel, stunned.

I don't remember much more about that trip, except it wasn't a trip. The weather *did* turn to crap after all, and we ended up running back in without hauling a thing. It was a complete bust—and to make matters worse, my brother was out a pillowcase.

Christmas wasn't far behind, though. I know we must have managed to squeak in another trip or two before the holiday. Traps were picked. Lobsters were banded.

And maybe—just *maybe*—Bradford actually cooked a meal.

Ah, well . . . here's to you, ol' Brad. We miss ya.

Merry Christmas.

Chapter 36

Cassie Pegs Out

*My youngest daughter Cassie just turned 21.
She's still dangerous at cards.*

≈

It's my deal on what almost certainly will be the last
hand of a Saturday night cribbage game between my
youngest daughter, Cassie, and me. Cass is no slouch
at cards for an 11-year-old (she routinely slaughters
me at games like Uno and crazy eights), but I'm pretty
sure I've got her this time. Cass is 20 holes away from
home while I only need four to peg out. She's still
smiling, though—a good sport to the end.

Off the deal, I'm holding 4,5,7, a pair of 9s and
an ace. I toss the 4 and the 7 in the crib; I'm holding
enough points to win.

Cassie's brow furrows slightly in thought, then she
slowly places a pair of cards in my crib. She's still putting plenty of thought into it, even though ol' Dad's
about to win. What a sport.

*I don't think the game of cribbage has any direct mari-
time roots, although I'm not sure of that. It seems, though,
that it's always easy enough to find a cribbage board around
the waterfront—along with someone who knows how to
use it.*

My first introduction to cribbage was by an older lobster-man who lived nearby to the first place I had on my own. Sometimes after coming in off an offshore lobstering trip with my brother Stevie, I'd go home and just zonk out solid, sleeping the sleep of the dead for a few hours.

And then I'd be wide awake, trying to place the sound that had stirred me. Ah—the ripple of shuffling cards. My neighbor Royal would be downstairs, waiting to play some cribbage. "Whatcha gonna do—sleep yer life away?" he'd greet me as I'd stumble into the kitchen, rubbing my eyes.

It wasn't until later on in life, once I'd played cribbage with other folks, that I realized that not only did Royal dole out most of the basics of cribbage to me, but he took some small delight in inventing a rule or two along the way: "You mean I don't get an extra couple of points for having a three of clubs and a seven of diamonds?" I'd ask my brother.

He'd just look at me with the pitying expression usually reserved for village idiots. "Another Royal rule?"

"Well, yeah . . ." I'd say. "But only because it's a Sunday." Stevie would shake his head.

Cassie cuts the cards for me and I turn over a 5 of hearts. Hey—a bonus I didn't even need. A couple more fifteens and a pair of 5s.

"Go for it, Cass."

She lays down a jack. "Ten."

"Gotta watch that—leadin' off with a ten," I say as I plunk down a 5. "Fifteen for two."

She nods her head slightly, then flips a 5 of her own onto the table. "Twenty for two." Her expression is still all business.

I lay one of my 9s down. "Twenty nine."

Cass shakes her head. "Go."

I play the ace for 30 and take my point for the go. One more and I'm home.

You take my brother Stevie: now there's a cribbage player. I can't say that he's ever laid a hand on me while we've been playing, but there's something about the intensity and fierceness of a round of cribbage with Stevie that makes it feel like a contact sport. You push away from the table exhausted and drained.

My brother can make a three-point hand seem like a grand-slam homer that's over the fence and out of the ballpark. He'll rake the peg wildly across the holes, sending the weak-nerved running for cover. These days, he gets in the occasional game with my Uncle Gene (that's "Handsome Eugene B. Eaton of Little Deer Isle, America" to you) and I haven't had the chance to sit in on one—but I bet it's a show.

≈

"Ten," says Cass as another jack hits the table.

There's a slight warning tingle in my head, but . . . I play my last card, the remaining 9. "Nineteen."

Cass's last card is another 5. "Twenty four," she says. "One for last card."

And now Cassie is grinning as she spreads her hand out and begins the counting process. I take in the fact that she has a pair of 5s and a pair of jacks—not to mention the 5 of hearts that was cut . . . and one of her jacks is a heart . . .

"Well, let's see . . . fifteen for two, fifteen for four, fifteen for six, fifteen for eight, fifteen for 10, fifteen for 12, fifteen for 14 . . . I think that's all the fifteens . . ."

"Yep," I say, sounding a bit dazed.

"So fourteen and then triple 5s for six makes it twenty; a pair of jacks is twenty two—and the right jack is . . ."

"Twenty three." I shake my head.

"That's right, Daddy—twenty three!" She runs the peg along the holes with a victory flourish unnervingly similar to her Uncle Steve's.

The little squirt has just smoked me, playing it cool and casual.

"Good game, Dad. I think I'll go to bed now," says the cribbage queen, transforming back to a pretty little 11-year-old as she heads off to brush her teeth.

"Me too," I say to Casper the cat, who has watched the game from atop his scratching post. "Me too."

Chapter 37

Pa's Ducks

This was written in 2001 after a long—but good—day on the road in the H&H Propeller van. "Stop and smell the roses," some say. "Take the time to watch the ducks" works for me.

≈

Late May, almost Memorial Day.

Bittersweet. Summer blooming (one good rainy weekend and suddenly everything's *green*), which is super. I can't help but think, though, that it's six years this month since we lost Pa—and missing him gets no easier.

It's early evening and I've taken a ride with a guy on his new lobster boat, meeting him after he's come in from setting a load of gear. He's tickled—and I'm tickled, too. As we ripped out of the harbor, right in the bucket, I stood over the lazarette and watched the water in the cups of the hatch cover. Not a ripple. Slightly overturning the propeller. He'd been a wee bit skeptical in the beginning of the project, but believed that I'd take care of things if we'd missed it on the sizing. And I appreciated that.

Now he's grinning. Life is good.

I'm heading up over the ramp as the guy heads out to his mooring to put her on the hook. A couple hours or so in the van will put me back home. I'm wondering what the cats have cooked for supper when—

The splash of a pair of oars gets my attention and as my head turns, my eyes take in the yellow before they see the row boat.

"Bead Yellow" it would say on the label of the can. But I know better. It was the color he adopted for his old powerboat for the last 15 or so years that he had her; his skiff was the same color; and so was the heavy, broad-beamed outboard that he was aboard as he finished off his years on the water.

The young boy rowing in circles in the head of the cove was oblivious to my wave as I saluted his choice of color for his skiff.

"Bead Yellow" be damned; *that's Pa's yellow.*

≈

A couple days later, I'm coming off Hopkins Point in Jonesport where I've delivered a prop. As I come over a little rise, I see a pickup hove to in the road.

It's easy to figure out what the driver, an older man, is looking at. To our left, holding court in a little pond that kisses the shoulder of the road, is a handsome mallard duck. His satiny colors reflect the late afternoon sun and he paddles easy, just being a duck. A lazy spiral; an elongated figure 8; a little burst of speed to check out something wiggling in the water close to the shore, but then throttle back to idle. *I am a duck*, he says, *and this ain't bad, boys, let me tell ya.*

The man in the pickup sees me in his mirror, and shifts around in his seat like he needs to get out of my way. But I'm holding back, trying to let him know that I'm in no hurry: *I want to watch the duck, too, Mister.*

'Cause, you see . . .

≈

It was what turned out to be the last time Pa and I crossed the causeway onto the Island together. I was bringing him home from the hospital; they'd done what could be done and there wasn't a whole lot more to it except to make Pa as comfortable as possible. And he wanted to be back home.

So we were in my car, me concentrating on going along easy and Pa, on the passenger side, looking tired and sick. We talked a little—but I knew he mostly just wanted to get home and lay down on his own bed and hold Marm's hand.

A transformation took place, though, as we started up the bridge over Eggemoggin Reach. Grabbing hold of the strap over the door, Pa hauled himself up straight in the seat.

Seconds before, he looked like a very weary 79-year-old man.

Now he looked like a king.

We crossed onto Little Deer Isle, then made the rock-lined causeway that leads onto Deer Isle itself. I slowed down, realizing that Pa was looking out over the water, taking it all in. He wound the window down, drawing in a deep breath full of the southerly wind that was coming in off the bay.

And then, just as we made the end of the causeway, he nodded toward the beach turnoff on our right and said, "Pull over for a minute."

I did—having no idea as to why he wanted to stop —and shut off the engine. We sat in silence. Small whitecaps rolled in easy, busting into foam on the sand.

Then Pa pointed out of the window on his side. "Look at those ducks," he said.

Stephen Harold Robbins Sr., 79 years old, lobsterman, scalloper, seiner, draggerman, and hook fisherman, had probably seen—what? Thousands? Millions?

Billions?—of gulls and hawks and eagles and geese and ducks over the years. Enough so that the average person would cease to see them; would put time and attention into other things and let all those gulls and hawks and eagles and geese and ducks just fade into the background.

But Pa still saw them. And still appreciated them. Enough so that on this day, when we were making our last crossing together, he had time to stop and look at the ducks on the water.

I'll never forget that—although sometimes I have to make myself take a second look and see just what's around me . . .

≈

So you see, Mister, you don't have to move on my account, I think as we sit alongside that little pond in Jonesport watching that mallard?—me in my van, he in his pickup.

I'm watching that ol' duck, too.

Chapter 38

The Black Crow: A Love Rained Out

I have some explaining to do here. First of all, there's the meteorite thing with Eddie Pluggs' boats, which was really an analogy for . . . aw, never mind—that was then, this is now. Eventually, Eddie returned to the column.

The part about Josh Bollard and Dottie Nickerson is just as true as true can be. They're doing great—even better than when I wrote this in August of 2001.

And, sadly, the inspirations for both the Black Crow *and* George Apple *are no longer with us. There'll be no replacing them.*

≈

Every now and then, someone will ask me about Eddie Pluggs, a fictional character who used to visit this space pretty frequently. We (and that includes *me*) haven't seen much of Eddie since a smoking meteorite fell on his boat (second meteorite, second boat) back in '99. But don't worry—Eddie's okay. He just hasn't been around, that's all.

(In fact, I'll let you in on a little secret: if you've *really* been hanging around here for a while, you might remember ol' Josh Bollard, a fictional character who first inhabited this space in 1988. Now, as far as the column goes, Josh's ashes were scattered out over the waters in December of '91, but don't you worry. Josh is actually doing fine and he and Dottie Nickerson are more in love than most folks ever know. It's just the way it is. The storyteller can only be responsible for so much.)

So I can't tell you where Eddie Pluggs is or just what exactly he's doing or if/when he'll be back on the water in a column sometime . . . that's up to Eddie.

In the meantime, ponder this: did you ever wonder about the name of Eddie's last boat—the *Black Crow*?

There really *was* a Black Crow (we'll leave proper names out of this—you either knew him or you didn't) who left an indelible mark on both my brother Stevie and me. The Crow's adventures were the makings of great early morning CB and VHF talk over the years. And there even was an occasion when the Crow made a trip offshore with us, under the watchful eye of the unsinkable George Apple.

I mentioned Josh and Dottie's love for each other. Well, we never really knew a whole lot about the Black Crow's romantic life—except for "The Incident At The Ferry Landing."

The usual suspects had gathered at George Apple's shop one afternoon and in the course of conversation, it was brought up that the Black Crow had been spotted spending a fair amount of time hovering around the ticket booth at the ferry terminal over town. And seeing how the Crow hadn't made any ferry trips to anywhere, it was determined that the lady in the ticket booth might be the object of his attentions.

"Well, we've talked about the weather and stuff," the Crow admitted once the gang poured him a little bit of primer.

George Apple got right to the point. "Does this

woman know what your intentions are?" he asked, chomping down hard on the plastic tip of his White Owl.

"Intentions?" asked the Crow. He looked into the bottom of his Dixie cup for answers, but there were none. Badly rattled, he reached for the jug.

"Don't worry," said Apple, waving one big paw. "We'll fix you right up." He barked orders to the gang like a platoon sergeant and off they sped, knowing that they only had a few minutes to go before the last ferry of the day made its run and the ticket booth closed. Just like Cinderella being magically transformed for the ball (sort of), the Crow was turned into a new man.

While he mildly protested between blasts of courage out of his cup, the Crow's salt-and-pepper hair was turned solid black with the help of a can of shoe polish. A bouquet of fresh flowers (still bearing a solemn ribbon reading "Rest In Peace") was presented for courting purposes. And, one of the boys donated his best wedding-and-funeral jacket, shirt, and tie—a generous action, not to be spoiled by the fact that the outfit was about 10 sizes too big for the Crow.

To top things off, a slightly battered tweed hat was placed upon his freshly polished hair. That, too, was a bit on the large side and fell over the Crow's eyes, but George Apple assured him it wasn't a problem. "We'll point you in the right direction."

The assembly piled into the cab and the back of George's pickup and sped down to the ferry terminal. They hove to within sight of the ticket booth and unloaded the Crow, flowers and all.

"Stay on course, now," said Apple, noticing that it was beginning to sprinkle. He gave the Crow a push to get him started.

What had taken only a few minutes to put together fell apart even quicker.

As the Black Crow wobbled unsteadily towards the ticket booth, the rain fell harder and the wind began to pick up. First to go was the hat (gull feather and all), exposing the Crow's shoe-polished scalp to the elements. The oversize jacket and shirt climbed up around the lower half of his face, giving him the look of a tortoise with its head halfway in its shell. And, sadly, the shoe polish began to rinse out in the rain and run down the Crow's face. By the time he was making his last tack toward the ticket booth, the Black Crow resembled something out of a minstrel show.

Up until that point, the object of his affections had been busily tallying the day's receipts with her head down. When she heard the feeble tapping on her window, the ticket lady looked up into the red-eyed coal-black face of a large, unsteady turtle and promptly screamed and fainted.

The Crow shrugged, tucked the flowers into the ticket slot, and stivvered back to Apple's pickup truck. He climbed into the cab, took a swallow out of an offered cup and sighed.

George Apple squinted at him through a billow of White Owl smoke. "Well?"

"Not tonight," said the Crow. "I think she has a headache."

Chapter 39

Somebody's
Always Out

I wrote this column in November of 2001, soon after Tigger and I had taken our first road trip to Cape Breton, Canada together. Discovering that our feelings were mutual as we watched the old eastern rig leave Cheticamp Harbor was no surprise, just more confirmation that what we had was meant to be.

≈

I know I've told you this before—and I'll probably tell you this again—but I want you to remember this one thing when you're sitting down to your big ol' holiday turkey, roast pork, or lobster stew: no matter what day of the year it is, or how bad the weather might be, *there's always somebody out.*

Somewhere, for whatever reason—whether it's looking ahead or just not wanting to look *behind* them— somebody is always out.

1994 marked my first Thanksgiving as a divorced dad and I wasn't doing very well with the prospect of being on my own that day. I knew my brother, Stevie, hadn't gotten out on an offshore lobster trip for a week or two prior to that. When you don't have a French

Foreign Legion enlistment office handy, you go off-shore. (I'd been in the relatively dry offices of CFN for six years at that point.)

"If you want to make a trip, I'll go," I said. "It doesn't matter when—let's go."

We left Thanksgiving morning; my brother, my nephew Stevie III ("Boris"), the unstoppable Timmy McGurl, and I. With Boris and Tim running the deck, I was just the extra set of hands, but that was OK. We burrowed up in the trip for the next few days and there was nothing else to think about. At the time, it was the best place I knew to be. Since then, I like to think I've learned to handle things better.

I guess that's one of those examples of going to leave something behind.

Recently I found myself standing on a hillside on Cheticamp Island on Cape Breton, Nova Scotia, flying a kite with my best friend Tigger. That's right: flying a kite. Everything in the world that could be done was done (except for the things we'd decided not to do), and the peace and serenity that surrounded us just cried out for, well, a kite to be flown. So Tigger magically produced one and we flew it. It was just that simple.

The Cape Breton weather on that particular afternoon wasn't all that peaceful, though; a northerly wind was squalling up in pretty good shape and at one point, a fairly fierce hailstorm descended upon us as if to say "What are you two fools doing flying a silly-colored kite up here? Stop that laughing *right now!*" We played for an hour or so, finally giving in to the weather and the approaching darkness.

Whilst reeling the wildly diving and swooping kite in, she parted her string (just like every one I'd ever flown when I was a kid—including the one my brother coaxed right out across the thoroughfare so that it seemed to hover over top of Russ Island). Tigger and I stood, shielding our faces against the weather, and watched the kite strike a course for the town of Cheticamp on the far side of the harbor from us.

It was Tigger who spotted the eastern rig first, pointing out the old classic as she eased away from the big dock in the middle of the village and headed for the mouth of the harbor.

We each knew the story without sharing a word. Most likely, the weather report and an old barometer in the wheelhouse were both calling for the wind to let go by morning—and by striking out for the grounds right then, this skipper was figuring to be fishing while the rest of the fleet was just starting to run off as it flattened out.

But there was no denying that it was going to be a lousy night aboard that old eastern rig. The weather was waiting just beyond the last pair of buoys that marked the channel out of the harbor. Rollers thundered and busted on the bluff shores of Cheticamp Island, daring anything to nose out into their path.

We cinched our collars tighter and drove our hands deep into our pockets as we watched the old girl catch the first mean one under her bow. Up, up, *up* she lifted . . . then settled her length right out on top of it— gracefully, but violently enough to make the spray fly as high as her masthead. It was the kind of fetch-up that makes every cupboard door in a fo'c'sle pop open, sending canned goods crashing into the floor.

The next two or three seas rolled under the eastern rig's bilges, but then another sharp, steep one took her right in the teeth—the type that drives the spokes of the wheel right into you. An oilclothed figure secured the deck, moving about with the easy surefootedness of a veteran of weather.

There were a couple of course changes in the first few minutes; we figured the skipper was eyeing the ride and plotting a destination. The reality was, the only comfortable ride was going to be the quick one back into Cheticamp Harbor—and that wasn't happening. One final bit of a swing and then it appeared she had her course and was headed, taking the weather more on the port bow.

We only watched for a few minutes more, then turned away purposefully to avoid seeing the old eastern rig disappear from sight (that's something you just don't do). And when we sat at the wood stove-cozy table that night, munching on smoked mackerel and cheese and crackers, we never said it aloud, but we both knew it.

Somebody was out.

Chapter 40

The Tunk of
the Caulking
Mallet

I don't know as I've ever left Wesley Lash's shop in Friendship, ME without something to think about. Although Wesley began his days in Friendship and intends to see them through there, he spent a few growing-up years on Deer Isle when his father Winnie worked at Billings Diesel. I figure he understands my roots as well as anyone.

It was Wesley who said once that it didn't matter where I called home these days: "You can take the boy off the Island, but you can't take the Island out of the boy."

I'm good with that.

This was written in early 2002 when three generations of Lashes—Wesley, his son Wes, and father Winnie—all had a hand in the building of a 42' wooden lobster/swordfish boat.

≈

Caulking a boat is just like cutting fish, ballroom dancing, or juggling chain saws—a person who's good at it makes it look easy.

Having said that, I still didn't feel like I could have taken the mallet and iron away from Wes Lash the other day and tackled a seam of the 42-footer he is building in his Friendship, ME boat shop, even though he surely made it look smooth and simple.

With a steady rhythm, Wes would make the first tucks of a length of cotton to be spaced so that the second pass with the iron would cleanly snuggle the caulking into the seam. The mallet would tunk the iron, driving the cotton strand into the seam; the iron would lightly rebound into Wes's loose grip; he'd flick his wrist so to pick up the hanging strand with the iron and tunk. Tunk. Tunk. Tunk.

When I said something about his technique, Wes raised an eyebrow and shrugged. "You know how long it's been since I did any amount of this?"

Tunk. Tunk. Tunk. Tunk.

"Too long."

Tunk. Tunk. Tunk. Tunk.

It's true that for the last 15 years or so as he and his crew (including one of his sons, young Wes) have been busy pumping a steady stream of custom-finished fiberglass hulls out the door. And it's also true that Wes Lash's mallet-handling of late has been limited to an occasional recaulking job on an older wooden boat. I'll tell you something, though: the man sure doesn't look rusty.

It's a simple pleasure these days to visit Wes's shop (Lash Brothers) or Pete Kass's shop (John's Bay Boat Co.) in South Bristol, ME, where the art of building a wooden lobster boat is alive and well. That same feeling filled Calvin Beal's shop down on Beals Island last year when he was building the wooden plug for his new 38' fiberglass hull—and J.O. Brown's out on North Haven a couple of years ago when Foy Brown got back to his roots with a new wooden lobster boat of his own.

Tunk. Tunk. Tunk. Tunk.

When you walk in through the door of a wooden boat shop, the aroma is the thing that grabs ahold of your head and heart—wood. That good smell that requires no respirator or high-tech fan system to exchange the air in the building every few minutes. Wood.

And wood shavings. Stuff that you can grab handfuls of and just bury your snout into. It's an old smell; a simple smell; a healthy smell.

After you come out of a wooden boat shop, yeah, you might brush the biggest part of the shavings off your clothes. But if a little bit of them are still clinging to your vest the next morning when you put it on, it's just a comfortable reminder of where you've been.

And the tunk of that caulking mallet . . . for me, that's the soundtrack in my head to a memory from a long time ago: back to Pa's seining days. I remember one winter when he worked in a shed made of clear poly sheeting over a 2 x 4 frame, recaulking the bottom of the old *Nicola C.* She was the bait boat for Colwell Brothers, and I suppose Pa was either trying to get caught up on or get ahead of his twine bill with them by working on the Nicola.

Tunk. Tunk. Tunk. Tunk.

And even on the coldest of days, once the sun got up and had a chance to work on that plastic, it was cozy in there. For a little kid, it was this neat little summery world, filled with hazy sunlight beating through the cloudy plastic.

Tunk. Tunk. Tunk. Tunk.

"You know why I always liked caulking boats?" said Wesley. "'Cause when you were caulking, that was your job—no digging timbers out of the snow and lugging them in; none of that. Your job was caulking seams and doing it right. I liked that."

Tunk. Tunk. Tunk. Tunk.

There's no doubt in my mind but that I'm looking at a man who enjoys what he's doing—and is lucky enough to realize it now, rather than later, after it's over and done with.

Tunk. Tunk. Tunk. Tunk.

My life has come full circle of late in many ways. There are simple joys to be had that have been lost for a long time—and some that have never existed. And there's tucked-away memories that I now know are safe to haul out of my pocket.

On a recent winter evening, sitting by a wood stove with a belly full of turkey pie, I was told the story of the final resting spot of the old *Nicola C*—she was the *Theophilus N. Winslow* when she was grounded out for the last time.

Pa's recaulking was long lost by then; the best of cotton can't hold wood that's just plain gone. The *Nicola* was a dying boat at that point and I don't expect there's much left of her to see these days. But even so, that's a little tiny part of me that I'd like to visit again if I could.

So I will.

Tunk. Tunk. Tunk. Tunk.

Chapter 41

Enjoy
The Blessings
Of Every
Single Day

*For a good, good friend who made me laugh just
about as much as anyone has in my whole life.*

≈

On the morning of Thursday, Feb. 14, 2002, my
close friend Ray Cronk sat beside me on the edge of
a hospital bed in Brunswick, ME and told me he had
cancer.

On the afternoon of Tuesday the 19th, 2002, I sat
on the edge of Ray's bed at his home on Westport
Island, ME with his wife (and best friend) Joyce and
saw him across the bar.

That's all it took—just a handful of days. But I
guess if I was going to make use of any of the lessons
I learned from Ramie over the years it would be to
never, *ever* discount the value of every single day.

If you attended any commercial fishing show in
New England since 1990, or any of the lobster
boat races sponsored by C.E. Shepherd during that

period, then you probably would have seen Ray. He was the little guy with the biggest grin in the world, who always took care of business, but never missed a chance to laugh, either.

My friendship with Ramie began when C.E. Shepherd brought him aboard in 1990 to manage the sales of their lobster trap wire throughout New England (along with Maritime Canada and Newfoundland). I was working at *Commercial Fisheries News* back then and Shepherd was one of my ad accounts. The first time that Ray came to the *CFN* offices in Stonington he warmed us all with his personality and left us looking forward to working with him.

From there, it didn't take long to get to know Ray as a friend. Over lunches, trade show weekends, and shared road trips, we discovered that we both had some offshore time in our pasts (Ray gillnetting with Hubba Bradford, myself lobstering with my brother, Stevie). We shared a weakness for good guitar pickin'. The northern latitudes fascinated both of us (we'd take Cape Breton over Orlando and Farley Mowat over Jimmy Buffet any old day of the week). We were equally as happy bellied up to the lunch counter at Moody's Diner as we were in any of your finer dining establishments.

And there was the humor. Ramie made me laugh just as hard as I did him. Sometimes it was choked-back giggles and sometimes it was helpless, teary-eyed and snotty-nosed gagging laughter that makes you just *ache* when it finally fades, leaving you gasping for breath and trying to wipe your face dry.

I'm sure there were very few waiters or waitresses that ever tended our table that didn't suspect, at least at the beginning of the meal, that they were dealing with a couple of crazy-ass drunks—but by the time the meal was done and there'd been no liquor served, it was probably pretty clear: the big white-haired guy and the little fella with the wicked grin were just chock full of foolishness . . . and, for the most part, our servers would be laughing, too.

Ray always had a joke or a story handy, but the funniest stuff he'd lay on me usually just seized the humor in the moment—right *now*—and most often was at his own expense. And that was one thing that anyone who ever found themselves the target of Ramie's humor would come to know if they were around him for any length of time: he laughed the hardest at himself.

Maybe the biggest lesson one could learn from Ray was the importance of *right now*; the ability to live in the moment and enjoy the simple stuff. Where a lot of folks need to surround themselves with material possessions, Ray could offer you half of a big ol' cookie and make you both feel like kings as you stood side-by-side on the dock chewing.

We made a bunch of trips up and down the coast during the years that I covered the boat races for the paper on Ray's 23' *For Play*, but some of the best trips came after I left *CFN*, when we went for a ride to simply "enjoy the blessings of the day," as Ray would often say. When he purchased a 32' Jim Day-built wooden boat in the spring of 2000, we became gentlemen cruisers, easing down the Sheepscot and savoring the simple pleasures of *right now*.

His wonderful wife Joyce was a part of the happiness—you couldn't be around the two of them together and not say to yourself "Now *that's* what every marriage should be: they *like* each other."

I was lucky enough to be able to share Ray and Joyce with all three of my kids over the years. And Tigger and I shared our first moment together on the water (after a *long* time of talking about it) aboard of

Ray and Joyce's *Patient Lady* last fall with my daughters, Cassie and Jess, at our side. That turned out to be my last boat ride with Ramie—but it couldn't have been a better memory to hold on to. And I'm thankful for that.

Damn it, Ray.

You weren't supposed to leave yet.

At least, not in *my* story. But none of us is really in charge of how the story goes—only telling it, right?

So the best I know to do is keep that smile you gave me handy—and enjoy the blessings of the day.

You rest for a bit, little buddy, and we'll take the watch.

Chapter 42

A Low-Budget
Peter Pan

This is a testimonial to just how much I trust my brother Stevie. Either that, or a testimonial to just how numb I am. Maybe both.

≈

I hate heights.

I *really* hate heights.

I'm not sure just how tall I am (maybe 6'4" or 6'5" at most, depending on the weather and my mood), but that's just about the maximum height I'm comfortable with.

This condition renders me utterly useless in many facets of everyday life. For instance, the only thing that would strike a greater fear into my heart than the question "Hey, Brian—do you want to go up on the roof and do some shingling?" would be "Hey, Brian—do you want to go up on the roof and catch some snakes?"

Imagine it: years ago, every time I slid a bait tub over the edge of a dock and lowered it down, I had to suppress the thought that I was surely going to be sucked right out into space myself by some unseen force.

One-handed climbs up rickety ladders at dead low water while clutching a sea bag were the sources of bad dreams.

And then there was the time that my brother, Stevie, tried to turn me into Peter Pan. You remember Peter Pan, don't you—the fellow who not only wanted to be a boy forever, but could fly as well?

It was 1984 and my brother's 54' steel offshore lobster boat *Stacie Vea* was hauled out on the inside railway at Billings Diesel & Marine in Stonington. The boat was only three years old at that point, but Stevie wanted to give her a good going over—from the bottom of her keel to the top of her mast. Literally.

Now, I'd actually gone up into the rigging before— I remember once climbing up to cut free a riding sail that had blown itself out and was giving the antennas on the crosstree a savage whipping. Somehow, that was different: for one thing, it was night; and once I was up there, I made myself fast with a length of $9/16$" groundline that was strong enough to pull Hell itself out by the roots. I wasn't giddy with glee about climbing up there, but I really didn't have time to think about it. It was just one of those things you do.

But there was something very frightening about the prospect of going up to the top of the *Stacie's* mast while she was propped up in the railway cradle— making her overall height (and the potential distance to fall) all the more intimidating.

Plus, there was paint and a paintbrush to contend with. Good Lord, I can get into enough trouble with such items on level ground. On a good day, it's best if I just take half of the paint made available to me and rub it in my hair and smear it on my clothes and get it over with. It's a given that there will be some horror show before the operation is all said and done.

It didn't look good, and I told my brother so.

"Ain't no way," I said.

"Sure there is," he replied.

"Yeah—right," I said. "Why don't I just *fly* up there?"

The look that came over Stevie's face must have rivaled the expression on Newton's face when the apple hit him on top of the head. He pointed up at the ceiling. I looked up there, but all I could see was the big hook hanging from the building's heavy-duty overhead hoist.

I suddenly realized what he was thinking. "No. No way. No friggin' way."

"Don't worry," he assured me as he began lowering the hook with the handheld control box. "I'll run it. All you have to do is ride up, paint the mast, and come back down. Piece of cake."

I love my brother and trust him completely. That's the only way I can explain to you how, just minutes after Stevie's idea was hatched, I was hanging from that overhead hoist in a homemade rope harness with a bucket of paint in one hand and a brush in the other.

"Give me a second to get the feel of this thing," my brother said, cigar clenched between his teeth. He picked me up a few feet and then set me back down. "Ready?" he asked. I made a squeaking noise and nodded weakly. The hook jerked me off the floor and I arose.

Stevie yelled encouraging stuff like "Lookin' good!" and "Relax!" as I slowly climbed. There was a slight bobble as he attempted to level me off at mast height. Then he scooted me sideways toward my target, which was about 50' away.

The unfortunate thing about lateral movement is the pendulum effect that results. Thus, the hoist stopped, but I kept on swinging. "Those doggone laws of physics," I thought (or something like that—remember, my mother reads this column) as I rocketed out by the top of the *Stacie's* mast. After about 30' to starboard, I began to swing back to port.

It flashed through my head that I could attempt to grab the mast on my way back by, but then I realized that I actually needed to use any and all available body English to avoid ramming said mast.

"Don't spill the paint!" my brother yelled up at me as I reached the outboard limit of another swing. "Quit showing off!"

I won't go on about this. The basic story is, eventually, we got things steadied up, the mast got painted, and nobody got hurt.

But I can honestly say that once his size 14 sneakers touched back down on the floor, Peter Pan never took flight again.

Chapter 43

And They're Off!

Another totally made-up lobster boat race report, which paled in comparison to reality.

≈

FRITTER HARBOR, ME—Everyone knows that Shepherd Lobster Wire has been a major supporter of the Maine Lobster Boat Races for years—now the first corporate-sponsored *individual* entry is about to join the circuit. Local lobsterman and performance enthusiast William "Binky" Willard has secured financial backing from Preparation H to fund his 2001 race campaign. Willard's 27' *Welcome Relief* looks to be not only a contender in her diesel class, but a candidate to possibly lay down some record-breaking speeds, as well.

"The Preparation H folks have bucks to burn," said Willard. "I wrote a letter saying I knew they'd been making a killing off us lobstermen up here in Maine pulling our insides out for years and figured it was time for them to kick a little back this way."

With a flashy paint job (featuring the slogan "We're right behind you") and three spare engines standing by ("The first couple's just so we know how far to turn the screw," said Willard), the 27-footer should be a real crowd-pleaser.

CRONK'S NUBBLE, ME—Veteran boat builder Hadley Osborne suffered a setback in his 2001 race campaign in early May when a seagull landed on the top of the wheelhouse of his 31'*Horndog* and flattened it "right chock to the deck," according to Osborne. The 31-footer was rumored to be built on the light side solely with racing in mind, but Osborne defended the *Horndog's* structural integrity.

"That cussed gull was *huge*," he told *Commercial Fisheries News*. "Biggest one I ever see."

Reportedly, Osborne beached the *Horndog* immediately after the accident so that he and his wife could carry it home to repair the damage. "We'll be there for the season opener," Osborne promised.

CLAM HEAD, ME—With the opening event of the 2001 season only weeks away, local lobsterman Hugh Jass is feverishly trying to gather a few more signatures for his petition to present to the Maine Lobster Boat Races Oversight Committee. Jass is seeking the sponsorship of one more class in the diesel ranks, defined as follows: "All vessels between 38'11" and 39'1" with bright red trim, black boot top, and orange bottom powered by an 8-cylinder engine with a decal on it that reads '250 hp,' and carrying a name on the transom containing 6 consonants and 4 vowels."

Jass's petition also suggests a prize for that particular class: "Maybe a nice wide-screen TV." Jass himself was unavailable for comment as *CFN* went to press; he was reportedly busy trying to get the orange bottom paint touched up on his 39' *Miss Sophie* while she was grounded out.

SOUTH DUMPLING, ME—In what appears to be the first serious merchandising scheme designed to cash in on the growing popularity of the Maine Lobster Boat Races, local businessman Winston Bunsen is offering an "Official Maine Lobster Boat Racing Cap." The recently introduced item has met some skepticism in the marketplace, however.

According to Bunsen, the headwear is "aerodynamically designed for high performance enthusiasts." Basically, Bunsen says the visor is already on the back of the hat, saving racers (and fans) the trouble of turning the caps around.

His critics point out that the plain red cap is just a regular hat that you put on your head backwards to begin with, hardly justifying the $99 price tag. Bunsen has scoffed at such statements. "They all laughed at Columbus, too," he says.

Reportedly, Bunsen also has plans in the works for a line of race-endorsed dried fish ("Quick Chaws"), scale model race boats ("Hot Waves"), and a feature film starring formerly retired motion picture star Belted Galloway ("Days Of Nitrous").

SHAG'S HEAD. ME—Race committee officials in this midcoast village are busy researching the claim by gas class contender Norm Gumption that his 26' *No Kiddin'* is powered by a 10-hp Tecumseh engine.

"It's awful big for a 10-hp motor—even with the supercharger taken off it," said race chairman Billy Bob Muncey. "And I got to be honest with you: not to call Norm a liar or anything, but I haven't been able to find any specs anywhere that show a V-8 Tecumseh lawn mower engine."

Gumption has claimed that the engine is a "detuned continuous-duty version . . . they only made a few of them. Mostly, you see these on riding mowers for *really* big lawns." Gumption denied allegations that he might be trying to pass off a high-performance racing engine as a lowball entry. "Don't be stupid," he told the *CFN* Sports Desk when interviewed in early May. "Look at those neat stickers on the valve covers—any dope can see they say '10 hp'."

Chapter 44

A Good Argument for Wearing Oil Pants

Did this really happen? What—would I lie to you?

≈

It is hot.

Hot?

Yes, hot. Some friggin' *hot*.

It's the kind of hot that you can't escape from; there's no sweet little afternoon sea breeze—there's nothing but *hot*. Gummy, sticky, thick-as-pogey-grease hot.

It's the kind of hot that drives folks to slinging bait forks at those who say things like, "It's not the *heat*—it's the *humidity*," or—and this is the absolute worst—"Hot 'nuff for ya?"

(Don't try to act innocent with me . . . you *know* you've come close to throttling someone before when they've said one or the other of those lines to you on a day when flies lay panting alongside the dogs. Don't be ashamed. It's a perfectly understandable reaction and would hold up as a legitimate defense in any court of law.)

It's a mean hot.

It's a no-escaping-it hot.

Remember: There's a limit to how many clothes one can take off when it's hot—especially when working on the water. Of course, the standards change in direct proportion to how far offshore one is, but there's still a limit.

It's inevitable that the worlds of the landlocked and the waterbound will collide now and then—sometimes it is not a pretty picture. And heat only complicates things.

I remember one bit of culture shock many years ago involving one of the locals from home and a charge of that particular summer's visitors to our rockbound coast.

There were a bunch of fellows over on the west end of town who had life pretty well figured out in a way similar to the characters in John Steinbeck's novel "Tortilla Flat." "Laid back" would be an appropriate phrase, I guess. They were all older men, but for the sake of telling the story, we'll call them The Boys.

The Boys didn't seem to get too wound up about what the wind or the tide was doing. If it wasn't much of a day to go to haul, that was OK—and even if it was a good chance weather-wise, well, that didn't mean you *had* to go, either.

"There ain't nothin' wrong with a long set . . ."

"No sense to bait on what they had—maybe there'll be some fresh herrin' tomorrow . . ."

"By Gawd, I oughta bleach the bottom of the old girl—although I guess I missed the tide today. Maybe tomorrow . . ."

"No sense to bait on that fresh herrin'—might just as well let the salt take hold of it. Maybe tomorrow . . ."

There was always tomorrow for The Boys. But make no mistake about it: they still managed to take the bull by the horns each day just the same. They were brought together over on the west end of town to mentally tackle what might be done tomorrow and debate the issues of the day by a common bond: **the grape.**

Ah, yes. Old Duke—a bargain-priced item at Vic's IGA that could be counted upon to cost the same each and every day of the year, rather than fall victim to some scandalous marketing scheme that might see the cost per gallon jug skyrocket around the holidays. No, there was none of that for Old Duke.

Most days there were enough of The Boys on hand to rally up some cash for a visit to Vic's by midmorning or so. Usually Mack (not his real name, but it worked for Steinbeck, so it's good enough for me) would be the designated walker (if he wasn't out to haul) for the first run of the day. And being a rugged man of good constitution, ol' Mack would usually make the bulk of the rest of each day's visits, too, one gallon at a time.

Now The Boys never got rowdy or violent—there was no gunplay or knife fights or anything like that. But they were capable of getting awful frigged up. Especially if it was one of those days when Mack made a number of trips down to the IGA.

It was a savage hot summer afternoon when Mack left the rest of The Boys deep into the Duke and stivered over to the shore to go aboard of his boat. She had a little bit of a leak to her and ought to be checked, he decided.

Mack politely weaved his way through the crowd on the lobster car, a thick mix of people fishing for mackerel and vacationing photographers recording the excitement.

At most, maybe half of the gathered mass paid any attention to the badly sweating, intoxicated man who rowed off to his little lobster boat on her mooring.

And even fewer of them noticed Mack disappearing down below for a long period of time, finally reappearing apparently shirtless and wearing his old Helly-Hansen apron.

And maybe a handful of observers watched Mack's attempts to bait a few pockets in the sweltering heat.

And only a couple of people at most saw Mack sort of roll down over the rail sometime later (still wearing the yellow bait apron) and make a zig-zag course in his rowboat back to the lobster car where he made her fast.

But by the time Mack weaved his way to the top of the ramp and stepped onto the wharf, he had the complete attention of the whole crowd.

For, as Mack started the long, slow, hot climb up the ramp (with his backside to the gathering on the float), it became apparent that he had not only shed his shirt when he was off aboard the boat, but his pants and underwear, as well.

I guess it wasn't the heat as much as it was the humidity.

Chapter 45

A Few Words
for Edward

Though I knew who Edward Myers was for many years, I didn't get to spend anywhere near enough time with him once Tigger and I were together as a couple. But I'm thankful for what time we had.

This was written after he passed away in September of 2002.

≈

*I*n the photograph, a man is in the middle of a dirt road. There are no signs to give away his location, but the exotic-looking foliage in the background tells you that it isn't coastal Maine, for sure.

He's far enough away and the slightly rumpled hat pulled down to the tops of his glasses hides enough of his features so you can't pinpoint his age. However, you get the sense that he's an older man.

A jacket is tied around his waist, letting the sun shine on his Oxford-cloth shirt with its rolled-up sleeves. "Who is this?" you might ask yourself. "A lawyer? A banker? A teacher?" Ah, but look farther down his solid frame and you'll note that his pants are tucked into a pair of rubber knee boots

> *... and, even from a distance, you can tell that he's*
> *quite at home in them. As exotic as the setting may*
> *be, you just **know** that this is a man of the water.*
>
> *But why is he dancing a jig in the middle of*
> *the road?*
>
> *And is that a flute that he's holding, offering a*
> *tune to the jungle around him?*
>
> *"What a funny picture," you might say.*

I normally fill this space up with words about boats and fishing. But tonight I'm writing what I feel, and although there's salt water in this column, it's not the main focus.

I only got to spend a year (almost to the day, in fact) around Edward Myers before he passed away on September 19 of this year. It was nowhere near enough time, for sure—but I'm thankful that I had what I had.

I certainly knew who Edward was prior to last year; and we'd actually had a conversation of sorts a number of years ago. I was still a full-timer at *Commercial Fisheries News* at that point and was hanging around our booth at the ME Fisherman's Forum in Rockport one early March weekend when an older gentleman in a tweed jacket and bow tie approached me. There was something familiar about him, but nothing I could nail down.

After a quick glance at my name tag, he got right to the point of his visit: "My daughter is apparently quite a fan of your columns," he said. "And I enjoy them myself from time to time. Keep up the good work." I mumbled something utterly forgettable as he shook my hand. And then he was gone.

I turned to one of my booth mates and asked, "Who was that?"

"Ed Myers," they answered. I immediately felt

my face and ears burn with a blush. The father of the one and only Tigger—a person who, once I'd met her, I would surely never, ever forget—had just complimented me and I had managed to do my best impersonation of an absolute oaf. (Edward told me last winter that he didn't remember me saying anything that day to embarrass myself, but he did take note at the time and sort of held it against me that I hadn't mentioned *his* columns in the *Working Waterfront*. He grinned while he said it, though.)

So life went the way it did over the years ... and the Great Spirit directed things to happen the way they were meant to. Therefore, Tigger and I have ended up together and that gave me a chance to spend a little bit of precious time around Edward Myers.

You may know him as the founding father of farm-raised mussels in Maine. Or maybe you knew of him as a defender of his beloved Damariscotta River. Or the Gulf of Maine. Or the world.

But me, I'll mostly think about things like the time that Wes Lash handed me a hunk of oakum when Edward and I visited his shop. The scent of the oakum was strong and good; and when I offered it to Edward he inhaled its perfume and smiled at me like we were sharing the greatest of treasures.

I guess in many ways we were.

≈

Edward was in his seventies when he made the first of two trips to Nicaragua with Witness For Peace, a group of like-minded people who were dedicated to the hope for world peace. They weren't missionaries, mercenaries, politicians, or soldiers—they were just regular folks who wanted to touch the far corners of this old world and let the people there know that hope did, in fact, exist.

On the day the photograph was taken, the group was tucked into the back of an old truck, making a flying run through a section of jungle road where sniper attacks and roadblocks manned by gun-toting rebels were common.

Something let go under the hood of the truck and it rolled to a stop. As the dust settled around them, the group felt very exposed and vulnerable. Maybe a simple repair would get them going, but who was going to bend over the front fender, knowing full well that a sniper's cross hairs might be trained on them?

Edward wasn't long in bailing out of the truck body, ignoring the words of his companions. "I'm the oldest," he simply said. Edward then quickly pulled out his trusty jackknife and cut a length of sugar cane by the roadside.

With his jacket tied around his middle, and his sleeves rolled up to his elbows, Edward began to dance a jig to the melody of his makeshift sugar cane "flute." There was no doubt: this silly-acting old man was certainly the center of attention in this patch of jungle road. His faithful old rubber boats kicked up the dust as he twirled to his tune and his jacket swung out from his hips like the skirt of a young girl at a Saturday night dance. Entranced, the rest of the truck's passengers forgot their fear for a bit while the repairs were made and the group was soon underway again with no further incidents.

But the photograph of Edward's jig remains.

Chapter 46

A Wish for Peaceful Waters

Though the nighttime-in-the-seineboat theme is a repeat from an earlier column, I think it's worthy of it. My vision of Pa and Edward together from January of 2003 still makes me feel good.

A side note: I've had the opportunity to speak with both Jorma Kaukonen and Jack Casady in the years since writing this. They're both good souls.

≈

Well, what are they doing in Heaven today?
Sin and sorrow are all gone away
Peace it flows like a river, they say
What are they doing there now?
*   —Traditional Folk Song—*

It was billed as "An Evening With Jorma Kaukonen And Jack Casady: The Original Hot Tuna." And it was good.

I'd been grinning and stomping my foot in time with the acoustic blues flowing from the stage all evening, but when Jorma and Jack eased into that particular song, I found myself just sitting quietly, wrapped up in the music like a well-worn comfy quilt. I held Tigger's hand with my left and my daughter Cassie's with my right and breathed a sweet, sad sigh.

"What *are* they doing there now?" I wondered.

I miss Pa every day of my life, but right then, at that moment, sitting in the Lebanon Opera House in Lebanon, NH watching those two 60-something-year-old guys pick and plunk was one of those times when I *really* missed Pa. And Tigger's dad Edward. And my buddy Ramie.

I guess it's part of the Christmas season to let down our guards a bit more than usual and allow stuff to seep in and out of us a little more freely. It's hard to explain but since Pa passed away in '95, one of the things I've wished I could do, especially at this time of year, is tell him that he's still loved and missed and that he's still an inspiration and a comfort.

I've written this before, I'm sure: I remember those occasional summer nights during Pa's stop twine seining years (I was just a little guy) when it would just be him and me out patrolling for fish. Looking back now, I don't know if he ever expected to find a single herring those nights that just the two of us went, but it was the greatest kind of adventure for me . . . and now I have to wonder if that wasn't part of the reason why he did it.

Once we'd get things straightened away aboard the old Lucky Star, there'd be a good seine boat snack—a sandwich, or maybe buttered Crown Pilot crackers and rat cheese—followed by a curl into our bunks while we waited for night to truly fall.

Then it was time to go in the outboard.

Once I learned what my job was, there weren't many words exchanged between us during the sojourns around whatever particular cove we were patrolling. I manned the motor (which, once I got older, I could occasionally yank to life on my own—nearly dislocating a number of major structural bones in the process, but no matter: I started the outboard *myself*) and Pa'd be in the bow with his feeler pole. I kept my eyes focused on the outline of his head and shoulders silhouetted against the night sky; when he wanted me to turn, Pa would lean to that side.

The motor chugged along easily and the feeler stick cut silently through the water. And I waged war with my little boy's attention span, forcing myself to stay locked in on my father's silent shadow in the bow of the boat.

He was my guide.

And he still is.

I'm not always aware of Pa, but during those times when I need to get my bearings, I know he's right up there in the bow. The lessons in patience and strength and humor that he passed along are right there, too—I can navigate my way through an awful lot of stuff if I just take the time to heed his courses.

So, sometimes now when I try to imagine a peaceful, pleasant setting for Pa, I envision him in the bow of a slow and steady open boat, slitting the water's surface with the feeler pole—not in an effort to find fish to shut off, but just to know they're there. These days I like to think of Edward maybe at the outboard—though my father and Tigger's never met, their souls were knit from a number of common threads (as well as a number of diverse ones). A love of the water was a shared feeling, for sure.

And Edward, being a master of the silent drift (allowing the senses to sop up everything from a bird's far-away call to the splash of a mackerel to the scent of a wild rose bush in on the shore to the perfect beauty of a hawk's dive) would be an ideal man to run the outboard: quiet and attentive and just plain happy to be there.

And wouldn't it tickle Edward to have a turn at the feeler pole, too: I can see the smile on his face as he feels the slender fish swim by . . . and Pa back at the motor, breathing in great chestfulls of salt air.

Yeah, that's what I see sometimes . . . when I wonder what they're doing in Heaven today, that's one of my versions of a pretty good time.

I hope it's like that.

Chapter 47

The Great Downhill Dory Ride

This one was inspired by a mid-winter phone conversation with my brother-in-law, Allen Myers. They never put a kinder, gentler person on the face of this earth than Allen. Plus, he's funny.

≈

Eddie Pluggs was 11 years old when he and Monroe Sinclair took their Great Downhill Dory Ride—years before Eddie grew into a highline lobsterman and Monroe was elected the Village Idiot.

Even back then, Eddie knew that any adventure he got into with Monroe Sinclair often resulted in some sort of trouble. But it was hard to ignore Monroe when he was making a case for The Thrill Of Doing Something, as he was on this particular February Saturday. The two of them stood at the foot of Rabbit Mountain, watching most of the town's population of children go sledding.

"You see what I'm talkin' about, Eddie?" asked Monroe. "That ain't nothin'." He gestured with a mittened hand at the slope filled with happy sledders. "I betcha that ain't even a *tenth* of the total height of the mountain," he said with a slight air of disgust.

Eddie watched a toboggan full of kids fly down the

well-packed snow and come to a gentle halt in the field at the hill's base. "Yeah, but—" Eddie turned to find Monroe walking briskly away. He trotted to catch up. "It's the best sleddin' spot in town and it always has been. Where else are you gonna go?"

Monroe was silent for a few minutes as they walked the road that both chased the foot of the mountain and led to the head of the harbor. They were abreast of the old sardine cannery when he stopped.

"There," Monroe said, pointing to the very top of Rabbit Mountain. Eddie, knowing that this would later be remembered as The Point When He Should Have Said Good-Bye, took a sight along Monroe's outstretched arm.

First, there was the big empty lot (now snow-covered) where the cannery's warehouse had stood until the previous fall, when it was torn down. Up in back of that was a big field where blueberries grew wild in the summertime. Farther up the slope, where there used to be acres of scrub pines, there was nothing but snow—a bad fire had leveled the area back on the 4th of July. Then Eddie's eye rose to the big clearing where the old homestead of some famous painter used to stand; the artist's heirs had the structure—barn and all—dismantled and re-erected somewhere in Oklahoma, according to the word on the waterfront. And above that was more field . . . and Eddie's eyes quickly reviewed the hillside and realized that the circumstances of the last year had opened up a never-before-possible opportunity: a sled run right from the top of Rabbit Mountain.

Except—"What about old man Hubbard?" asked Eddie, squinting up at the house sitting at the peak.

"Gone to Florida," grinned Monroe. "And left his seinin' outfit behind. Come on." And he set off up the road that led to the top of Rabbit Mountain.

The seining remark didn't make any sense to Eddie until they arrived in Mr. Hubbard's dooryard at the peak. There were mounds of twine and a dozen or so dories strewn around. Monroe slapped the bottom of a particularly weathered-looking dory that was over-turned and leaning against a tree. "Here's our ride," he said, eyes slightly glazed.

Eddie found himself helping Monroe overturn the thing onto its bottom. And then he realized that they were perfectly lined up with the open run stretching all the way down to the factory parking lot—and poised right at its very beginnings. Destiny could not be denied—and with a couple of good pushes and heaves over the side, they were off.

Monroe took the bow while Eddie lurched back aft. It dawned on Eddie that they had no way to steer the now-speeding dory and he opened his mouth to ask Monroe about it when—WUMP!—the dory launched off a little knoll and landed pretty hard, dumping Eddie into a heap in the bottom. "Wow!" yelled a wild-eyed and grinning Monroe.

Eddie was beginning to feel concerned when they hit about seven knolls in a row—WUMPWUMPWUMPWUMP!—and that's when the plank came off the bottom of the dory.

"Hey!" yelled Eddie just as the snow started rooster-tailing up through the opening in the bottom of the wildly careening boat. Monroe, braced off in the bow like a crazed Captain Ahab, hollered, "Hang on, Eddie—we've stove a plank off her!" As they rocketed down the slope, Eddie was pinned in the stern by the rapidly growing snowdrift; within seconds he was buried.

Monroe was still upright, hanging onto the painter with the wind ripping at his clothes and screaming,

"YEEEEEEEEHAAAAAAAA!" at the sky. He was oblivious to the situation back aft.

The dory was probably going 50 miles an hour when it hit the parking lot of the cannery, skidded across its icy surface, fetched up on a frozen snowbank, and exploded. Monroe somersaulted into the air and landed in a snow-laden apple tree. The drift Eddie was buried under acted more or less like an airbag and he ended up atop the frozen snowbank with the wind knocked out of him, big time.

There was dead silence for about a minute. And then Monroe said from the upper reaches of the apple tree: "Wanna do it again?"

Chapter 48

Just leave
a message . . .

I've been without a television for almost 16 years now. But somehow I acquired a cellphone along the way. This column was written about the time that I began to question whether it was a step forward or backward. I'm still not sure.

≈

There are a lot of things in life that are just like slipping on a banana peel. In a sick way, it's humorous if it happens to someone else. If *you* are the victim, however, there is nothing funny about it.

So there we'd be in the wheelhouse, listening to the ruination of some poor slob's homelife over the single sideband radio, the only connection any of us had back in the 1970's between offshore and the mainland. Usually the conversation would be through the marine operator, rather than radio to radio.

The occasion would be whatever it was: a birthday; an anniversary; the evening of a daughter's first dance recital; the afternoon after a son's first Little League homerun; Valentine's Day. It didn't make a difference.

We'd be there like an offshore version of a family from the Golden Age of radio, only instead of Jack

Benny, we might, for instance, catch an episode of "The Missed Anniversary":

"I just wanted to see if the flowers came. Over."

"What? I couldn't understand you . . . are you there? Can you hear me?"

"Yeah, but you need to say 'over' when you're done talkin' so I know when to press my mike button and start talkin'. Okay? Over."

"-have a microphone."

"What? Over."

"I said I don't have a microphone. I'm on the telephone here in the kitchen."

"Yeah, yeah, I know you don't have a microphone in the kitchen . . . I was just wonderin' if you got the flowers I sent. Over."

"-not stupid, you know."

"What? Over."

"I said I'm *not stupid.* You don't have to talk to me in that tone of voice."

"But I -"

"—not my fault if —"

"—sary. Over."

"You *better* say you're sorry."

"Sorry for what? I didn't say I was *sorry*; I was tryin' to say 'Happy Anniversary', fer chrissakes. Over."

"—listened to my sister way back when."

"Look—I can't hear a friggin' thing you're sayin', if you're talkin' when I'm talkin'! I just want to know if you got the stupid flowers or didn't you?"

"You didn't say 'over'."

"Oh, to hell with it. *Over.*"

It didn't always erupt into some dreadful horror show between the parties involved, but at best, there would be the repeating of phrases and words—usually a key sentence, which would totally lose its clout after a few dozen times.

"I miss you. Hurry home. Over."

"The dog's got worms? Over."

"No, I said I miss you . . . *I miss you.* Over."

"The kids got the flu? That's too bad. Over."

"No, no—*miss you.* **Miss . . . you.** Over."

"The fish got the flu, too? Better clean out the aquarium. Over."

Oh, for the ability to just call home, we thought. Wouldn't it be something when the day came that you could just dial a number and talk like a human being instead of a mildly-retarded robot. (Let's face it: even the most eloquent of emotional outpourings loses something when it's ended with a pause and then the word "Over.") What a blessing it would be to have some sort of mobile phone.

Yeah, right.

Here we are, the best part of three decades later. These days, *everyone* has a cellphone, it seems. And not just to get a critical message through to the mainland, either. Ha! That's the least of it.

What's that annoying noise behind you in the movie theater? That's a ringing cellphone—and thank the Lord that fellow has it with him because now he can give the person on the other end a complete recap of what's happened so far in the film and a preview of what *might* happen. Neat.

Why is that man talking to the jars of peanut butter in the supermarket? Wait—he has a cellphone pressed to his ear, reading the labels to someone who just needed to know what the contents were of the leading brands. How nice.

Hey—I confess. I have a cellphone, although it usu-ally stays right in its cradle in the H&H Propeller van. I hate the cussed thing, but I have to have it . . . it's as simple as that. There's no way I could tend on things up and down the coast if I was trying to rely on occasional stops at payphones, that's for sure.

And when it works, the cellphone's a great thing. But when it doesn't . . .

At least it has voicemail, which is one of those things that seems like it's an impersonal annoyance, I know. But, hey—between being in and out of the van, in and out of good reception areas, and in and out of other phone conversations, it's the only way I know of to keep track of who needs to talk to me.

So if you call me—or anybody—and opt to just hang up and not leave a message, that's okay. But when you do finally talk to me, don't say "Jeez, you're a hard guy to get ahold of." Just don't. I've tried wrapping a towel around my head and sitting cross-legged on the floor trying to imagine who might have called and hung up without leaving a message, but I can't do it. (Do you know how happy we would have been to have voicemail back in 1978? And while you're at it, eat your vegetables.)

Hang on a second; the phone's ringing.

There, I'm back. It was Tigger saying she was on her way home.

Or maybe she's found a banjo with a nice tone.

She might have said she had a trunk full of loam.

I couldn't tell for sure . . . she was on her cellphone.

Chapter 49

Our Fathers' Oakum

This may not mean as much to you if you've never smelled oakum. Then again, maybe that's not the important part.

Thank you, Wes.

≈

Just a box of rain, wind and water
Believe it if you need it, if you don't just pass it on
Sun and shower, wind and rain
In and out the window like a moth before the flame

And it's just a box of rain, I don't know who put it there
Believe it if you need it, or leave it if you dare
And it's just a box of rain or a ribbon for your hair
Such a long, long time to be gone and a short time to be there

(from "Box of Rain" by Robert Hunter and Phil Lesh)

It's been just a year since Tigger's dad Edward passed away. In the relatively short time I had to spend with Edward as part of the family circle, we had fun. I made

244

him laugh and he made me think. And sometimes *I* made *him* think and *he* made *me* laugh.

We had a good time together—we just didn't get to have enough of it.

Two afternoons in particular stand out in my memory when I think about Edward and the time we had to just be friends. The first was in the spring of 2002 when Edward rode over to Friendship with me to pay a visit to Wes Lash's shop.

I was happy for Wes; he had returned to his roots and was in the middle of building a *wooden* 42-footer . . . something you just don't see enough of anymore (unless you visit Pete Kass' shop in South Bristol). Simple pleasures were the best in Edward's world and that afternoon was chock full of them: the beauty of a plank fitted to the shear; the graceful curve of a bilgeline; the rhythm of the caulking mallet; and the smells—ahhh, the *smells*.

The aroma of the wood that filled the shop was one thing, but there were also the more subtle scents that either meant something to you or they didn't.

Wes knew that day how to make Edward grin the biggest kind of Edward grin: he passed him a wad of oakum caulking and Edward buried his nose in it like a bouquet of roses and drew in a deep breath.

"Ahhhhh," he sighed, "that's a good, old, *real* smell." He passed the oakum back to Wes and almost shyly said, "Thank you."

There was a common thread of caulking running through the second special afternoon that I shared with Edward. I can see him now in the stern of his beloved flat-bottomed outboard *Marisco* with a full crew of us aboard: Tigger and I, her mom Julia, and my youngest daughter Cassie, plus our faithful Chesapeake Bay Retriever Chelsea and Edward and Julia's doleful-eyed Bassett Hound Willie. We took an easy chug down and around the Damariscotta River with gentle commentary from Edward.

At one point we circled Peter's Island which lay about 2 miles downriver from Edward and Julia's home in Clark's Cove. When Tigger pointed out the bones of an old wooden boat grounded out in on the beach, I immediately had a lump in my throat.

It was the old *Nicola C.*

When I was little, Pa worked one winter in a shed made of clear poly sheeting stretched over a 2 x 4 frame, replanking and recaulking this same boat. Back then she was a small sardine carrier owned by Colwell Brothers and Pa was probably trying to either get caught up on or get ahead of his twine bill with them by working on the *Nicola*.

Years later that same boat was renamed the *Theophilus N. Winslow* by her new owner, Edward Myers. The name was a nod to his Belfast-born grandfather, and the 45' boat was now to be used to tend Edward's mussel lines. Tigger herself had spent one winter assisting in the labor of love to keep the old boat's bilges tight by recaulking and painting her once again. Edward kept *Theophilus* active as long he could, but finally even he had to admit that she was too far gone to keep afloat.

The little cove on Peter's Island became *Theophilus'* final resting spot. As we drifted by in *Marisco* that day loaded with members of our newly-formed family, it was amazing to think that the bones of that old boat represented a link between our fathers that neither Tigger nor I knew about until years later.

My father had passed away in 1995. And a few short months after that ride in *Marisco,* Edward was gone, too.

Recently, as the first anniversary of Edward's death approached, plans were made for a small family memorial service. A headstone of Deer Isle granite was to be placed; and if anyone wanted to contribute some memento of their relationship with Edward, they were welcome to.

The items brought to the gathering on that handsome September morning were as diverse and interesting as the man himself. Little bits of love and deep thought and humor and the water were offered up and all were perfect.

With a puff of salt air stirring through the trees bordering the cemetery, Tigger and I added our things to Edward's pile.

A shackle that represented long quiet moments for father and daughter, tending to the hardware of the waterfront.

A length of oakum from Wes Lash's shop.

And some old cotton and a few bungs from the *Theophilus N. Winslow,* formerly the *Nicola C.*—the boat that both our fathers' hands hand touched.

Tigger and I (and Chelsea) had taken a moonlit ride aboard *Marisco* a few nights before that and visited the old boat to gather some gifts to Edward.

On the way back upriver, we shut down the motor for a bit and let the boat drift.

And our fathers sat with us as we silently rode the moonbeam on the incoming tide.

Chapter 50

Shirley V. Robbins
1923–2003

Stevie and I had the greatest parents in the world.

≈

There's a part of me that doesn't much care if I write this column or not. I will, of course, because I've promised that I would. But there's an awful emptiness inside me as I sit here in front of this screen.

For the first time in my life, I know that my mother isn't going to be reading these words. She won't be calling my brother Stevie to share a laugh over one of these foolish stories, or giving one of us a mock scolding over some retold memory of our years fishing (and acting up) together.

And no matter how many times a day I go to dial her number . . . or how many times my brother reaches for the microphone aboard the boat to call her . . . she's not going to be there to answer.

Our mother and friend, Shirley Robbins, is gone.

I don't know how Pa knew all the things that he knew; he just knew them.

He could handle a feeler stick and work it through a body of herring in the middle of a summer night, making it talk to him just as easily as a fiddle would sing in those same hands on a wintry afternoon by the woodstove.

He knew the best recipe for mixing up pine tar to coat a deck and he believed in starting just about any recipe atop the stove with an onion.

And he knew just how many turns of wire it took around a riding sail mast at such-and-such height to make a radio antenna that would that would send out a signal capable of blowing a CB base set right off the kitchen table.

For much of my childhood, that's how my folks conversed with each other for a good percentage of the time—over the airwaves. Pa wasn't a trip fisherman, but during the herring seining season, he'd be up all night looking for fish. By morning, unless they had a shutoff, Pa'd be headed down the bay to haul his lobster gear. And then when the winter months came, there'd be long days scalloping.

Don't get me wrong—there were some quiet times at home, too. But the radio was an important part of Marm and Pa's relationship.

When I was little, Pa's lobster boat was painted Newport Green with a white house and trunk. Her name was the *Fireball*—in total contrast to Pa's measured and patient approach to all things. Later on, the old *Fireball's* hull took on a coat of Bead Yellow and people began to call it the "Banana Boat" on the CB. The home set, however, remained "Fireball base."

If Pa and my brother Stevie were the captains in the family, then I guess Marm was the shore engineer.

My earliest memory is of a big shortwave radio on the kitchen table; that was replaced by a much smaller CB; and then a VHF was added. Our mother didn't get out much, and she never held a driver's license—but her voice was known by many people up and down the coast. Anyone within range of the signal put out by one of Pa's homemade antennas knew Shirley Robbins.

When Stevie and I first went offshore back in the 70's, you could just say the words "Fireball base" over the microphone—any hour of the night—and, if you were close enough to land to get a signal through, one of them would answer. If it was a technical issue, Marm might have Pa come to the set. And if there was any message to be taken, Pa'd usually have Marm do the writing.

When Pa passed away in 1995, Marm kept it all going. She went from being a fisherman's wife to a fisherman's mother to a fisherman's grandmother when my nephew Steve III teamed up with my brother.

Marm was the contact point when there was a mechanical or electrical problem; she might have to help line up a trucker or ask a lobster dealer to unlock the car in the middle of the night; bait, fuel, grub and crew were all rounded up by Marm; and over the years, she was responsible for the first news of who won the presidential election, the World Series, or the state basketball finals.

No, Marm didn't get out much, but she brought the world to the rest of us so we could keep on doing what we were doing. She never had much, but she gave us everything we could ever want. That's what she was all about.

> *This morning I counted three times before the tea water boiled that I was going to reach for the phone to call Marm. Every time I do it, it's like something inside me comes undone and I have to coil it back up.*

Life has changed—it's as simple as that.

As I sit here with the wind ripping out of the northwest, I can see the sun's reflection on the water through the trees. Those aren't choppy bay waters, though; it's a fresh-water lake.

This is home. Life has changed.

So Stevie and I can't pick up the phone or the microphone and talk to either Marm or Pa anymore. I think we're both awful lucky to be able to know that there was nothing left unsaid; nothing we wish we'd shared with them before it was too late.

And when the Northern Lights set the sky afire a few nights ago, I couldn't help but think that Pa'd somehow taken a few extra twists of copper wire around a mast up there to let us know that he and Marm were together and everything's all right.

When it comes right down to it, that's all that matters.

Fireball base out.

Chapter 51

Roots: Some Lost and Some Found

As you'll read, Uncle James was 93 when I originally wrote this just after Christmas of 2003. As of this writing, he's 99 and still sharper than most of my peers. Sadly, Harold is no longer with us . . . we'll talk about that in a few chapters.

≈

Pretend you're in a hot air balloon over top of the town where I grew up: Stonington, Maine. Standing in the basket of your balloon, if you face the water, you'll see a road that chases the east end of the thoroughfare off to your left. That's the Indian Point Road—Clam City, to those in the know. That's where Marm and Pa lived.

It was a great place to be a kid. There was a big ledge alongside our house that was the perfect setting for a young boy's adventures. Down the road a little ways further was Ames' Pond, chock full of lilies in the summer and skaters in the winter. And there was the beach down below Doc Brown's house next door to us. I spent a lot of time playing on that beach when I was little—either there or up in the field above it, whose western bluffs overlooked Stonington Harbor. From my burrow amongst the tall grass and lupine, I'd keep a sharp eye out for German U-boats and pirate ships. None got by me.

Lately, with Marm and Pa both gone, that end of town seems gone, too. Sure, the ledge, the pond, the beach, and the bluffs are still there, but they're not the same. (Or maybe they are . . . and *I'm* not.) The old house we grew up in is gone; I can't pronounce half the names on the mailboxes down that road any more.

Whatever the reason, it feels like my roots never got any deeper than the thin layers of soil atop the granite that our old house sat on . . . and they've just faded away.

Now let your balloon drift to the west end of Stonington, past the end of the village proper, up over Green Head Mountain. Now you'd be looking down on Moose Island, where Billings Diesel has stood for a long time. On the chart, the water tucked between Moose Island and Green Head itself is referred to as Allen Cove, but for those who live around those parts it's known as Green Head Cove—and that whole area around it is called Green Head.

That was the setting for the other half of my childhood—the long summer days when Pa was either out to haul or tied up with a shut-off of herring and Marm was working in Genesta Cleveland's laundry, ironing the summer folks' clothes and bedding.

And I guess if I have any roots left, that's where you'd find them.

I spent my days with Nanny and Gramp Robbins, whose house sat at the head of the cove. With my pockets jammed full of Nanny's biscuits and my head full of Gramp's stories, I had a fine time.

Above them lived Bob Quinn, the only adult I knew who could wear a coonskin cap and look *right* in it. (Bob lived alone and was pretty self-sufficient when I was little—sort of a mild-mannered Grizzly

Adams—and he was living proof that a fella could get by just fine on his own. When the day came that he got married, it was a blow to my boyhood vision of the world as it should be. But Helene was nice and just as real as Bob . . . I reevaluated my outlook on life to include girls.)

To the east of Nanny and Gramp were Ruth and Isabel, whom everyone called the "Old Maids." I never gave their lifestyle any thought when I was little; I just knew that they treated me like gold. I discovered the joy of homemade spaghetti sauce at Ruth and Isabel's house; they took me on my first train ride; and Ruth taught me how to swim. And maybe most of all, without me realizing it, they taught me that it's the soul that counts.

If you head west from Nanny and Gramp's, you soon come to the dock that Pa and my Uncle James (Pa's brother) shared at the head of the causeway leading over to Moose Island. That dock was the launch point for my adventures in Green Head Cove, many of which involved my dumboldgirlcousin Julia and the rowboat that Pa built for me. Back then I acted like I could just barely tolerate Julia's company, but I was heartbroken if she wasn't around.

Julia's folks, Joan and Harold, lived across the road from the head of the Moose Island causeway. And beside them were my Uncle James and Aunt Ethel.

And that's just how big my world was for a number of years. It was a pretty good life.

Ruth and Isabel have been gone for a long time; so have Nanny and Gramp—and their home, as well. The house where Bob and Helene lived still stands, but they've lived year-round on Eagle Island for years now.

But Joan and Harold still have their spot at the head of the causeway, as do Uncle James and Aunt Ethel.

And even though Uncle James took up his last load of lobster traps four years ago, he's still pretty limber for *93*.

About any day you can drive by Uncle James' little shop that still stands on the dock at the head of the cove and see smoke coming out the stovepipe. You'll find him in there building boats—wooden models of everything from dories to three-masters. I hadn't really seen any of them close up until I went down for a visit shortly after Marm passed away at the end of October.

I sat by the woodstove in Uncle James' little shop and let that good old feeling wash over me . . . if I looked out the window, I could almost imagine Pa's yellow-hulled Fireball off on the mooring.

I'm sure my wife Tigger and I talked about my visit that evening over dinner, but I don't recall her showing any unusual interest in Uncle James' models. Of course, I'm not that sharp, either.

As near as I can tell after interviewing all the co-conspirators, Tigger placed a call to Joan, whom she'd known years ago. Joan's mission was to talk Uncle James into building a model (boat to be of his choice) for Tigger to give me for Christmas. It was a struggle, as Uncle James doesn't build to order now—he just *builds*. Somehow, though, Joan convinced him. With Harold sitting in as design consultant, Uncle James built a model of Pa's old Fireball—nicknamed the "Banana Boat" after he painted her hull yellow in the mid-70's. And I was oblivious to the whole conspiracy until the boat was sitting in my lap on Christmas Day.

I look at that little boat every morning while waiting for the tea kettle to boil and grin at all the things it represents.

Roots don't need soil, just a little love.

Chapter 52

Eddie & Monroe: Aground

Some wise man once said, "The only man that never ran aground never left the mooring." I'm not sure what that same fellow would've said about this mess.

≈

"DO YOU HEAR THAT?"

A simple question, Eddie Pluggs had to admit later, but that was when everything took a turn for the weird: when Monroe Sinclair, Eddie's stern man for the day, stuck his wet nose in Eddie's ear and yelled.

It was 3:30 on a handsome, flat-arse calm late summer morning. Eddie was at the wheel of the *Black Crow II*, lost in his thoughts and oblivious to Monroe, who was back at the bait box filling bags. Monroe, the incumbent candidate for the post of "Village Idiot", was always on standby for whenever Eddie's longtime stern man/brother-in-law Ross missed a day.

For all his strangeness, Monroe was actually a good man on the boat. Unfortunately, it seemed like he had a knack for making things go awry just when they seemed to be coasting along smoothly. Most people in the harbor wouldn't consider taking Monroe down the bay, but Eddie had been putting up with him ever since they were little kids and—even though he'd suffered through more of Monroe's stunts than anyone—had developed a certain level of tolerance. Every now and then, however, Monroe would push Eddie over the edge. Knowing he'd gone too far, Monroe would keep out of Eddie's sight for a period of time (adjusted according to the offense). Then, as the incident in question (and the emotions following it) began to fade, Monroe would come around again and Eddie would sigh, shrug, and let bygones be bygones.

On this particular morning, Eddie rammed his skull into the ceiling of the wheelhouse when Monroe bellowed into his ear.

"CUT IT OUT!" yelled Eddie, his hat driven down over the tip of his nose, and his hands flapping wildly as he tried to grab the steering wheel.

Monroe leaned in close to Eddie's head yet again. "I SAID, DO YOU—"

"I HEARD YOU THE FIRST TIME!" Eddie pried his hat off his face and yanked the throttle back to an idle. "What's the friggin' problem?"

Monroe crossed the arms of his "Smokey's Greater Shows" carney jumpsuit and shook his head. "You know, Ed, maybe you oughta consider decaf in the mornin'. You ever thought about that?" Eddie's eyes narrowed, spurring Monroe to talk faster. "Didn't you hear that noise back aft? I don't know if we got somethin' in the wheel or what, but it sure sounds funny."

Eddie raised an eyebrow and cocked his head to one side. "Hear what? I don't hear anything."

Monroe shook his head. "Naw—not now. You gotta open her back up."

Eddie hit the throttle and waited a few seconds. "I still don't hear anything."

"You gotta stand back aft," said Monroe, shooing Eddie away from the helm. "Then you'll hear it."

Without thinking, Eddie went back aft and stood with his eyes closed, leaving Monroe alone at the wheel. He didn't feel a tremor or a shake, nor did he hear a rumble or a noise of any kind. He turned to walk back forward and ran square into Monroe, who was standing right beside him in the dark. "See what I mean?" said Monroe.

"No!" said Eddie. "There ain't a thing wrong back here! Just forget about it and bait some bags and-" Eddie's words fetched up in his mouth as he realized that with both he and Monroe back aft, no one was at the wheel. He lunged for the bulkhead.

Eddie's fingers were only about six inches from the throttle when the *Black Crow II* bounced up over the ledge known as "The Old Maid's Boil". With a little more water, the Crow would've slipped off over the other side, too, but it was not to be. She fetched with her bow floating and her stern high and dry.

Eddie found himself in a heap on the floor with Monroe on top of him. The engine was revving up in pretty good shape, the prop obviously spinning freely below the stern, which was now jacked up in the air.

Monroe scrambled to his feet first, grinning. "Neat!" he said. "Now we can look at the wheel and see if we got anything in it!"

Eddie made a mental note to choke Monroe later as he pulled the throttle back and threw the gear into neutral. A quick pacing from rail to rail told the tale: the *Black Crow II* was pretty tiddly, but a little muscle might free her from her perch.

There was no time to lose—the tide was falling. Eddie started to peel off his stuff, not wanting to spend the day in wet clothes just in case they could continue on down the bay. "Okay," he said, "I'll do the pushing. She feels like she's right on the verge of sliding off. Throw me a line once you drift clear and then I'll try to pull you close enough to climb aboard." With that, he slipped off over the side and onto the submerged end of the ledge.

Eddie braced and grunted and pushed and strained and nearly passed out, but he couldn't quite do it. He was gasping for air when a jumpsuit-less Monroe Sinclair splashed into the water beside him.

"Come on, Ed, let's give her one more big one together!" hollered Monroe, putting a shoulder to the transom. Eddie, chest heaving, did the same.

The two of them nearly lost their balance when the Crow suddenly slid clear and refloated. Wheezing, they staggered up onto the dry end of the ledge, thankful that they hadn't fallen overboard. As is too often the truth, neither one of them could swim.

Once Monroe got his breath back, he shook his head. "Boy, she sure looks pretty floatin' off in the moonlight, don't she?"

Eddie nodded in agreement. "Sure does. Now pull her in."

Monroe turned to Eddie, looking puzzled.

"With what?" he asked.

Later, as the sun was rising, the first boat on the scene found the two nearly-naked men (they were both wearing hats) running round and around the dry end of the ledge, one desperately trying to get his hands around the neck of the other.

Chapter 53

Tap Tap Tap

I'm not a gadget sorta guy, but a good weather-glass? Now you're talking.

≈

It was the last of Tigger's presents to me that I opened on my birthday: a box you could hold in one hand, but very heavy for its size. "Tap tap tap," read the tag.

I surveyed the spread of gifts from her that I had already opened: some books, some music, some silly stuff, a neat shirt that I'd mostly likely break in at the Fishermen's Forum. Then there were the presents from the kids and the case of kipper snacks from my brother—breakfast for weeks to come.

Looking back at the package in my hand, I sighed. "This has got to stop."

"That's all—just one last little thing," Tigger laughed. "Go ahead," she coaxed. "Open it."

I did.

Over the years, Marm and Pa both enjoyed the simple comforts of their early morning rituals—if uninterrupted by frozen pipes. Cups of tea and toast with jam, with the old Hellicrafter short-wave boat radio on (replaced over time by the CB and then the VHF)—or when I was little, the standard broadcast radio with WRKD tuned in, giving the morning reports of which sardine factories would be cutting fish that day.

One early morning memory stays with me, stronger than any other: in the little house where Stevie and I grew up, Pa had an old barometer that hung by the kitchen door. At some point— usually just as he was getting ready to leave—Pa would reach up and

tap tap tap

that barometer, then offer a quick synopsis like "Boy, that glass is fallin' " or "Prob'ly come around nor'west later on." I had no idea how the barometer worked or how it told Pa what the weather was going to be. But that sound, that

tap tap tap

is embedded in my memory from childhood, like the mournful whistle on Mark Island or the screech of gulls when a bait boat was unloading at the co-op.

Pa's great big hand with one finger crooked:

tap tap tap.

It was a small, brass-cased barometer; solid, heavy, and very beautiful, and I told Tigger so.

"Where do you want to hang it?" she asked.

"Oh, man," I said. "I don't know . . . we'll have to find the place."

We set it out on the wooden-topped island in the kitchen, on standby for the right spot.

On the boat—on both the 44' Shirley & Freeman and the 55' Stacie Vea, actually—we had a barometer that originally belonged to Gramp Robbins. I'm no expert on these things and I suppose, in a world where everything is perfectly calibrated and synchronized, all barometers should move the same in a given location, as barometric pressure in a given area at a given moment is a number—not a feeling or an emotion.

Having said all that, I can only tell you that Gramp's weather glass didn't have a big range of movement—but when it did move, it told the truth. When the hand began to drop—

tap tap tap

—set your watch. You had eight hours before the wind struck. If you knew how the low was moving in relation to where you were, you could figure the direction of the blow and make a decision on what you needed to do.

We got the tar beat out of us plenty over the years by listening to weather reports that missed the mark. And more often than not, Stevie would snort and curse himself for doubting Gramp's barometer. Whether it was what you wanted to hear or not, it was the truth—

tap tap tap.

I got up about twenty past three the next morning. From her dog bed, Chelsea peeked up at me, then clamped her eyes shut and curled into as tight a ball as her old bones would allow. Chesapeakes, even those going on 14 years old, are most happy when they have a job to do, but even they draw the line on a cold February morning. "You snooze a little while longer, doggie," I said softly. "I'll tell you when it's time."

Walking out into the living room, I could see coals glowing through the glass in the door of the wood stove. I hove a couple of sticks in and opened the damper a little to get a good fire going for Tigger.

I headed for the kitchen stove to light the tea kettle. The barometer lay face-up on the island and as I was about to light the gas burner, I reached over—

tap tap tap

—and I felt something halfway between a chill and a hug and I knew Pa was right there. I froze, finger poised above the glass face of the barometer, not wanting that feeling to leave just yet. If I could have got out a second cup and tea bag for Pa and had him sit for a while, I would have. But, of course, he wasn't there—just as he never left us, either. Sometimes he's just closer than others.

It was a wonderful moment, just the same, realizing that such a simple gesture—

tap tap tap

—could bring on such a powerful feeling. That particular barometer probably sat on a shelf with many others just like it—beautiful in its own right, but with no connection to my family or my past. But that half-asleep early morning act had transformed it into a little time machine, capable of bringing to life so many memories with just a

tap tap tap

and I wanted to go back in and wake up Tigger and tell her all about it.

But I didn't. I waited until it was time to go and Chelsea had uncurled herself with a yawn and a very stiff stttrrrretttccchhh and was waiting for her orders to climb into the van for the long day ahead.

I leaned over, kissed Tigger and whispered "Thank you."

Chapter 54

A Big Piece of
a Little Place

For Julia and Joan.

≈

A question:
How many pieces can you chip out of a place until it ceases to be the same place?

Or maybe the bigger question is, how much of the people who live somewhere make it be what it is? If everyone who had lived in a neighborhood for years was suddenly gone forever, would it be the same place?

And if those same people settled somewhere else, would that place be the same as the original neighborhood?

Green Head, the part of Stonington, ME where I did a lot of my growing up (not where we lived, in Clam City over on the east end of town, but where I spent my summers and where I learned how to swim and row and run an outboard and ride a bike and bait a pocket and skip a rock) just got smaller.

Harold Robbins passed away.

Pa and Harold were some sort of cousins, although it was a coincidence that their last names were both

Robbins, as the connection was on their mothers' sides, as I understand it. The one time I asked, it was explained to me that the term was officially "half-assed cousins" and I didn't want to repeat that for fear of getting in trouble for talking bad, so I just accepted the fact that Harold and Joan were my uncle and aunt and their daughter Julia was my dumboldgirlcousin whom I pretended to barely tolerate but actually loved very much.

Julia was my playmate, my adventure buddy, my rowing navigator.

My Aunt Joan was tough as nails with a heart as big as Green Head Cove itself.

And Uncle Harold (Pa and Uncle James always called him "ol' John" although they both had him beat by a decade or more) was one of the Green Head fishermen like Pa and Uncle James and Uncle Toot and Bob Quinn. He could do a little bit of everything and therefore did a lot of things to earn his living, but the common denominator was always the ocean. And just about every workday, be it to haul his lobster gear or take a crew out to one of the islands where he was the caretaker, began with a row out to his mooring in Green Head Cove.

> *Green Head ran on tea when I was a kid. Oh, there were coffee drinkers for sure, but it seemed like Nanny and Gramp Robbins' house was the center of the universe with everything orbiting around that old oil-fired Clarion stove that was always roaring in the kitchen and the tea kettle that was always on.*
>
> *Everyone who came in the door was offered tea and a chair and a chance to sit and talk over the day's haul or the high-running tides or the body of fish that was laying just outside the cove up at*

Freese's Island or the stone that was being cut over at the quarry on Crotch Island.

So, I ask you another question: is there tea in heaven?

Is there a white enameled Clarion in a cozy kitchen where sits Nanny and Gramp and Pa and now Harold?

And is it still the center of the universe?

Harold was an easy grownup to be around when I was little. He had a good sense of humor; he didn't put the questions to you; and he talked to you like you were grownup, too—even if it was about a very simple little kid subject. To me, Harold always wore his manner the same as he wore his clothes: he was comfortable.

It's a blowy, raw fall day as I sit here writing this and it's easy to picture how Harold would be dressed if you saw him over around the shore at Green Head: a couple of well-worn shirts layered over each other with the collars turned up to cut the bite of the wind; a pair of dark-colored work pants with maybe a few spatters of yellow and white buoy paint, and a pair of low-cut workboots, loosely laced so that you could just step in and out of them.

I don't know that Harold ever actually owned any clothes just like that, but that's how his memory feels to me: comfortable.

When the ocean is inside you; when you've made yourself part of it and it's part of you; when the rise and fall of the tide and the beating of your heart are as one, then you go back to that ocean in the final hours and finish up. That's what I think, anyway.

During his final days in the hospital, as his body was shutting down, Harold went back to the ocean to get things squared away.

Pa showed up for a cup of tea, just like old times. And they nailed a big shutoff of herring; carrier after carrier full. ("17 boats" Harold said at one point, "but some of 'em's old wrecks.") They worked hard on those fish, Harold and Pa and the gang. And when the fish were loaded and gone and the twine was flaked aboard the dories and everything was secure, it was okay for Harold to rest. My Aunt Joan told him so.

And Green Head got a little smaller.

In memory of Harold L. Robbins 11/27/23—10/21/05

Chapter 55

Eddie, Monroe, and the Trap Hauling Contest

I often hear in my travels (when talk turns to lobster boat racing) the opinion that "if they can't haul a trap, they ought not be allowed to race." Me, I don't want to get into it—as a reformed race junkie, I try to steer clear of such debates.

This was another column inspired by a visit with Foy Brown out on North Haven.

≈

"This, Cap, is gonna be a piece of cake," said Monroe Sinclair, the holder of the title of "Village Idiot" for at least a couple of decades (there are no term limits imposed on the Village Idiot post). "A friggin' piece of cake."

Eddie Pluggs tugged his ever-present long-billed cap even further down over his eyes and shrugged. "Don't get too cocky," he said to Monroe. "You're just temptin' fate when you say stuff like that."

Monroe snorted and gestured toward the harbor in front of them. "Look at 'em out there! The poor buggers are rippin' and tearin' and they ain't gettin' a thing done! It's takin' them forever to haul through that string!"

Monroe was pointing at one of the many entries in the town's annual trap-hauling contest—an event which had heralded the beginning of summer each year for a long, long time. The speeding lobster boat was whipping the harbor's waters into a white froth as it spun in a fierce frenzy around the contest course.

The rules were simple enough: each boat entered had to have a crew of two. Each team was given a bucket of colored bricks by the judges. At the starter signal, the team would charge down the ramp to their idling boat tied to the float below. Lines had to be untied (not cut) and then the competitors raced to the awaiting string of five single traps where they would exchange their bricks for five differently colored ones. Once the string was hauled through, the boat returned to the float and tied up. The team then ran back up the ramp with their bucket of bricks and their time was recorded.

Eddie Pluggs and his faithful sternman/brother-in-law Ross had entered the contest a couple of times in the past, but had never won. (It was hard for Eddie to fight the urge to turn on the bottom machine and try to find a good-looking nook or cranny to set back in.)

A bad back had laid Ross low for a few weeks and forced Eddie to rely on his eccentric friend Monroe for sternman duties down the bay. (Fortunately, Monroe's position as Village Idiot meant he was usually unemployed and available whenever Eddie needed him.) Eddie had no interest in that year's trap-hauling contest, but when Monroe got all teary-eyed while pleading for a chance to participate in the event, Eddie gave in.

And now, as the team before them raced up the ramp with their bucket of bricks, Eddie and Monroe got ready to take their turn.

As one of the judges passed the bucket of dripping bricks to Eddie, Monroe dug a large tube of grease out of one of the many pockets of his faded, dirty "Smokey's Greater Shows" jumpsuit. He popped the end cap off and reached around behind him, slathering most of the tube's contents over the rear end of his coveralls. The crowd gathered on the dock roared. Eddie grabbed Monroe by the collar.

"You promised, Monroe—no weird stuff! Remember?"

Monroe patted his friend gently on the shoulder with one hand while prying Eddie's fingers clear of his neck with the other. "Don't worry, Ed. Trust me."

Those two words had always led to trouble since Eddie and Monroe were little boys, but there was no time for Eddie to reflect upon that fact now—the judges' cap pistol had fired.

Eddie was first to start down the ramp, but he was soon passed by Monroe, rocketing down the handrail on his well-greased bottom. With a crazy war-whoop, Monroe hit the float running and had the boat untied before Eddie reached the toe rail. With a mighty push, the Black Crow was clear and roaring for the first buoy. The crowd went wild as Eddie and Monroe ripped the first trap aboard, picking and re-bricking it in a flash. And then someone yelled out, "They're takin' them all on!"

Sure enough, the Black Crow was headed to the next buoy with the first trap simply slid aft. The idea to take on the string had been Monroe's and Eddie had had to admit that it sounded like a good one. Once all five singles were aboard, they'd set them out as they raced back to the float.

"They're makin' wicked time!" yelled one onlooker.

"Yeah, but don't forget—he's got Monroe aboard there," said another.

The plan was going flawlessly as the last trap hit the rail. Eddie swung the Black Crow around towards the float and laid into the throttle.

"FEED HER BREAKFAST, CAP!" Monroe yelled as he turned to launch the first trap. The smell of victory was strong in Monroe's hairy nostrils. Unfortunately, the wob of grease did not have a strong hold on the seat of Monroe's coveralls. The grease plopped onto the deck just a split second before Monroe's work boots stepped into it.

The crowd ashore gasped as a wildly flailing Monroe cleaned Eddie off his feet, leaving the speeding Black Crow with no helmsman. They then watched the coveralled Monroe do a triple backflip and disappear below the level of the washrail, knocking several of the traps overboard in the process. The ensuing snarl hauled the remaining traps overboard, as well. The Black Crow skimmed around in a broad circle, heading over top of the massive snarl. Eddie was just getting to his feet and reaching for the throttle when the prop took a bite on a ball of rope as big as a 55-gallon drum, stopping the roaring engine dead.

The crowd stood in shocked silence. All was quiet aboard the Black Crow as well. And then they could hear Monroe Sinclair ask, "What was our time up to that point, Ed?"

The Coast Guard later fined Eddie Pluggs for the large slick he caused when he threw Monroe over the side.

Chapter 56

For Chelsea

Let me tell you something right now: when it comes to dogs, you can't go wrong with a Chesapeake.

≈

Someone once said (and I regret to say I can't remember who) that when you get to heaven, all the pets you ever loved will come running to meet you. That's a wonderful image, but brings another question to mind: who will be there to greet them?

Any dog who's 15 years old, if they've had their health and someone to love them, has had a pretty darn good run. I know that to be true for Chelsea, our Chesapeake whom we recently lost. She had a pretty darn good run, but then again, so did we, and all who knew her.

I've always loved dogs, but none ever stole my heart like that old girl.

She was something else.

It strikes me that dogs are like the caulking in the planking of our lives.

There are all the big things; our families, our jobs, birth and death, love and loss. Throughout all that, the companionship and devotion of a dog remains a constant, unaffected by the weather, stock market reports, the rising price of diesel fuel, Hollywood scandal, or bad breath. You can come home feeling like the biggest loser the world has ever known and a dog will greet you just the same as if the stretch limo had just brought you from the party where you collected your Megabucks winnings.

When a dog has left your life, you realize how many cracks they filled. The early morning rituals; the one-sided conversations; the evening ear rubs.

It's not the big void—it's all the seams.

If there was one phrase to best describe the nature of a Chesapeake, I believe it would be this: Chesapeakes need a job.

That's definitely the way it was with Chelsea. Don't get me wrong; she had a lot of fun in her life, but—at least in her mind—she had work to do. If a boat was being bailed, someone had to jump overboard and try to catch the flung water. Dock lines needed to be grabbed and rendered through her jaws as she swam for shore, cleaning off any accumulated rockweed. Gulls and crows were potential troublemakers; one had to know just how close to let them get and when to drive them off. A lawn couldn't even be mowed properly without a Chesapeake; who would chase the sticks when the mower spit them out or the human tossed them out of the way? She went from Massachusetts to Cape Breton, Nova Scotia in the H&H van and was the best co-pilot you could have.

Sure, Chelsea loved every minute of it, but in her mind, how would the world get along without a Chesapeake to take care of such details?

Since she's been gone, that's a hard question to answer.

Hold me to one memory, one Chelsea story that would best sum up who she was and what she was all about, and I'd have to tell you about the Peter's Island picnic swim.

Tigger's family had always enjoyed picnics on Peter's Island, about two miles downriver from their home in Clarks Cove on the Damariscotta River. The first 4th of July after Tigger's father Edward passed away, her mother Julia thought it would be fitting to get the family together and head downriver to Peter's, as Edward loved to do.

Tigger and I were going to paddle down in our kayaks, and in her younger years, Chelsea would've tucked into the after hold of a boat and been fine. But Chels didn't bend quite as easily as she used to, and the plan was for us to scoot along the shoreline and let her follow us by foot along the beach.

But we hadn't taken the status of the tide into account and just how bold that left a lot of the shoreline as we started downriver. It made for hard going for Chels. The rest of the family had gone ahead with Edward's old big scow, so hitching a ride wasn't a possibility. It didn't take long for Chelsea to decide her plan of attack: forget scrambling and slipping up and down slippery ledges—she was going to swim. Into the river she went.

If you'd flown over our little convoy on the 4th of July, 2003, you would've seen a blue and a yellow kayak threading their way downriver through the thick array of multi-colored potbuoys. And off the starboard quarter of the yellow kayak you would've seen a copper-colored Chesapeake with a greying muzzle looking proud and bold and strong.

Chelsea swam the two miles to Peter's Island, shook herself off when she hit the beach, announced her presence with a "roo-roo" and then looked for something to eat.

The vision of her swimming that day will stick in my mind forever, as she looked simply majestic.

Last night we walked the Dodge Point trail down to the shore of the Damariscotta River. The sand told the tale of the day's activities: many doggies of various sizes had left happy circles of paw prints while chasing sticks and rocks. A number of choice fetching sticks lay at the water's edge, awaiting the next toss.

We sat and watched the river for a little bit as evening came on. It was quiet on the Damariscotta. We were too far upriver for any lobster gear; besides, with the summer hauling law on, it was too late in the day for anybody to be working. The afternoon's playboaters were all home with grills going or out to eat enjoying what they would tell the folks back in Iowa was a "real Maine Saturday night dinner—just like the natives eat all the time!"

Chelsea did not suffer fools gladly; she was oblivious to titles and trends and what was in and what wasn't. Chesapeakes need a job and if she had been there on the shore, Chelsea would not have cared about tourists or Saturday hauling laws. She would have pawed the sand and roo-roo'd until a stick was thrown.

Without a word, Tigger and I got to our feet, each picked up a stick from the sand, and flung them out into the Damariscotta.

There was the sound of the sticks hitting the water. But that was all.

So, if it's true that when you get to heaven all

the pets you had in your life come running to meet you, who greets them when they go there before you?

Call it Heaven, the Great Beyond—call it whatever or don't call it anything at all—I hope that wherever Chelsea's soul is now there's a stick to chase and plenty of swimming to be done.

See you later, old girl.

Chapter 57

Calendars You'll Wish Existed

Willy Spear already gave me a ration of crap once about this column when it first came out (of course, he was grinning when he did it). He's probably forgotten about it by now—might as well do it again.

≈

It happens every year at this time.

I'll get out of the H&H Propeller van, walk into a boat shop and I'll be met with the same question, time and time again: "You got any new calendars on board?"

"Well," I'll say, "the new H&H tide calendars ought to be here any day now."

"Tide calendars?" they'll say, shaking their heads. "Who wants a tide calendar? Doncha have any calendars with nekkid women on 'em? Most companies do."

"Oh," I'll say. "Well, no, I don't."

"Hmm," they'll answer, looking disappointed. Then they'll brighten a little and, looking hopeful, ask, "How about calendars with *half*-nekkid women on 'em?"

"Nope," I'll answer. "Don't have any of those, either."

277

"Huh," they'll answer. There'll be a period of silence—just long enough to let me know that I've failed—and then we go on from there.

Every year . . . the same thing.

I know it's a red-blooded American tradition of sorts to use temptations of the flesh to sell various products and services, but I always get caught up in the practicalities of the situation.

For instance, when I see an ad for an arc welder featuring a woman wearing a garter belt and welding goggles, my first thought is, "Jeez—look out for sparks!" Or a 4-color display of a thonged lady offering up chicken nuggets hot out of the fry-o-lator makes me shudder with thoughts of disfiguring burns and skin grafts.

Besides that, I don't want any misunderstandings and unmet expectations. I wouldn't want someone thinking that the farmer's daughter-looking girl jumping out of the hay (sans overalls) on the July page of a calendar came with the cutless bearing they were about to buy. (Plus, there's all the unanswered questions, like why is she naked in the haystack with a cutless bearing? On a farm? In Iowa? See—the practical stuff just gets in the way.)

But don't worry; I'm not here to offer up a problem without a solution. I'll be right up front about it—I haven't run these ideas by anyone else, but we're all friends here, right? Right.

So consider some of my ideas for future calendars:

Darn Good Dried Fish—Hold on, hold on—don't go buggy on me. I wasn't even going to bring up my scratch 'n' sniff idea for this one, just some neat scenic shots along the coast. Think about it: a nice scrod cod laced with pepper hanging on a clothesline off on Fantasy Island with the harbor in the background. Or maybe a pollock drying in the rigging with the skyline of Portland, ME artfully placed behind it. If you want the human element added in, you could have, say, good ol' Willy Spear gnawing on a hunk of that same pollock with a big grin on. (Now that would be a good thing as far as I'm concerned, 'cause when Willy grins, you can't help but grin back. Heck, the whole family could be grinning with Willy—even your grandmother with whom you might be ashamed to share the calendar featuring the three nude NFL cheerleaders and the pressure washer. Think about it.)

Classic Pickup Trucks—Again, don't jump to conclusions; I'm not talking about these soulless chromed-up tricked-out things coming off the lots left and right these days. Sure, they're pretty, but they don't stick with you like the real classics we all grew up with. Right off the top of my head, I'd like to see my brother Stevie's old 1960-something short-bodied Ford roaring through town on two wheels headed to the shore at 3:30 in the morning with the radio stuck on WWVA ("Comin' to ya live from Wheelin' West Virginny! Yeehaw!"). Or maybe Melvin Bridges' pickup with the windshield perpetually fogged over. (He never got it up to running temperature between his house and the wharf in the morning, so there'd just be a few whiffs of lukewarm air threading their way up between the Skoal cans on the dash. As I say, that's a true classic.)

Shelling Knives—Okay, okay . . . not for everybody, I know. But—I can still remember the first time I got the Bulldog tape built up just right on the handle of the old ground-down butter knife Pa'd rigged up for me to try. When you picked it up, you didn't have to scrunch down to get a grip—it almost hung onto you. Now somebody else might have picked up that same knife and immediately said, "How the hell can you work with that?" So what I'm saying is, you take a dozen scallopers, you've probably got a year's worth of customized shelling knives. See?

Hats—Left up to me, I wouldn't even have them on heads. I'd just go for the artistic layouts, catching all the glory of a visor bent just so (not from some dopey visor-molding gizmo in a store at the mall, but from repeated adjustments and tugs by a gurry-soaked glove). I suppose if one was trying to push the subliminal ad message, they could be caps emblazoned with the logo of the calendar sponsor, but any cap worth its weight in dog snot shouldn't even be readable in real life. And whatever you do, don't be washing it.

I can tell some of you are ready to slide this column right under the parakeet without giving any of these ideas a fighting chance. I don't understand it, either. Is it the lack of nudity?

Well, okay . . . if you're going to be that way about it, how about this: Willy Spear could be naked gnawing on that hunk of dried fish.

Just thought I'd throw it out there.

Chapter 58

I'm Telling You– It's No'theast

The Mr. B advice column became a neat way for me to rave about something under the guise of being helpful. This one was written one evening after a long—and I mean long—day of hearing people jabber about an impending "nor'easter."

≈

Hey now!

Greetings, ladies and gentlemen and children of all ages—it's your ol' buddy, Mr. B. Who would've even dared to dream that our initial pass at Mr. B's guide to shipboard etiquette back a few years ago would stir up the response that it did?

It's been a life changer for me to be faced with the responsibility of setting so many of you straight when it comes to the ins and outs of getting along with your crewmates and the world at large. Yessir, there's times when I can honestly say I know how Mother Teresa must've felt when I finish one of these columns, knowing that I've been able to take one of you (or maybe hundreds—or *thousands* of you, who knows?) by the rubber insulated glove and lead you down the path to clarity and happiness.

"But Mr. B," you may ask, "how did you come to be blessed with all that wisdom and insight at such a relatively young age (even though you admittedly do look to be at least 20 years older than you really are)?"

Well, it's all a matter of letting yourself *see* and *hear*, poor pitiful one, not just *look* and *listen*. Don't worry, lost sheep, ol' Mr. B has paid his dues along the way, including that nasty topple the length of the stairs at the Pier II Restaurant in Portsmouth, NH in August of 1979.

But, we won't get sidetracked on that right now—we'll save that stuff for Mr. B's upcoming self-esteem class. (You wait; once you've made it through the final exam where you have to dig furiously through a wooden box full of rusty tools, blown running light bulbs, and wooden lobster plugs [yes—it was a long time ago: *plugs*] while my brother Stevie bellows at you, "Hose clamp! Hose clamp! *Hose clamp! Hose clamp! Hose clamp! HOSECLAMP!!!*" without having some sort of breakdown, you'll feel altogether different about yourself.)

(Wow . . . I just reread that paragraph—where the hell did *that* come from?)

Anyway, let's quit wasting time and space and get on with our first letter.

> *Dear Mr. B—*
>
> *You must've heard it just like I and everyone I know did: the wall-to-wall media coverage of the recent blow that ripped through New England. Every time you turned on the TV or the radio, there it was: "**Nor'easter!**" this and "**Nor'easter!**" that.*
>
> *I know that just because you hear something on the radio or see it on TV doesn't make it so, Mr. B, but after a while, you can't help but get to wondering, "Is that how you're really supposed to say it?"*

I need your help, Mr. B.

As I write this, we're getting ready to leave on a trip. Hopefully, by the time we get back, you'll have an answer for me. Until then, just call me . . .

Perplexed On Platts

Dear Perplexed—

I know where you're coming from. In my humble opinion, the only folks who refer to a gale of wind that blows from a direction of approximately 45 degrees magnetic as a "**nor'easter**" have probably never been caught in one.

Perplexed, my friend, "**nor'easter**" is brought to you by the same folks who put up signs touting "**lobstah dinnahs**." I'm not condoning violence or destruction of property, folks, but it's really hard not to imagine driving the length of Route 1 with a chain attached to the rear bumper, gleefully uprooting every offensive billboard and dopey magnetic sign offering specials on "**clam chowdah**." (But you probably shouldn't.)

Write this down, Perplexed: **no'theaster**. This is the proper term for a wind that blows out of the **no'theast**. In fact, while we're at it, let ol' Mr. B take you on a quick phonetic trip around the compass rose:

Northerly—"Naw-ther-lee"
No'theaster—"No-thees-ter"
Easterly—"Ees-ter-lee"
Southeaster- "Sow-thees-ter" (See? Now, doesn't that work nicely with no'theaster?)
Southerly—"Su-ther-lee"
Sou'wester—"Sow-wes-ter"
Westerly—"Wes-ter-lee"
Nor'wester—"Naw-wes-ter"

Drop out the "r" and stick the "th" onto the beginning of the second syllable to launch it with: **no'theaster**.

If you notice, Perplexed, you've got to have a consonant (or a couple of the rascals) to push that second syllable out there. You just can't have that "r" hanging out in the wind—nothing good can come of it. If you don't believe me, go stand in front of a mirror. Watch and see what happens to your face when you try to pronounce "nor'easter." See how numb you look curling your lip up to get that second syllable out with no "th" to push it? The only way I can do it is to make a face like a really bad Elvis impersonator. That's gotta be telling you something.

I believe the above list, properly trimmed with scissors, will fit nicely taped to the underside of a cap visor, Perplexed. Stick it under there now, my friend— I guarantee that long before it's faded and yellowed, you'll be saying the proper terms naturally without any prompts.

And if anybody questions you on it, you tell them to call ol' Mr. B.

So, until next time, folks, remember: keep your pants hitched up so that your "r"s won't be hanging out.

Happy trails,
Mr. B.

Chapter 59

Eddie & Monroe:
The Tale of
the Tape

My buddy Dan MacCaffray has been the inspiration for more than one Bearin's column over the years—usually the thought-provoking ones. Thanks for the tape measure, Danny—and everything else.

≈

Eddie Pluggs first heard the noise as he was rowing ashore from the *Black Crow*. Although he couldn't identify the source, he would have been willing to bet with anyone who cared that it had something to do with newly-re-elected village idiot Monroe Sinclair.

Sure enough, Monroe was sitting on a stack of crates at the head of the ramp, wearing his ever-present "Smokey's Greater Shows" carney jumpsuit and a tattered Australian bush hat. As Eddie walked up the ramp, he identified the source of the sound: a battered banjo with only two strings. Unfortunately, there was no way to walk by Monroe without acknowledging him.

Monroe spoke first. "Hey, Eddie! Let's start a band!"

"Right." Eddie tried to squeeze by him and get to his truck.

"No, I'm serious, Ed. You need a hobby or somethin'. I'm worried about you. You never have time for *anything*."

Eddie stepped back as Monroe jumped down off the crates and dug into a pocket, hauling out a tape measure.

"Here," said Monroe, passing the end of the measuring tape to Eddie as he began to walk backwards holding the bright yellow body of the measure. "You stand right there and hold that."

"What are we measurin'?" asked Eddie. He scanned the immediate area of where he was standing to see if anybody was looking as Monroe backed away slowly. "This is stupid. There's nothin' here to measure."

Monroe, concentrating on the numbers as they reeled out of the housing, grunted. "That's what *you* think, Ed." Monroe slowed to a stop when he got about eight feet away from Eddie. "Now, tell me how long you figger on livin'."

Eddie leaned slightly towards Monroe and squinted. "*What*?"

Monroe shrugged, staring cross-eyed at a grease spot on his nose, which he wiped at with an even greasier sleeve. "Don't get weirded out on me, Ed. Just take what you know about statistics and family history and stuff and give me a number—the average life expectancy of a male Pluggs."

"Oh." Eddie straightened up, clearing his throat and slowly reaching up to rub his chin. "Well, I dunno . . . never thought about it, I guess."

"Well, take your Dad, fer instance," said Monroe. "See, that's where you got an advantage over me—you knew *your* folks. Me, I never knew mine. All I got to go by is what I've found out over the years—my father went on sardine carriers in the summer and went south in the winter with the circus." His gaze wandered off to a far point on the horizon. "Nobody knows for sure, but they think it was a bad incident involving a midnight tryst on a faulty ferris wheel with the bearded lady that got him. What's the chances of that happenin' to me?"

The tape began to droop between them as Eddie cocked his head and stared at Monroe. "I'm sorry, but I don't want to hear this."

"And, supposedly, my mother was a sword swallower—"

"Monroe, shut up."

"—and that comes with its own occupational hazards, like hiccups and-"

"MONROE!"

Monroe's eyes lost their glaze and he refocused on Eddie. "Anyhoo, spec out a number for me, Ed."

Eddie's gaze lingered on Monroe for a minute, and then he shrugged slightly and sighed. "Okay, okay . . . let's get this over with. Well, Pa was 79 when he died. And actually, the Old Man was in great shape for his age when he passed away—heart, blood pressure, all that stuff. It was prostate cancer that got him, and that was probably 'cause it had gone too far before they knew it was there. The rest of the Pluggs family lived well up into their 80s and some went longer than that."

Monroe gave Eddie a dirty thumbs-up and displayed a checkerboard grin. "There you go, Ed. Now, was that so hard? So," Monroe began slowly feeding the tape back into the housing, "how about if we go with . . . 85? How does that sound?"

"85?" asked Eddie, the tape almost touching the ground as he leaned towards Monroe, trying to figure out what the point was.

"Woah, woah," Monroe waved Eddie back. "Keep the tape tight. 85 years old—that sounds like a pretty fair estimate of how long you might live, right?"

"Oh, okay. Yeah, I guess so. So what?"

"So . . . how old are you now?"

"49, almost 50."

Monroe whipped a tiny pair of greasy vice-grips out of a pocket of his jumpsuit and snapped them shut on the tape at the 50" mark. "There you go, Ed!"

Eddie Pluggs cocked his head and stared quizzically at the yellow tape stretched between them. "Huh?"

Monroe shook his head slowly. "Come on, Ed—get with the program. Your end—the beginnin' of the tape—that's a chubby-cheeked newborn Eddie Pluggs. Where the vice-grips are bit on is *right now*, Ed. That's you, almost 50. And this end," Monroe wiggled the fingers of his free hand in greeting as Eddie's gaze came to rest on him, "is our estimate of your lifespan: 85 years.

"So, Ed, let's review what we got here: from your end to the vice-grips is what you've lived so far. From the vice-grips to me is what we're estimatin' you've got left. And if you don't mind me pointin' it out, note the difference in distances. Think about it."

And Eddie did. He didn't dwell on it, but he never forgot it, either. Did it change his life? Well, no. But it did help him to chew his time a little slower. And from that day forward, there were two other things that he never forgot:

Always keep a tape measure handy, and

For a crazy person, Monroe Sinclair was pretty smart.

Chapter 60

Serial Mooners: Stalking The *Roseway*

This was all very unfortunate. That's my story and I'm sticking to it.

≈

The first time we mooned the *Roseway*, we weren't even trying to. It just happened. Honest.

The *Roseway* was one of a number of independently-owned windjammers that would (and still do) make Stonington Harbor one of their stops during a several-day tour cruise along the Maine coast. Marm and Pa called them "party boats"; some of the men around the waterfront called them "skin boats," but I never dared to in front of Marm. I didn't know what would happen, but I wasn't about to test the situation.

You could usually tell when the party boats were in town, even if you couldn't see out across the harbor: the mass of folks moving sheep-like down the middle of Main Street, oblivious to local traffic and wrapped in their newly-bought oilskins was a dead giveaway. The less-patient locals who were trying to carry on with their regular working days would curse loudly, shake their fists, and gun their engines at the meandering bright-yellow-clad crowd choking downtown Stonington.

The shops would sell some trinkets (in those days, usually something involving old worm-eaten laths) and postcards; photos of the natives would be taken ("Excuse me—could you stand closer to those lobster traps while you do that?"); copies of the *New York Times* would be sold. Then the herd would be led aboard the launches and taken back out to the *Mattie* or the *Victory Chimes* or the *Mary Day* or the *Adventure*.

Or the *Roseway*. Even to those unfamiliar with the windjammer fleet, the *Roseway* was easy to distinguish from the rest of the pack. 137' in length, her black hull and dark red sails were hers and hers alone. A visit from the *Roseway* meant a pack of three dozen wide-eyed Kodak-toting visitors clad in L.L. Bean foul weather gear.

Anyhow, as I mentioned earlier, the first time we mooned the *Roseway*, she was actually just a victim of circumstance. Honest. We were headed across the bay to Vinalhaven aboard my brother Stevie's 54' offshore lobster boat *Stacie Vea* to get bait before leaving on a trip. Snyder, Hogg, and I were busy out on deck when Stevie called to us from the wheelhouse. "Look!"

Heading on a course to pass a boatlength or two off our starboard rail was the 83' sardine carrier *Pauline*. When you spoke of the *Pauline* back then, you spoke of her two-man crew as a unit—"Henry and the Swede." (For those wanting to be politically correct—including me—make no mistake about it: the Swede's name was a term of endearment . . . as awful-acting a thing as he could be, we all loved him, and Henry, too. Those were the days, my friend.) And there they were—Henry leaning out of the wheelhouse doorway and the Swede atop a pile of saltbags, both shaking their fists and grinning as only true pirates can.

We never hesitated; there was no battle plan on standby; we just automatically did the first thing that came to mind: we ran to the rail, dropped our trousers and mooned the *Pauline*. Henry and the Swede immediately put their hands over their hearts in salute.

What Stevie had neglected to point out to us from the wheelhouse—and what we hadn't taken in from the deck—was that the western bay was a busy place that handsome summer's day. Converging on the scene at the same time—clear of any threat of collision, but, unfortunately, within view of the mooning, was the *Roseway*. There was much pointing and camera-clicking going on as the paying customers who happened to be on deck at that exact moment witnessed the age-old ritual in action.

That was mooning #1—a total accident. Honest.

Mooning #2, I'm sorry to say, was totally on purpose—though not pre-meditated in any way. We'd just finished unloading a trip of lobsters at the Co-op on a foggy morning and were securing the deck while jogging to the mooring. Suddenly, the fog parted and there she was, close on the port side: the *Roseway*. Did we have a personal vendetta against the black-hulled windjammer? Certainly not. Why then, did we all automatically drop our oilpants and britches and wave our pale-white arses at the shocked early-morning risers on deck? I don't know . . . because it was there, I guess.

I won't go into detail about moonings #3, #4, and #5, but it really got to be a compulsive reaction: you'd see the poor *Roseway* somewhere and the next thing you knew, you were at the rail with your rearend pointed at them.

It took us awhile to realize that we'd become part of the Maine coast experience for *Roseway* customers. I'm not saying that we were listed in the brochures or anything, but by mooning #6, we realized that passengers were lining the rail as soon as they saw the *Stacie*, *waiting* for us to drop our laundry. "This has gone too far," we decided. "We're not pieces of meat." Or something like that.

Anyhow, the moonings came to an end.

These days, the *Roseway* is a floating school owned by the World Ocean School and takes part in outreach programs for young folks in Boston, MA and (during the winter months) the U.S. Virgin Islands. These programs give kids from all walks of life a chance to build their confidence and self-esteem while learning how to work a windjammer.

In fact, Tigger thought she caught a glimpse of the *Roseway* from our crazily-weaving taxi bus as we rocketed from the airport in St. Thomas to catch the ferry to St. John this past February.

For the record, there was no mooning involved. Honest.

Chapter 61

Bonnie:
A Chesapeake
Smile

After we lost Chels, a number of months went by before either of us felt like even saying out loud, "Would you ever think about . . . ?"
When the time was right, we did.

≈

It's been just a year ago today since I sat at this desk and wrote a goodbye to Chelsea, our beloved Chesapeake, who'd just ended her nearly 15-year run on this earth. At the time, the best words I could find to express the loss included these:

It strikes me that dogs are like the caulking in the planking of our lives.
There are all the big things: our families, our jobs, birth and death, love and loss. Throughout all that, the companionship and devotion of a dog remains a constant, unaffected by the weather, stock market reports, the rising price of diesel fuel, Hollywood scandal, or bad breath. You can come home feeling like the biggest loser the world has ever known and a dog will greet you just the same

293

> *as if the stretch limo had just brought you from the party where you collected your Megabucks winnings.*
>
> *When a dog has left your life, you realize how many cracks they filled. The early morning rituals; the one-sided conversations; the evening ear rubs.*
> *It's not the big void, it's all the seams.*

I've made observations and expressed my views on things from this space for almost 20 years now; you could easily find plenty to disagree with me about in that time . . . but I believe the words above to be the stone solid truth.

So, for quite a while, we couldn't even talk about having another dog in our lives. We needed to feel the lack of a dog first: there were all the thrown sticks with nobody to chase them; the unanswered early morning thoughts-out-loud (even in her later years when Chels' hearing left her, she still knew you were talking to her and would respond appropriately, even if it was only with a demand for another Milk Bone); the fact that there were no more welcome-homes with that big ol' Chesapeake smile.

Did I ever tell you about that Chesapeake smile?

Maybe the thing that makes it so special is the fact that, by nature, Chesapeakes are convinced that they are on this earth to make sure things get done. Go ahead, look 'em up by whatever means you prefer— Google or hard cover tome, it makes no difference— somewhere it'll tell you: Chesapeakes need a job. Again, I did the best I could to explain it last year:

> *If there was one phrase to best describe the nature of a Chesapeake, I would believe it to be this: Chesapeakes need a job.*
> *That's definitely the way it was with Chelsea.*

*Don't get me wrong; she had a lot of fun in her
life, but, at least in her mind, she had work to do.
If a boat was being bailed, someone had to jump
overboard and try to catch the flung water. Dock
lines needed to be grabbed and rendered through
her jaws as she swam for shore, cleaning off any
accumulated rockweed. Gulls and crows were
potential troublemakers; one had to know just how
close to let them get and when to drive them off. A
lawn couldn't even be mowed properly without a
Chesapeake; who would chase the sticks when the
mower spit them out or the human tossed them out
of the way? She went from Massachusetts to Cape
Breton, Nova Scotia in the H&H van and was
the best co-pilot you could have.*

*Sure, Chelsea loved every minute of it, but in
her mind, how would the world get along without
a Chesapeake to take care of such details?*

*Since she's been gone, that's a hard question to
answer.*

Knowing the work ethic of the breed makes a Chesapeake grin all the more special. For all her focused attention on what might need to be done at any given moment, Chels could look like she was about to explode with happiness at the sight of you. She wasn't a jumper—there was a whole body wag that started at the hind end and worked its way to her snout, blossoming into a huge smile. Sometimes it was an Elvis-like lip curl; many times it evolved into a full-blown Ray Charles teeth-baring grimace chock full of joy.

So we put in a long winter with no Chesapeake smiles. Winter turned to spring mud and with all the miles and long hours of the average work week (leaving no time for anything except planning for the following week), there still seemed to be a void that needed filling; some caulking between those fore-mentioned planks. We were ready to talk about another dog.

A Chesapeake, of course.

We made a connection with a breeder in York, ME ending up with pick of the litter with the first-time momma due in mid-June. By the summer solstice, there were 13 chubby pups, each vying for a teat of their own.

We knew which pup we wanted when we first visited them at 5 weeks. We just did. The next visit a couple of weeks later showed us a little bit more of her personality: a cuddler, for sure, but with a mind of her own nevertheless.

By the time we went to pick her up yesterday, we'd been referring to her as "Bonnie" for a couple of weeks.

So, yes, life has changed a lot in these last 24 hours. For sure, we just gave up a lot of freedoms that we've known in the last 12 months.

But you know what?

When Bonnie came trotting up to greet us yesterday, she offered us up the greatest of gifts: her little snout began to wrinkle up on the right side and then there it was—a Chesapeake smile that Chels would've been proud of.

If there were any doubts, they vanished . . . Tigger and I were goners.

So, that's the news around these parts for now.

And if you'll excuse me, it's time for our Sunday morning walk.

Chapter 62

A Pre-Christmas
Run to Canada

I've met a lot of characters up and down the coast over the years whom I'm lucky enough to be able to call friends. Boat designer Spencer Lincoln is one of them.

To paraphrase the old "Dragnet" show, the story you are about to read is true. No names have been changed to protect the innocent, however—especially Spencer's. He's ***never*** *innocent.*

≈

I was rolling up socks—enough for five days in Canada—and stuffing them into my seabag when a wave of déjà vu curled, broke, and washed over me. All of a sudden, it was a few years ago and I was starting from a different launch point, but the scenario was the same: work-related trip that needed to happen and Christmas right around the corner . . . now or never; pack yer bag and go. Or, in the words of the immortal Dickie Betts: "Git out on the highway an' let 'er roll on . . ."

Oh, and my friend Spencer went with me on the original trip—this time it would be just me and Bonnie the Chesapeake (at 6 months old, already an accomplished road dog).

I got to thinking about the original pre-Christmas

Nova Scotia run; it made for sort of a nice holiday story: bits of tension and intrigue; setbacks on the part of our heroes; impending doom; a miracle of sorts— and a happy ending. Oh, and snow. There was lots of snow.

So let me take a few minutes and share this log of my Yuletide journey to the North Country with Spencer Lincoln. (And remember, kids: don't try this at home. We were professionals.)

DAY ONE

9:07 PM—I arrive at Spencer's house, figuring on a good head start in the morning. After string of long road days in the H&H Propeller van, I'm already beat. Spencer greets me at the door with an opened can of kippers. *"Eat up – you'll be needing your omega 3s!"* The local community radio station's reggae program blasts from the speakers.

DAY TWO

1:23 AM—After losing a few minutes to a debate over how many hours it had to be past midnight to actually qualify as the next day, we're on the road. It's snowing. It's snowing hard, in fact—but we need to press on as there's a boat launch to make. (A quick note of explanation—and there's no intended endorsements here; just the facts, ma'am: we were headed to Nova Scotia for the launch of hull #1 of one of Spencer's designs. The 37' hull was built by a Brooklin, Maine company, but this first one to hit the water was finished by a shop in Petite Riviere [think Lunenburg] and was due to hit the water in a couple of days. I was headed up to offer a choice of propellers for Spencer's new baby.)

DAYBREAK (FAINTLY)—Spencer's snoring gives the guard at the border crossing a start. There's an unsure moment when it seems that the customs officials are considering taking a cutting torch to the van, but we are eventually released, free to continue into the blizzard.

10:18 AM—"NO FERRY TO DIGBY TODAY" reads the sign on the door of the terminal in St. John, NB. As we read the message through our ice-glazed windshield, a gust of wind takes hold of the sign and peels it clear, probably carrying it halfway to Digby. Guess we're driving around. *"I'm ready for wheel watch!"* announces Spencer, rubbing his paws together while knowing that, nothing personal, I'll never abandon the helm. "Thanks—I'm all set," I say, fishtailing out of the parking lot. "Got any quarters for the toll?"

SOMETIME AFTER SUNDOWN (WAS IT *EVER* UP?)—We've made the slow crawl around (at times the only vehicle on the road) and rolled into Bridgewater. Dull and weary, we trudge into the only establishment open on the main drag, the River Pub. Life takes a turn for the weird: "Looky here—it's the propeller men! How's ya doin', luv?" yells the barmaid. As two frothy mugs are slid the length of the bar, halting perfectly in front of us, Spencer and I exchange baffled looks, asking *"Have you ever been here before?"* in unison and then answering *"No"* in the same fashion. Our suspicions of great psychic forces at work are proven false later on—turns out that, because of the H&H Prop logos on my vest and Spencer's hat, we were mistaken for reps from the Propeller Brewery. So what? They liked us all the same and it was warm and dry there.

11:33 PM—In our room at the Comfort Inn. The "Local on the 8s" says snow continues tomorrow. Spencer is snoring.

DAY THREE

6:24 AM—Steaming cups of Tim Horton's best in hand, we creep south to Petite Riviere. Spencer says we ought to take a ride on the LaHave River cable ferry today. I can't even tell that there's a river through the snow.

NOON—Warm reception at the boat shop. Project supervisor Colin O'Toole's eyes twinkle when Spencer mentions that I've brought my guitar for the combined launch/shop Christmas party. Some questions for Spencer, then we decide to get out of the way; there's nothing we can contribute 'til launch tomorrow. We head out in the snow with intentions of visiting some boat shops on the south shore.

DAY FOUR

NOON—Yes, I know: a bit of a gap in the narrative. It's been a tough 24 hours. Some highlights: snow drives us into the Loyalist Inn in Shelburne; we take a walk around town, discovering a neat museum (good idea) and the Sea Dog Saloon (bad idea); back on the lawn of the museum early evening, the older curator lady flailing a broom trying to drive us off as Spencer throws snowballs at her; leaving the local hardware store in a hurry when an errant slapshot (Spencer was Christmas shopping—don't ask) sends a puck through a display of stacked teakettles. Now it's the next day and we're watching the 37 float clear of the trailer. It's still snowing. Thank God for the LaHave Bakery and their coffee.

MIDNIGHT—A happy ending. More highlights: Spencer at the helm, landing the 37 perfectly crosswind/crosstide after our maiden run; 5-blade prop we've brought fits the bill; many congrats all the way around and then we're off to the party; holed up with Colin in the kitchen of the hall where the get-together is, 12-string face-to-face with mandolin, playing and singing "Dead Flowers" wide-open; Spencer dancing with every woman in the house.

We go outside for some fresh air. The snow has stopped. There's a full moon. My fretting fingers hurt.

All of a sudden, it feels like Christmas. I'm ready to go home.

Chapter 63

No Rowboats
in Castara

Truth be known, Tigger and I feel the pull of the northern latitudes the strongest. But every now and then, a little bit of elsewhere is good.

*I am **so** glad we had pulley lines and rowboats when I was a kid.*

≈

7:00 AM on the 14ᵗʰ of February, 2008—Valentine's Day—found Tigger and me barefoot in tees and shorts, sitting with steaming mugs on the deck of our little cottage ("Fisherman's Lodge" read the hand-painted sign by the door, and that's what it was—a converted fish shack) on a hillside overlooking the village of Castara, Tobago.

Prior to going there, any question put to me about Tobago would most likely have been answered with, "Yeah, it's good sprinkled over eggs, but don't get it in your eyes," showing off my natural ignorance of all things geographical. Now that I've been there, I could probably point it out on a map to you—or tell you where to look: plop your fingertip on Cuba and start chasing the curved string of islands that border the eastern end of the Caribbean down towards the South American coast. When you're about to jab your fingertip into Venezuela, stop: off the Venezuelan shore, you should see the island of Trinidad; NNE of that lies Tobago. There, now you know everything I know about the islands of the Lesser Antilles. You want more details, ask Tigger.

Me, I'm just trying to get across the point that it was **warm**.

And the whole point of telling you it was warm has nothing to do with rubbing in the fact that back at home it was snowing (I happen to like our home *very much*, thank you, even in the middle of February)—I just need you to understand why the Castara fishing fleet has no rowboats.

They just walk down the beach in the morning, wade in, and swim off to the mooring.

Yup.

The cove that the village of Castara wraps around is home to a fleet of 15 or so open outboard boats 22' to 24' long. The hulls are all basically the same style: a vee entry flattening into a hard-chine hull. Yamahas were popular power choices, with a sprinkling of Mercs and Mariners thrown in; horsepowers ranged from 40 to 90.

The names were painted in many different styles and colors along the sides of the hulls—no black block letters for the Rastafarian fishermen of Castara . . . no way, mon. Names you could read easily from a distance: *"Brighton Rock"*. *"Spice Girl"*. *"Heaven"*. *"Saltlee"*. *"Vibot"*. *"Black Fox"*. *"Why Worry"*. *"I Wish"*. *"Blessed"*.

Though the hulls were mostly white, the names dominated the side of the hull and, along with the trim and bottom color combos, gave each boat its own look: bright red bottom/bright red trim/royal blue (and I'm talking Jonesport-Beals blue) cockpit; dark blue bottom/yellow trim/dark blue cockpit; deep red bottom/light blue trim/pink cockpit . . . no two were alike.

The Castara fleet was hook fishing—going for stuff like snapper, pompano, and tarpon—although we heard at times it wasn't unusual for them to shut the cove off with one of the boatloads of twine that sat waiting on a mooring (just like Pa and Uncle James in the old stop-twine days, except the Castara guys will just stand on the shore and haul the net right up onto the sand and empty it out).

Once we got a feel for the rhythm of the village, it became part of our morning to watch the fleet leave from the low cement-walled co-op building which sat on the edge of the sand. The pattern was always the same, choreographed naturally by years and years of things done the way they're done, hard work accomplished at an easy pace . . . no worries, mon, no worries: the skipper would wade into the surf (there were anywhere from 2' to 6' rollers constantly while we were there) and dive in, swimming off and swinging himself easily up over the gunwale of the boat. Now, keep in mind that these weren't all young bucks who regularly hang out at the health club—don't bother to look; there aren't any health clubs on Tobago—the Castara fleet has the same demographics as any coastal village in the world. There were some older men who have been at this every working day for a long time . . . and I don't know about you, chummy, but even when I was at my physical peak, I know *I* couldn't make climbing in over the rail of a boat from the water look that easy.

While the motor warmed up, the skipper would hit any place missed the evening before with a scrub brush—and there usually weren't many places missed; the boats were all super clean—and stow any loose gear. Then he'd cast off, run in toward the beach, and swing the boat around sharply with just enough water to keep the prop from grinding into the sand, bow pointed into the rollers. That particular hull shape was ideal—they'd ride the surf like eider ducks.

So the skipper would be there, standing at the tiller of the outboard, maybe eating a piece of fruit or having a morning smoke, giving the throttle a twist now and then to keep things comfortable. In the meantime, the helper would wade out with buckets and gear, tossing them into the boat. An ice chest would be floated out on the last trip and the two of them would ease it up over the rail. Then once the helper swung himself aboard, they were off—usually gone until late afternoon, when the process would be repeated in reverse and the day's catch could be purchased right there on the beach if you had a hankering for fresh fish.

This is how it went, with one exception: we called him Inner Tube Mon.

Inner Tube Mon left just as early as the rest—and put his days in, too. His boat was just as brightly painted—and he caught as many fish as the rest of his fellow Rastas.

But if I had to guess, I'd say that maybe Inner Tube Mon couldn't swim.

Each morning he'd carry an oversize inner tube down to the surf, wade out a ways, then plunk himself down onto it, paddling with his hands. He'd make boarding his boat from a prone position look easy, tie the inner tube off like you would a punt, then let the mooring go and head back to shore to load on his helper and gear. In the afternoon, once the day's catch was landed, he'd put the outboard back on the hook, ease over the side onto his inner tube, and paddle back ashore.

That was Inner Tube Mon. He made it work.

So, if anyone asks you, tell 'em I verified the following facts:

Tobago is a place, not a bottled hot sauce.

The cove in Castara has never been froze in.

The fleet has no rowboats.

They work hard and make it look easy.

And there's only one Inner Tube Mon.

Chapter 64

For Lydia: Welcome to the World, Little One

Since starting the Bearin's column in 1988, I've been getting away with writing about almost anything as long as I mentioned the word "boat" or "lobster" or "fish" somewhere in the process. I think this one did have the word "boats" in it— other than that, it's all Lydia.

For the record, the now much-talkative Lydia refers to me as "Pops"—as in, "Let's go to PopsTiggerBonnie's house." And she's been joined by newly-arrived little brother Mason. He'll have to wait 'til Pops' next book to get his own chapter.

≈

I am a grandfather.

I know, I know, we just got done talking about the turning 50 thing a couple of months ago, but that's just a number—this is a new chapter. No—this is a whole new *story*.

At 10:27 PM on April 8, 2008, Lydia Paige Carter came into this world, daughter of Jessica (Robbins) and Caleb Carter. At 9 lbs., 4 ozs. she was well shy of her great-Grampa Robbins' claimed weight of something like 16 lbs.—but we weren't ever able to verify Pa's figures, to tell you the truth. As Jess has put it more than once, with a shake of her head: "How would you ever know *anything* about the Robbins family history? Anything you could *believe*, anyway?" And then she rolls her eyes and laughs.

It's true: our family tree is firmly rooted in foolishness and music and storytelling.

Oh, Lydia . . . are you ready for all this?

My grandfather Eaton—Marm's father—was a good man; I just didn't see a lot of him. In fact, I can't honestly remember seeing him outside of his plumbing and heating shop in Deer Isle, ME. Grandpa lived in the back of the shop; I remember he was big on gunning—and without a woman's touch handy (he and Grammie Eaton had separated before I was born) Grandpa's living quarters had the atmosphere of a year-round hunting lodge. Sadly, about all I have in my head of Grandpa is the way his eyes would crinkle at the corners when he'd talk to me. And Canada Mints—seems like there would always be Canada Mints for a treat when I'd visit with Grandpa Eaton. I can't tell you a lot more than that—it's just the way it was.

And then there was the Robbins side: Nanny and Gramp—Pa's folks—who lived on Green Head on the western end of Stonington. I was around them more, just by virtue of their house being at the head of the harbor where Pa, my brother Stevie, Uncle James, Uncle Harold, Uncle Toot, Bob Quinn—everybody in my world as a kid, it seemed—kept their boats.

It was the hub of the universe when I was little.

There was the never-ending pot of black tea going.

And, of course, there were always stories. Plenty of stories.

We had some conversations early on, once we knew Lydia was on her way, about what Tigger and I would like to be called by the next generation. "Tigger" it seemed, needed little or no variation; what kid wouldn't want to have an elder they could snuggle with for a read whom they could call "Tigger"? As far as I was concerned, it wasn't as definite: "Gramp"? "Grampy Bear"? "Pops"?

And then we sort of let it go, remembering that at some point in her early years Jess had begun calling her grandfather on her mother's side "Buff" for no reason obvious to any of the rest of us—he remains Buff to this day . . . and a great Buff, at that.

And a great-Buff, too.

So we'll just let Lydia decide.

> *Gramp Robbins was a neat mix: when stirred up, he could be absolutely fiery—but I remember there always being a twinkle, too. He'd say stuff that ranged from fierce observations about someone's integrity ("When he died, they had to screw him into the ground, he was so crooked!") to totally irreverent statements about life itself, and say it all with such conviction that nobody ever questioned him (in my presence, anyway) except Nanny Robbins.*
>
> *My brother Stevie has a lot of Gramp in him, for sure, from the humor to the fire; if you want to know what our grandfather was like, spend some time with my brother. Being 14 years older than I am, the beginnings of Stevie's working years overlapped with the tail end of Gramp's.*
>
> *Me, I spent summers at Nanny and Gramp's house when I was little while Marm was work-*

ing at a local laundry and Pa was down the bay. They were good summers, full of Nanny's biscuits, the smell of the humongous wild rose bush that pushed up against the front door, and many, many circles around the cove rowing with my dumbold-girlcousin Julia.

*Even though Gramp was fairly old, to me, he wasn't like other "old men"—he was funny; he was lively; even when his days were spent mostly in his rocker knitting trap heads, there was plenty going on. He'd plague Nanny (never mean, but definitely pushing her buttons) and I'd be trying not to laugh, thereby being branded by Nanny as a co-conspirator. But when Gramp would look over at me and give me **that look**: eyebrow raised, a twinkle in his eye . . . I'd lose it every time.*

I can't wait to do that to Lydia.

At one point, when all the checks and weighings and measurings and hugs and smiles and laughter and tears had quieted down and we were preparing to leave parents and newborn to themselves, I looked over at Jess and Lydia.

At that moment, exhausted, her red hair piled up behind her head against the pillow, sleepy-eyed and smiling at her daughter, Jess looked just like pictures of her Grammie Robbins as a young woman.

Beautiful.

Both of them.

All of them.

Tigger and I were holding hands when we walked out of the hospital into the night air, a generation richer than when we walked in.

Chapter 65

The Brothers Robbins Unwrapped

I admit it: the sole reason for taking this one out of chronological order (by a few years, nonetheless) and placing it at the very end is to leave you with the vision of my brother described within. Why? Because it's funny, that's why. If you've gotten this far and didn't know that by now, then something ails you.

≈

At different times in your life you come to conclusions about yourself, accept them, and move on.

For instance: I have had to come to grips with the fact that I'll never be able to support myself as a male model.

I know, I know, there will be a number of you out there who know me who'll be staggered by this revelation. "Oh, but Brian," you'll say, "what company wouldn't *kill* to have a prematurely gray-headed guy with a chest that sticks out like a 55-gallon drum and absolutely no rear end whatsoever—all supported by legs usually seen beneath an ostrich—model its fall line of clothing?"

Well, don't try to change my mind. I'm not budging on this. The die has been cast; Fortuna has spun her wheel: no modeling jobs for ol' BR.

To tell you the truth, the male Robbins physique has been a source of amusement for my brother Stevie and me for years. I remember one night back during the offshore years when we were laying over somewhere and shared a motel room. Stevie'd already showered and was sprawled back on his bed with a big towel wrapped around him. When I came out of the bathroom after my shower, he started to snort.

"Nice legs," he said.

"Hey—I don't see *you* wearin' any short skirts yourself," I said, feeling a little defensive.

He looked thoughtful. "Probably if you weren't so awkward, your legs wouldn't be so banged up—that would help."

"Listen," I replied. "You are a 300-pound human—and 290 pounds of that is above your friggin' hips. Your legs are a marvel of modern architecture; if they could build bridges that could stand with so little for support, the world would be a better place."

We fired verbal salvos back and forth for a while until Stevie snapped his fingers, looking like he'd just come up with the Theory of Relativity. "It just struck me what you look like."

"What?" I said, crawling into my bed.

"A bottle-assed squid!" he said, totally collapsing in a heap of gagging, choking laughter.

Later, I tried looking it up, but could never find a "bottle-assed squid" mentioned anywhere, let alone a picture of one. Anyhow, that ended the debate for the evening—Stevie was the victor.

I was able to avenge my loss the very next trip, however—although the situation was sculpted by the hands of fate and my brother was simply a victim of circumstance.

It was early morning as we made our approach to the mouth of the river, returning to Portsmouth, NH to offload our lobsters. It had been an aggravating trip full of snarls, hard-running tides, and fogfogfogfog-fogfog. Oh—and fog *slop*, the cussed deep chop that just makes everything one notch more contrary.

Now it was just flat calm and foggy; maybe the mess would burn off while we were unloading. Stevie gave me the wheel, with a bearing on the bell at the mouth of the river. He disappeared below, coming back up a minute or two later laden with scrub brush, wash cloth, soap, toothbrush, toothpaste, Listerine, Witch Hazel, a couple of towels, and who knows what else.

Stevie answered my quizzical look firmly: "I'm gonna wash some of this damn trip off me." He then went aft, peeled off his clothes, turned the deck hose on himself, and began to lather up while bellowing "Mamas Don't Let Your Babies Grow Up To Be Cowboys" at the top of his lungs.

"Stunnin'," I said to myself and concentrated on the radar. The target that had to be the bell was starting to sprout some extra dots. Nothing big, but fairly steady . . . rod 'n reelers! No doubt, I realized—it was Saturday morning and every living soul who had a fishing rod and something that would float was sitting in the mouth of the river, hovering around the bell. They had every right in the world to be there, but they didn't have any fear, either. The roar of the *Shirley & Freeman's* 12V-71 Detroit in the fog wouldn't even cause them to look up. I'd need to be paying attention as we made our approach.

Meanwhile, my brother was back aft tearing up "Desperado" by the Eagles with a vengeance, slathered with shampoo and soap.

The bell was getting close, with enough pinpoint targets darting around the screen to cause me to reach for the throttle. Just as I laid my hand on the handle, however, a neat thing occurred. The gray wall that had encased us for a week parted—*I could see!*

Sure enough, there was everything you could think of for small craft clustered around the bell. Punts, outboards, fancy I/Os, rubber Zodiacs, canoes, kayaks . . . you name it, it was there. And each one of them was loaded to capacity with people, rods, and coolers.

And then I realized that the biggest part of the people were staring and pointing at us. Not with the natural curiosity one would apply to a 44' lobster boat steaming in from offshore, but with a mix of shock and disbelief.

Suddenly it hit me: if *we* can see *them* . . . *they* can see *us* . . . and . . .

"DESSSSSSSPERADOOOOOO, Why don't you come to your senses . . ." my brother roared, eyes closed tight as he stood stark raving naked in the stern of the boat, running the deck hose over his head.

I gave a jaunty Prince Charles wave to the assembled masses as we rounded the bell and swung up river.

"The revenge of the bottle-assed squid," I said to myself.

Glossary

The fact is, these stories were originally written for the pages of Commercial Fisheries News. *And even though the subject matter varied from fact to fiction and from birth to death, there was always some little trickle of salt water that ran through it all. I was pretty confident that the reader either knew what I was talking about when I mentioned putting on a barvel or tying a becket . . . or they'd have someone nearby who could explain it to them, at least.*

The good folks at North Wind Publishing pointed out the fact that, with any luck, someone might be reading this book who isn't going out to haul lobster gear in the morning. Good point. We can only hope.

Thus, some definitions (mine, not Webster's):

bander—The tool used to slip a rubber band over each of a lobster's claws. Also used by cooks to make annoying clicking noises just out of arm's reach of the captain.

barvel—Basically, a water-proof dress. These days, oilpants and knee boots are the norm; I grew up with barvels and hipboots. Great for curtseying on deck.

bearin's—When you're on the water, the act of figuring out where you are and what's going on is known as "getting your bearings." The same applies to life itself. In the Northeast, we often don't fuss around with the letter "g" at the ends of our words. Therefore, "bearin's."

beckets—A length of rope made fast to one end of a lobster trap that the main line ties into.

davit—On a lobster boat, the davit is the arm that swings out over the side you haul traps on. Some folks also refer to the sheaved block that hangs from it as a davit (pronounced "davey" where I come from).

drags—The iron-framed dredges used to . . . well . . . drag up scallops from the ocean floor. Some folks use one large drag known as a "sweep"; others use multiple small drags (in our case, six drags 2-½ feet wide each) attached to one main frame or "bale."

dubs—Clumsy, know-nothing oafs. Or worse.

feeler stick—A wooden pole shaped somewhat like a long, very narrow oar used to "feel" a school of herring in a cove. An experienced man with a feeler stick could get a pretty good idea of just how big that body of fish was. As I've mentioned, Pa was a good man with a feeler stick.

fog slop—That sort of short, steep, chop that seems to come from all directions at once on a foggy day sometimes—just to be despisable.

glomming—Awkwardly attaching oneself to, either literally or figuratively. You can "glom onto an idea" just as well as you can "glom onto an oar."

highliners—The folks in the fleet who do well and have their act together. Which, in theory, is why they do well.

hogshead—The age-old way of measuring herring. Since you asked: one hogshead equals 6.76751483 bushels. Yep.

humming tight—Ever seen a piece of rope stretched to the point where you can literally play a tune on it? Well, that's humming tight.

lobster car—A wooden-framed planked-up float used to keep lobsters in after they're caught.

longliner—A boat that catches finfish on long trawls with baited hooks.

low-drainer tide—A lower-than-average tide around the time of full moon.

oakum—A tarred fiber used in caulking the seams between the planks of a wooden boat. If you've never smelled oakum, well, you should.

peapod—A double-ended rowboat. There's nothing sweeter than a pretty peapod. Except my wife.

pennant—The main rope on a mooring that goes to the bow of the boat.

plotter—A piece of electronic navigational equipment that we never had during the offshore years but somehow got by without.

poly—Polypropylene rope. Don't be bugging me for a chemical breakdown, okay? It floated.

pot warp—The rope (at the time, both float and non-floating) used on lobster traps, also known as lobster pots.

rail—The gunwale (pronounced "gunnel" where I come from), or top edge of a boat's hull.

scrump—A little, tiny bit of something. Me, I like the phrase "stove to a scrump," which means something was damaged to the point of being just tiny little bits of its former self.

scupper—A hole or vent in the side of a boat that lets water on deck run overboard.

seabag—The bag that you tote your clothes aboard the boat with. It can be made of anything. As long as the clothes make it aboard, who cares? We used to refer to the standard green or black plastic garbage bag as "offshore Samsonite."

shucking—In the case of scallops, cutting the meats clear of the shell.

spilings—Interchangeable with "pilings" in my book—you know, the tall wooden posts around the perimeter of a wharf. Not interchangeable, you say? I can't help it if you grew up wrong.

stivvering or stivvered—Sort of like staggering, only not with the big, broad changes in course.

stupe—Someone not that bright.

The glass was rising—The barometer was showing a rise in atmospheric pressure.

wicked—Really, really, really neat.

wob up—To gather up in a disorderly fashion.

wooden four-footers—4' long wooden lobster traps, used before the much lighter wire lobster gear became popular. Our wooden four-footers used to weigh well over 100 lbs. apiece. That explains a lot.

Bearin's: The Book

ISBN-13 978-0-9830780-5-0

This collection of stories from Brian Robbins is available direct from the publisher, or can be ordered through your favorite bookstore or most online book sellers. To order by credit card, call the publisher at 207-542-0180.

To order direct from the publisher send $17.95 for each copy. Add $6.00 shipping and handling for the first copy, plus another $1.00 for each additional copy. Maximum shipping costs $30.00. Maine residents add 5% sales tax.

Please send ____copies to:

Name: _____

Address: _____

_____

_____

Phone number (optional) _____

e-mail address (optional) _____

(Phone numbers and e-mail addresses will be used for customer service only. Information will remain private.)

Total amount enclosed:_____

Please send check or money order to North Wind Publishing, P.O. Box 8, Belfast, ME 04915.

As Brian says in the introduction, if you are reading a borrowed copy, it's probably been read in the bathroom. Wouldn't you rather have your own copy?